WASTE-TO-ENERGY
IN THE UNITED STATES

WASTE-TO-ENERGY IN THE UNITED STATES

A Social and Economic Assessment

T. RANDALL CURLEE,
SUSAN M. SCHEXNAYDER,
DAVID P. VOGT, AMY K. WOLFE,
MICHAEL P. KELSAY, and
DAVID L. FELDMAN

QUORUM BOOKS
Westport, Connecticut • London

Library of Congress Cataloging-in-Publication Data

Waste-to-energy in the United States : a social and economic
  assessment / T. Randall Curlee ... [et al.].
          p.   cm.
  Includes bibliographical references and index.
  ISBN 0–89930–844–9 (alk. paper)
  1. Refuse and refuse disposal—Economic aspects—United States.
  2. Waste products as fuel—Economic aspects—United States.
  3. Energy development—Economic aspects—United States.
  4. Incinerators—Environmental aspects—United States.   I. Curlee,
  T. Randall.
  HD4483.W37   1994
  333.79′38′0973—dc20   93–26467

British Library Cataloguing in Publication Data is available.

Library of Congress Catalog Card Number: 93–26467
ISBN: 0–89930–844–9

First published in 1994

Quorum Books, 88 Post Road West, Westport, CT 06881
An imprint of Greenwood Publishing Group, Inc.

Printed in the United States of America

The paper used in this book complies with the
Permanent Paper Standard issued by the National
Information Standards Organization (Z39.48–1984).

10 9 8 7 6 5 4 3 2 1

Contents

Illustrations   ix

Foreword   xiii

Preface and Acknowledgments   xv

Abbreviations   xvii

1. Introduction   1

    1.1 Municipal Solid Waste and the Role of Waste-to-Energy   1

    1.2 General Approach   5

    1.3 A Preview of Following Chapters   7

2. Why Is Waste-to-Energy So Controversial?   9

    2.1 The Issues   9

    2.2 Uncertainties About Potential Environmental and Health Risks   10

    2.3 Legislative and Regulatory Uncertainties   17

    2.4 Uncertainties About the Future of Alternatives to WTE   25

    2.5 Uncertainties About WTE Technologies   29

    2.6 Potential Failures in the Decision-Making Process   33

3. An Overview of Waste-to-Energy in the United States   37

    3.1 Introduction   37

    3.2 The Adoption of WTE in the United States   37

3.3 WTE Industry Structure in the United States   41

3.4 The Potential for Energy Production from MSW
     Combustion   44

4. Waste-to-Energy in the United States and Key
   Socioeconomic Factors   63

     4.1 Introduction   63

     4.2 Analysis of Communities with Waste-to-Energy
          Initiatives   64

     4.3 Summary and Conclusions   92

5. A Focus on Financial Issues   97

     5.1 Introduction   97

     5.2 Some Background on the Cost of Environmental
          Management   98

     5.3 Potential Financing Mechanisms   98

     5.4 The Increasing Costs of WTE Facilities   106

     5.5 Federal Tax Policy   108

     5.6 Other Financial Constraints on Local Jurisdictions 120

     5.7 Adjustments in the Financing of WTE Projects   121

     5.8 Summary and Future Outlook   130

6. Case Studies: Community Decision Making   135

     6.1 Introduction   135

     6.2 Methods   140

     6.3 Broward County, Florida   144

     6.4 Oakland County, Michigan   156

     6.5 Knox County, Tennessee   171

     6.6 Monmouth County, New Jersey   183

     6.7 Analysis   197

     6.8 Summary and Future Outlook   211

7. The Socioeconomics of Waste-to-Energy: Conclusions   215

     7.1 The Motivation for This Study   215

     7.2 Why Is Waste-to-Energy So Controversial?   216

     7.3 An Overview of WTE in the United States   218

7.4 The Socioeconomics of WTE from an Aggregate
     Perspective   220

7.5 A Focus on Financial Issues   221

7.6 A Focus on the Decision-Making Process: Case-
     Study Results   224

7.7 Summary Conclusions   227

Appendixes

Appendix A: Air Emissions for Common Waste
             Management Strategies   231

Appendix B: Case Studies: Waste-to-Energy Facilities
             Protocol   233

Bibliography   239

Index   251

Illustrations

FIGURES

3.1	Historical and Projected MSW Quantity	48
3.2	Per Capita MSW Quantity	50
3.3	Historical and Projected Heat Value of MSW: 1960– 2015	55
3.4	The Percentage of MSW Combusted with Heat Recovery	57
3.5	Estimated and Projected Energy from MSW Combustion	59
4.1	WTE Initiatives by County Size	67
4.2	Counties with Existing and/or Planned WTE Facilities	68
4.3	Counties with Scratched WTE Facilities	69
6.1	Case-Study Site Locations	142
6.2	Broward County, Florida	145
6.3	Oakland County, Michigan	157
6.4	Knox County, Tennessee	171
6.5	Monmouth County, New Jersey	184

TABLES

3.1	Vendors of WTE Facilities in the United States: 1990	43
3.2	Historical and Projected MSW Quantity	47
3.3	Per Capita MSW Quantity	49
3.4	Historical and Projected Composition of MSW: 1960–2000	52

3.5	Historical and Projected MSW Btu Value: 1960–2000	53
3.6	Historical and Projected Heat Value of MSW: 1960–2015	54
3.7	The Percentage of MSW Combusted with Heat Recovery	56
3.8	Estimated and Projected Energy from MSW Combustion	58
3.9	Comparisons with Other Projections of Energy from WTE	60
4.1	Distribution of Counties by WTE Status	65
4.2	County Population Density	71
4.3	County Population Size	72
4.4	County Rural Population	73
4.5	County Population Growth	74
4.6	County Population with High School Degrees	77
4.7	County Per Capita Income	78
4.8	County Population at Family Formation Age	79
4.9	County Industrial Base	80
4.10	Recycling Programs	81
4.11	Access to MRFs	82
4.12	Access to Landfills	83
4.13	Availability of Landfills	84
4.14	County Municipal Solid Waste Disposal Expenditures	85
4.15	Membership in Conservation Groups	86
4.16	Local Environmental Quality	87
4.17	State Waste Management Policies	88
4.18	State Environmental Policies	89
4.19	Summary of Significant Differences of Means: Comparison of Counties with WTE Initiative to Counties with No WTE Initiative	90
4.20	Summary of Significant Differences of Means: Comparison of Counties with Operating WTE Facilities to Counties with Scratched Initiatives	91
4.21	Multiple Indicator Analysis of All Counties	93
4.22	Multiple Indicator Analysis of WTE Counties	94
5.1	Percentage Ownership of Municipal Bonds: 1975–1990	102

5.2	Waste-to-Energy Facility Adjusted Capital Costs: 1982–1990	107
5.3	WTE Facility Design Capacities: 1990	108
5.4	Private Activity Bond Volume as a Percentage of Total Bond Volume (1975–1986)	109
5.5	Yields on Corporate and Tax-Exempt Bonds and the Yield Ratio: 1965–1990	111
5.6	State Private-Activity Bond Volume Caps: Totals and Per Capita: 1989–1991	114
5.7	State Tax-Exempt Private-Activity Bonds: Percentage of Cap Used, 1989–1990	116
5.8	U.S. Volume of Long-Term Tax-Exempt Debt	119
5.9	Waste-to-Energy Capital Finance: Historical Trends of Finance	122
5.10	Alternative Methods of Finance: Advanced-Planned and Existing WTE Facilities: 1984–1990	123
5.11	Waste-to-Energy Capital Finance Mechanisms: 1990	124
5.12	Location of Scratched/Abandoned Facilities by State: 1986–1990	126
5.13	Waste-to-Energy Capital Finance Mechanisms at Scratched/Abandoned Facilities: 1986–1990	128
5.14	Waste-to-Energy Capital Finance Mechanisms at Scratched/Abandoned Facilities by Finance Amount: 1986–1990	129
6.1	Summary of Decision-Making Context	198
6.2	Summary of Decision-Making Process	200

Foreword

During the course of researching and writing this book, the authors became keenly aware of the tremendous controversy that surrounds the incineration of municipal solid waste (MSW). Incineration with heat recovery, commonly called waste-to-energy (WTE), is a topic about which there is no lack of emotion, no shortage of opinions, and no want of issues around which controversy thrives. Environmental questions, regulatory uncertainties, financial risks, technology reliability, the relative costs of alternative approaches to waste management, the potential for those alternatives to manage different segments of the waste stream, and the decision process itself are often debated by opposing sides that label themselves as opponents or proponents of WTE. And the resolution of these key issues has all too often been hindered or blocked by the strategic positioning of the opposing sides. Both sides harbor a concern—even a fear—that the results of studies will be taken out of context and the use of certain terminology will bias the public and decision makers in a particular way.

This book does not take a position of either opposing or promoting WTE or any other method to manage municipal waste. Rather, the authors have strived for neutrality in addressing the complex social and economic issues that are often central to decisions about particular WTE projects and that will play a key role in determining the overall viability of WTE in the future. Although the focus of the book is on socioeconomic issues, background information is presented on the key technical, environmental, and health issues that, in part, fuel the current controversy. Great care has been taken to summarize the various arguments, not with the purpose of assessing the accuracy of the arguments about health and environmental impacts or technology constraints—which is beyond the scope of this study—but simply as background on the social and economic sources of the controversy.

It is hoped that this book will be viewed as a dispassionate assessment

of the social and economic issues surrounding WTE and will serve to encourage additional objective work in the area. The current divided and often
heated debate over the future of incineration with heat recovery requires
no less.

Preface and Acknowledgments

What should we do with all of the garbage we generate? The issue of municipal solid waste disposal looms over many communities and has acquired national prominence in recent years due to decreasing landfill capacity and widely publicized local problems. Perhaps the issue is felt most strongly within communities that are facing the prospects of having their landfill closed or meeting state-mandated goals for recycling and source reduction. Other communities face challenges to proposed waste-to-energy facilities. Planning for municipal waste disposal is driven by pressing needs for which there are no simple solutions. No disposal alternative is free from technological, economic, environmental, health, regulatory, or social problems; and choosing among the options is difficult indeed.

This book was inspired by these difficulties. It also was inspired by the everchanging context of solid waste management—new and amended local, state, and federal regulations; escalating costs; technological developments; and evolving public and political attention and opinions. The book started with the premises that decisions about solid waste management are made within this changing context and that social and economic influences on decision making frequently are overlooked. Therefore, our goal is to understand how social and economic factors affect communities' decisions about municipal solid waste disposal by examining in detail one option, waste-to-energy.

The authors wish to thank the many individuals who, in one way or another, contributed to this book. Scott Rickard, an economics graduate student at the University of Tennessee, contributed excellent data and graphics support. Cynthia Coomer developed the maps for the chapter describing case studies. Cynthia Moody, Kathy Ballew, Judy Burns, and Glenda Hamlin provided industrious and timely secretarial support and helped in meeting an ambitious delivery schedule.

Special thanks go to all the individuals who made the case-study segment of this work possible. We greatly appreciate their time and valued insights into how the decision-making process works. Our thanks also go to those individuals who provided background data and information, in particular Dr. Roosevelt Allen of the Tennessee Valley Authority, Steve Brown of the Council of State Governments, Dr. Dwight Connor of the National Conference of State Legislatures, Dr. Peggy Douglas of the University of Tennessee, Jim Glenn of *BioCycle* magazine, Dr. Booker Morey of the Stanford Research Institute, and Steve Teslik of the Partnership for Plastics Progress.

We also benefited greatly from many reviewers' thoughtful comments on draft manuscripts. Participants in the case-study research provided valuable clarifications, corrections, and additions to sections of the book pertaining to their site. Individuals who reviewed the entire manuscript included Dr. Johnnie Cannon and Emily Copenhaver from Oak Ridge National Laboratory, Jean Peretz from the University of Tennessee, Jim Glenn of *BioCycle*, and several individuals associated with the waste-to-energy industry. Of course, the authors take full responsibility for the final product.

Finally, we thank our families for their continued support throughout this endeavor.

Abbreviations

AMBAC	American Municipal Bond Assurance Corporation
AMT	alternative minimum tax
BACT	Best Available Control Technologies
BDT	Best Demonstrated Technology
BIG	Bond Investors Guaranty Insurance Corporation
Btu	British thermal unit
CAA	Clean Air Act of 1970
CAAA	Clean Air Act Amendments of 1990
CFR	Code of Federal Regulations
COP	certificate of participation
CSWS	Council for Solid Waste Solutions (now Partnership for Plastics Progress)
DER	Department of Environmental Regulation (Florida)
DNR	Department of Natural Resources (Michigan)
DRA84	Deficit Reduction Act of 1984
EIA	Energy Information Administration (U.S. Department of Energy)
FGIC	Federal Guaranty Insurance Company
GAA	Government Advisory Associates
GNP	Gross National Product
HUD	U.S. Department of Housing and Urban Development
IDB	industrial development bond
IGAs	intergovernmental agreements
IRB	industrial revenue bond
kWh	kilowatt hour

LOC	letters of credit
MACT	maximum achievable control technology
MBIA	Municipal Bond Investors Assurance Corporation
MBtus	millions of British thermal units
MCRC	Monmouth County (New Jersey) Reclamation Center
MKSWA	Metropolitan Knox Solid Waste Authority (Knox County, Tennessee)
MRF	material recovery facility
MSW	municipal solid waste
MW	megawatts
MWC	municipal waste combustor
NJDEP	New Jersey Department of Environmental Protection
NPS	U.S. National Park Service
NSPS	New Source Performance Standards
NSWMA	National Solid Wastes Management Association
OTA	Office of Technology Assessment, U.S. Congress
PAB	private-activity bond
P&C	Property and Casualty Insurance Firms
PCDD/PCDF	dioxin/furan
PURPA	Public Utility Regulatory Policies Act of 1978
PVC	polyvinyl chloride
RCRA	Resource Conservation and Recovery Act of 1980
RDF	refuse-derived fuel
RECA	Revenue and Expenditure Control Act of 1968
RISWMC	Rhode Island Solid Waste Management Corporation
RRRASOC	Resource Recovery and Recycling Authority of Southwest Oakland County (Michigan)
SERI	Solar Energy Research Institute
SOCRRA	Southeast Oakland County (Michigan) Resource Recovery Authority
SWM	solid waste management
TLDA	Tennessee Local Development Authority
tpd	tons-per-day
TRA86	Tax Reform Act of 1986
TRB	taxable revenue bonds
U.S. EPA	U.S. Environmental Protection Agency
WMI	Waste Management, Inc.
WTE	Waste-to-Energy

WASTE-TO-ENERGY
IN THE UNITED STATES

Chapter 1

Introduction

1.1 MUNICIPAL SOLID WASTE AND THE ROLE OF WASTE-TO-ENERGY

In 1987 the public of the United States was awakened to its growing municipal waste problem when a barge of New York State garbage wandered for five months in search of a disposal site. The barge with more than 3,000 tons of municipal solid waste (MSW) aboard was rejected by several disposal facilities along the Atlantic Coast and in the Caribbean and was eventually returned to the New York area and burned. More recently a trainload of New York City garbage—commonly referred to as the "P.U. Choo Choo"—roamed the Midwest in search of a home. After traveling for more than a month through a number of towns in Illinois, Kansas, and Missouri, the train was returned to New York's Fresh Kills landfill in July 1992, and the waste was buried.

Media coverage of these and other similar events and related reports on the status of garbage in America have elevated MSW to one of the most visible and, in the eyes of the public and many government leaders, most problematic environmental issues of our time. Polls routinely find that MSW ranks near the top of the public's environmental concerns, and a recent survey found that solid waste management is the top environmental priority among state legislatures.[1] Municipal waste management is also the focus of intense debate within the U.S. Congress and executive branch as different views about the problem, potential solutions, and the appropriate role of government clash.

In many ways the severity of our municipal waste problem has been overblown, and in some cases real problems have been overshadowed by hype over trivial concerns. Referring to the problem as a "crisis situation" is not appropriate at this time.[2] However, if recent trends continue, municipal waste management could very well be at a crisis level within a decade.

Several key trends suggest that MSW management will become more problematic. First, quantities of MSW have grown rapidly in recent years, and further growth is all but a certainty in the coming one to two decades. While the United States produced about 88 million tons of MSW in 1960, quantities increased to some 128 million tons in 1975 and 196 million tons in 1990. In per capita terms, U.S. waste generation increased from about 0.49 tons per year in 1960 to 0.78 tons per year in 1990.[3] Projections of future waste generation depend on assumptions about, for example, growth in economic activity and the success of initiatives to reduce the quantity of MSW at the source. However, under realistic conditions—2 percent real growth in gross national product (GNP) and a 0.5 percent reduction in waste generation per year due to source reduction—quantities of municipal solid waste are likely to reach 218 million tons by the year 2000 and increase to 249 million tons by 2010.[4]

Recent and projected increases in MSW quantity are made more problematic by recent trends in the number and costs of landfills. Landfills have historically been the primary means of managing MSW in the United States, accounting for 81 percent of all MSW in 1980 and 83 percent in 1985. In recent years landfilling has decreased and accounted for only 67 percent of MSW in 1990 as recycling and waste-to-energy have become more popular. And although landfilling is expected to remain the dominant management option in the coming decade, recent trends suggest growing barriers. For example, the number of U.S. landfills has decreased from about 8,000 in 1988 to about 5,800 in 1991 (a 27 percent drop). Landfill numbers are expected to continue to decrease as new environmental controls force the closure of facilities not in compliance with environmental regulations and as larger regional landfills are adopted to take advantage of significant economies of scale. Trends in U.S. landfill capacity are controversial, with some experts claiming capacity has deceased, while others suggest that small landfills are simply being replaced by more efficient and larger-scale landfills. What is less controversial is that certain areas of the country do have problems with landfill capacity. As of 1991 the United States had about 12.5 years of landfill capacity remaining. However, 5 states had less than 5 years of remaining capacity and 22 states had less than 10 years.[5]

While landfill numbers and capacities are certainly of concern, the more challenging problems involve growing landfill costs and the inability to site landfills at virtually any cost. Nationally, landfill tipping fees are about $26.50 per ton, although tipping fees vary significantly from region to region. For example, tipping fees in the New England states approached $47 per ton in 1991, with Connecticut averaging $65 per ton. The mid-Atlantic states averaged about $46 per ton. At the other extreme are the Rocky Mountain states with an average of below $9 per ton and the Midwest averaging below $13 per ton (Glenn, 1992b). Most analysts project that landfill costs will rise in future years as recently enacted and more environmentally restrictive landfill rules are put in place. The U.S. Environmental Protection Agency (U.S. EPA) estimates that landfill costs under the new rule will be about $48 per ton (40 Code of Federal Regulations [CFR] Parts 257, 258).

Perhaps more problematic than landfill cost escalations are (1) the public opposition that communities and landfill operators face when attempting to site a facility and (2) the difficulties that communities often face when forming and operating regional compacts to build and manage the larger landfills that can take advantage of scale economies. Additional problems are presented by recent proposed legislation in the U.S. Congress to allow states to restrict the importation of MSW into their states.[6] States that have historically exported a portion of their garbage may soon have to manage their own wastes within their own state borders.

The most popular public alternatives to landfilling MSW, i.e., recycling and source reduction, also face uncertain futures. Recycling programs are currently on the rise in the United States, with total curbside programs having increased from about 1,050 programs in 1988 to more than 3,900 in 1991 (a 250 percent increase).[7] Composting programs for yard waste have also increased rapidly, and programs designed to compost the decomposable portion of MSW have been adopted in several communities. As a result, the percentage of MSW managed by recycling increased from 7.7 percent in 1975 to 14.9 percent in 1990. The percentage of municipal waste managed by composting went from 0 in 1975 to 2.1 in 1990. Source-reduction activities—i.e., measures to reduce MSW quantities through, for example, product redesign and packaging reduction—are also producing positive results, although those results are difficult to measure precisely. Many states have voluntary or mandatory goals of managing 25 to 50 percent or more of their MSW with one or more alternative management practices—i.e., recycling, composting, and source reduction.

Recycling efforts have been particularly ambitious and successful in some states, with three states (Minnesota, New Jersey, and Washington) claiming to have recycled more than 30 percent of their MSW in 1991. However, most of those states with recycling goals currently recycle 10 to 20 percent of their MSW; and many states recycle well under 10 percent of their MSW. At this point in time, the future of recycling and composting is quite uncertain, with many experts fearing that the 25 to 50 percent goals cannot be reached in the foreseeable future. Four particular problems arise. First, the cost of recycling programs, including the value of the collected materials, is proving to be quite high in some communities. The costs of collecting and processing materials for recycling are commonly in the $100 to $200 per ton range. Second, some markets for recycled products have been weak— e.g., recycled paper, glass, and more recently recycled plastics. Low and uncertain prices for recycled goods are forcing firms in the recycling business to proceed slowly. Third, there is increasing concern that recycling may not be as environmentally benign as once thought. Collection, storage, and the recycling processes themselves pose their own environmental risks that must be compared with the risks posed by alternative management options. Finally, there are questions about the percentage of the MSW stream that is amenable to recycling. While certain segments of the waste stream are definite candidates for recycling—e.g., newspaper, soda bottles, and milk jugs—there is technical and economic uncertainty about the extent to which recycling can be expanded. For example, can paper recycling be expanded to include the majority of paper products entering the waste stream? Can plastics recycling expand beyond the limited resins and product lines currently being targeted to a commingled plastics stream with numerous resins and product types?

If landfilling is becoming more limited because of costs and siting difficulties and, if, in fact, recycling, composting, and source reduction are limited by excessive costs and other problems, communities will be increasingly pushed toward incineration with heat recovery. Incineration, primarily without heat recovery, has been used as a means of managing waste for literally hundreds of years and as of 1960 was used to manage almost 31 percent of all U.S. MSW. However, the use of MSW as a fuel has occurred only recently. As of 1960 there was essentially no waste-to-energy (WTE) capacity in the United States, and by 1975 only 0.5 percent of MSW was burned to retrieve its heat value. The 1980s saw tremendous growth in WTE capacity as the percentage of MSW managed by WTE increased from 1.8 percent in 1980 to 15.2 percent in 1990 (U.S. EPA, 1992a). During the mid–1980s most analysts expected WTE to continue its growth well into the next century and projected that WTE would soon account for more than 50 percent of the waste stream. Backing up these projections were seemingly favorable relative costs and the fact that WTE was already being used in many European countries to manage more than 50 percent of their municipal waste streams (many, such as Switzerland and Sweden, with strong environmental legacies).

However, like landfilling, recycling, composting, and source reduction, waste-to-energy now faces a very uncertain future. In fact, recent WTE project cancellations suggest that the future of WTE is most difficult to predict of all MSW management options in the United States. A total of 248 WTE projects in various stages of planning were canceled between 1982 and 1990. Only 8 projects were scratched between 1982 and 1984, while 207 were abandoned between 1986 and 1990. To put these cancellations in perspective, consider that there were 140 operational WTE facilities in the United States in 1990. Further consider that the WTE capacity that was canceled between 1986 and 1990 (in excess of 114,000 tons per day) exceeded the total WTE capacity in 1990 (about 92,000 tons per day).[8]

These cancellations have been of concern to proponents of WTE, sent many communities "back to the drawing board" to select and develop new approaches to manage their MSW and raised questions about the future of WTE in the United States. Experts have revised their projections concerning WTE due to recent trends. For example, the U.S. EPA recently projected that WTE will account for less than 21 percent of all U.S. MSW in the year 2000, as compared to their 1990 projection, which put WTE at 26 percent of the waste stream in 2000 (U.S. EPA 1990b, 1992a).

Why have WTE projects been canceled and what, if anything, do these recent cancellations tell us about the future viability of WTE as a means of managing MSW in the United States? These questions are the primary targets of this study.

1.2 GENERAL APPROACH

Waste-to-energy in the United States is commonly known to face several significant barriers and uncertainties that may have contributed to recent project cancellations and that may suggest something about the long-run viability of incineration with heat recovery. Among these barriers are disagreements about potential environmental damages, legislative and regulatory uncertainties, the future cost and availability of alternative management methods, constraints and uncertainties about financing methods, questions about the reliability and applicability of existing technologies, and failures in local decision-making processes. There are, in fact, many papers and reports on these issues, referred to in this work, that have speculated on specific factors that have hindered the further adoption of WTE. Unfortunately, there has been very little work that has addressed these issues, especially socioeconomic factors, in a comprehensive and rigorous fashion. Information and data limitations have been particularly severe.

The approach used in this work was to first collect and assess all publicly available information and data on WTE in the United States and the various socioeconomic factors that may have played a role in recent project cancellations. Given that current information and data are better in some areas of concern than in others, a three-pronged approach was selected to utilize available information most effectively and cover the widest range of socioeconomic factors.

The first prong of our three-pronged approach is referred to as an "aggregate socioeconomic analysis." The basic question in this part of the work is whether communities that complete WTE projects differ significantly from communities that cancel projects with regard to state and local socioeconomic and other conditions. To some extent we also explore how communities that complete or plan a WTE facility differ from communities that have not yet actively considered WTE. Factors considered within this part of the work include per capita income, population density, metropolitan versus non-metropolitan areas, population age, education level, and type of industrial/commercial base. Also included within this work segment are the availability of alternative local management approaches (e.g., landfill and recycling), effects of state legislation, and local environmental conditions. This part of the work addresses these issues in the aggregate, or, in other words, relevant information was obtained for the entire population of WTE projects—both those that were completed and those that were canceled at some stage of the planning process.

The second part of this work focuses on financial issues. More specifically, it investigates whether altered financial conditions have played a major role in recent decisions to abandon WTE projects. This section looks in particular at recent sharp jumps in WTE capital costs, the effects of the Tax Reform Act of 1986, and the development and adoption of innovative financing methods that help to overcome the financial hurdles placed in the way of communities attempting to finance what may very well be their most expensive public-works project. As with the first part of this study, the financial section examines information from the entire population of WTE facilities, both built and planned.

The last part of our analysis takes a case-study approach to assess the degree to which the decision-making process itself contributes to the community's decision about WTE. The case-study approach also allows an investigation of issues that are not amenable to study at the aggregate level because of data or other limitations. Case studies were done at four sites. At two sites—Oakland County, Michigan, and Broward County, Florida—a WTE project was approved, and in the case of Broward County two WTE facilities are now operational. At the two other sites—Monmouth County, New Jersey, and Knox County, Tennessee—planned WTE facilities were abandoned. Questions of particular interest in the case studies include the sequence of decision events; the participation of different groups in different steps of the decision process; the degree of agreement at each decision step; the effects of mitigation and compensation at different stages of implementation; the effectiveness of different siting procedures; public attitudes about WTE technologies, costs, environmental impacts, and decision-making processes; and any difficulties that may arise when several governmental jurisdictions are forced to cooperate or form compacts to site a facility.

A note about the scope of this work is appropriate at this point. Although this study recognizes that WTE faces technology and environmental questions (which are discussed in brief in the following chapter), it is not the purpose of this study to assess these questions. The focus of this study is on socioeconomic factors that have had an impact on the selection and viability of WTE as a management option. Technology and environmental issues enter this analysis only to the extent that they alter actual or perceived socioeconomic conditions.

1.3 A PREVIEW OF FOLLOWING CHAPTERS

The following chapter gives an overview of the major issues that have made WTE such a controversial method to manage waste. In the first section a layman's perspective is given of the environmental issues associated with WTE. The environmental debate has been focused primarily on atmospheric emissions of heavy metals, furans, and dioxins; the disposal of ash; and concerns about the hazardous waste segment of the household waste stream. A lesser degree of concern has been raised about nitrogen oxide emissions. The second section reviews the legislative and regulatory uncertainties that face communities when making a decision about WTE. Of primary concern are recent amendments to the Clean Air Act of 1970 (CAA), the implementation of numerous state laws and regulations, and uncertainties about the future of the Public Utility Regulatory Policies Act of 1978 (PURPA) and the Resource Conservation and Recovery Act of 1980 (RCRA). Proposals to allow states to limit the importation of MSW into their states may also be important for some communities. The third section reviews the costs and availability of alternative management options—i.e., landfill, recycling, and composting. A brief discussion of financial uncertainties is followed by an overview of WTE technologies. The chapter concludes with a brief discussion of the barriers posed by the decision-making process itself.

Chapter 3 presents additional background on WTE in the United States. Topics include a history of WTE adoption; a description of the industry that designs, manufactures, and operates WTE facilities in the United States; a detailed discussion of the quantity and composition of MSW; and an assessment of current and future projected energy production from the combustion of municipal waste.

Chapter 4 presents the results of this study's aggregate socioeconomic analysis of WTE and recent project cancellations. Results of our financial analysis are presented in Chapter 5 and are followed by case-study methods and results in Chapter 6. The final chapter integrates the results of this study's three-pronged approach to assess the root causes of recent project cancellations. The final chapter also includes speculations about future trends and how those trends are likely to affect the long-run viability of WTE in the United States.

NOTES

1. See *Solid Waste Report*, 1992a.

2. For a broad overview of our municipal waste problems and an informative but witty discussion of common myths about garbage and its management, we recommend *Rubbish!* by William Rathje and Cullen Murphy. A more academic perspective on the problem is found in the Office of Technology Assessment's ex-

cellent 1989 book entitled *Facing America's Trash: What Next for Municipal Solid Waste?*

3. Estimates are derived from information in U.S. Environmental Protection Agency (1992a).

4. A detailed discussion of historical background and future generation of MSW is contained in Chapter 3.

5. See Glenn (1992b) for a detailed discussion of landfill numbers and capacities in the United States and in the various states.

6. At the time of this writing, only the Senate has passed such legislation. The House of Representatives is yet to vote on legislation similar to the Senate version.

7. Some argue that a distinction must be made between (1) recycling that includes the collection and reprocessing of materials into new products and (2) programs that collect recyclables but do not necessarily result in the production of new products. In some cases recyclable materials have been collected and then disposed of due to a lack of demand for those materials.

8. Statistics are derived from information given in several issues of Government Advisory Associates' *Resource Recovery Yearbook*.

Chapter 2

Why Is Waste-to-Energy So Controversial?

2.1 THE ISSUES

In the late 1980s, waste-to-energy projects became the target of intense public debate at the local, state, and national levels. A technology that had been seen by most technology experts to be a "safe" and "reliable" means of managing municipal waste was increasingly viewed by the public to hold unacceptable risks and uncertainties. Local groups were formed to challenge almost every WTE project in the planning phase. National environmental organizations provided support for local organizations and came out strongly against further adoption of WTE. Some environmental groups and members of the U.S. Congress even argued for a national moratorium on the construction of any new WTE facilities.

As a result, the WTE industry was placed increasingly on the defensive in arguing for specific projects and WTE in general. In addition, many local decision makers became very risk-averse toward WTE, as decisions about WTE projects were delayed or communities adopted more popular options, such as recycling and composting programs. Public confidence in WTE was eroded, and many WTE projects in the planning stages were abandoned.

Many issues have been at the heart of the debate about WTE. For example, are the environmental consequences of WTE severe, and how do those consequences compare to damages resulting from other approaches to waste management and other commonly accepted technologies? Will future legislation and regulations at the national and state levels alter the attractiveness of WTE? Should communities delay any decisions about WTE until pending environmental and financial rules are finalized? Will a facility built today be robust to future changes in rules regarding environmental emissions? Will alternative technologies—e.g., landfilling and recycling—be less costly during the life of the WTE facility? What percentage of the waste stream can those alternative technologies handle, and will public concerns about those alternatives limit their availabilities? How technically reliable are current WTE technologies? Is the technology evolving rapidly, and will any facility a community adopts today be archaic tomorrow? Will the community be assured of a market for the energy the facility produces? What price will that energy fetch, and will the facility's—and possibly community's—financial position be jeopardized if energy prices are below expectations or if unexpected financial problems arise? Is the credibility of current information about WTE so suspect and information so inadequate to make any decision about WTE too risky for a community that is possibly considering the most expensive project in its history? Is the decision process itself so filled with "potholes" and "booby traps" and so susceptible to conflicting information that WTE is essentially a non-starter?

These issues are but a subset of those facing communities when making decisions about WTE. Subsequent chapters of this work will assess these and other issues in terms of their potential contribution to recent project cancellations and the overall socioeconomic viability of WTE. However, before turning to those assessments, this chapter provides a brief overview of these key issues to help explain why WTE has become so controversial. The reader is also referred to other documents for more detailed assessments of these important concerns.

2.2 UNCERTAINTIES ABOUT POTENTIAL ENVIRONMENTAL AND HEALTH RISKS

Most individuals knowledgeable about WTE will agree that a primary obstacle facing the further adoption of WTE in the United States is public concern about the potential environmental and health consequences of waste incineration. These issues are numerous, complicated, and controversial; and while this chapter does not attempt to verify or refute the various arguments about potential health and environmental effects, the main arguments and concerns are summarized.

WTE health and environmental issues can be divided into three main categories: environmental and health risks associated with (1) atmospheric emissions; (2) ash management alternatives; and (3) alternative approaches to MSW management.

2.2.1 Atmospheric Emissions

Emissions from WTE facilities are a function of the composition of MSW, the process by which waste is burned, and the type of air pollution control equipment used. Some familiar materials in the waste stream, such as commonly used papers and plastics, may be responsible for the creation of problem emissions, such as furans and dioxins, if the waste is burned improperly. Some emissions may result when incineration releases materials such as heavy metals, which are contained in batteries or used in small quantities as additives in commonly used household items. Other emissions may result when household hazardous wastes—which make up about 1 percent of all MSW by weight—are burned without proper controls.[1]

Gaseous emissions from MSW incineration can be grouped into three main categories—emissions generally considered to be carcinogenic, those generally considered non-carcinogenic, and acidic gases. Although technologies exist to capture a large percentage of each emission—discussed further in Section 2.5.4—there is general agreement that some of these potentially damaging pollutants will escape, particularly if good combustion practices are not used, and can pose environmental and health consequences. There is disagreement, however, about the severity of those risks. Some authors suggest that while the environmental and health effects of WTE are small in relative terms, WTE should be adopted only when alternative waste-management approaches have been fully utilized.[2] Most authors argue, however, that the health and environmental risks associated with WTE are minimal if available technologies are adopted and operated correctly.[3]

Trace emissions from WTE that are commonly considered carcinogenic include furans, dioxins, and several metals—e.g., arsenic, cadmium, and chromium. Non-carcinogenic emissions include lead, mercury, particulates, sulfur dioxide, and nitrogen oxides. Acidic gases, which can result from emissions of, for example, hydrochloric acid and hydrogen fluoride, have not been the target of great debate.

The extent of atmospheric emissions from current WTE technologies and their impacts on the environment and human health are primarily a matter of perspective. For example, Kiser and Sussman (1991) conclude with respect to mercury emissions that WTE facilities "operating in the U.S. contribute less than one percent of the total mercury being released by man-made sources, resulting in health risks to the most exposed individual that are 10 to 100 times less than established regulatory threshold" (p. 41). They go on to conclude that even when scheduled WTE capacity is considered, WTE will "contribute less than one-half of a percent of total mercury emissions being released in the environment by man-made sources" (p. 44). The authors further point out that mercury in the waste stream declined by 33 percent between 1984 and 1989 due to source reduction and materials substitution, and by the mid–1990s quantities of mercury in the waste stream will decrease by another 65 percent. For a description of the atmospheric emissions from all forms of solid waste management, see Appendix A.

In another recent study (Macoskey, 1992), metals emissions from a typical 500 tons per day (tpd), mass-burn WTE facility were compared to emissions from a 250 megawatt, pulverized-coal power plant. That study found that for four carcinogenic metals—arsenic, beryllium, cadmium, and chromium—emissions from the WTE facility were an order of magnitude lower than the emissions from the coal plant in the worst-case human health risk. The study further noted that if the best available control technology is used, carcinogenic and non-carcinogenic risks from metals emissions would be several orders of magnitude below U.S. EPA acceptable risk levels.

The United States Conference of Mayors (1990) concluded "that given present composition of the MSW, it is confidently expected that the risks associated with metals in the effluents can be kept to levels below regulatory concern when proper design, maintenance, and operation of facilities (inclusive of residue management) is ensured" (p. 3). The report continues, however, that

possible exceptions thought to warrant attention were mercury and hexavalent chromium.... MSW incinerators can be a major source for the report of mercury to the environment. Although some data provides evidence that efficient removal of mercury in emissions has been realized in some instances, routine control of mercury emissions from MSW incinerators does not appear to be satisfactorily established (p. 3).

Concern has recently been expressed about the emissions of nitrogen oxides, which can lead to the formation of photochemical oxidants, such as ozone. Ozone can adversely affect human health, vegetation, and materials exposed to the environment. Although WTE is known to result in emissions of nitrogen oxides, most evidence suggests those emissions are minor when compared to other sources of that pollutant. For example, Clarke (1989) reports that only 0.4 percent of nitrogen oxide emissions come from solid waste incineration—i.e., 0.1 million tons per year. Transportation and fuel consumption (primarily for electricity generation) account for an estimated 9.3 and 11.3 million tons, respectively. Further, if WTE is viewed on the basis of emissions per unit of electricity generated, WTE produces lower emissions than coal-fired plants and equal to or slightly higher than natural gas or some oil-fired systems. Clarke reports that WTE produces between 0.27 and 0.57 pounds of nitrogen oxide per million Btus of electricity produced (lb/MBtu), whereas coal-fired plants produce between 0.50 and 0.80 lb/MBtu, natural gas facilities between 0.10 and 0.20 lb/MBtu, and residual oil between 0.20 and 0.40 lb/MBtu.

Serious concern has been raised about emissions of furans and dioxins, which are widely considered to be highly carcinogenic.[4] Their potential linkage with the incineration of plastics—in particular polyvinyl chlorides (PVCs) that are often used in packaging—has been the subject of particular public debate. However, the majority of scientific reports written on the subject reject the notion that plastics make a significant contribution to the production of furans and dioxins and reject the assertion that WTE contributes a large percentage of all furans and dioxins.[5] For example, Travis and Hattemer-Frey (1989) report that while combustion sources *in general* (including steel mills, copper smelting plants, motor vehicles, pulp and paper mills, and MSW incinerators) are major sources of PCDD/ PCDF (dioxin/furan) input in the environment ... environmental concentrations of PCDDs and PCDFs around operating MSW incinerators are not substantially elevated ... and ... 99 percent of human exposure to PCDDs and PCDFs is from background contamination, even for individuals living near a modern MSW incinerator (p. 91).

Others have tried to place environmental and health risks that result from MSW incineration in relation to common everyday activities. For example, *Waste Age* (November 1989) reports that the risk of contracting cancer from eating one peanut butter sandwich per month for 15 years is about 500 times greater than the risk of contracting cancer from the emissions of a particular WTE facility in Pennsylvania. In another article, Jones (1987) compares the estimated health risks from WTE facilities to several common activities and concludes that the risks associated with furans and dioxins are lower than, for example, having one chest X ray, drinking one diet soda per week for five years, or being exposed to the radiation resulting from traveling 50,000 miles by jet aircraft. The United States Conference of Mayors (1990) concluded that "the incineration of MSW in the United States should never provide more than 0.5 percent of all *combined* air emissions" (p. 2).

Although the majority of scientific evidence suggests that atmospheric emissions from WTE are not severe when compared to other commonly accepted health and environmental risks, some environmental groups warn that WTE can pose problems if technology is not used properly. Studies have shown, for example, that furan and dioxin production can increase when incineration temperatures are not maintained at design specifications. Concern was also raised during the 1980s that some U.S. WTE operators may not be trained properly to monitor and minimize emission levels (United States Conference of Mayors, 1990). Others warn that WTE is not appropriate for the entire municipal waste stream. For example, Denison and Silbergeld (1988) argue that "incineration is ill-suited to manage the municipal waste stream in its entirety.... Targeted removal of critical items ... can increase the safety and utility of incineration for the remainder of the waste stream" (pp. 343, 352). Removal of products that contain heavy metals, such as batteries, is particularly important.

2.2.2 Ash Disposal

Another controversial environmental issue is ash disposal. MSW incineration is usually successful in reducing the volume of waste by 80 to 90 percent, with the remaining ash typically going to a landfill. The primary controversy is over what type of landfill should be used for ash disposal.

About 47 percent of incinerator ash is currently sent to sanitary landfills along with other municipal waste, and the remaining 53 percent is sent to specially designed monofills that only accept ash (Government Advisory Associates, 1991). Also at issue is whether incinerator ash should be classified as a hazardous waste and be landfilled at sites with even more stringent standards and designs—and, of course, much higher disposal costs than conventional municipal landfills.

The modern WTE facility has a variety of air pollution control devices to collect emissions before they reach the atmosphere. A recent study found that the most common device is an electrostatic precipitator that removes most particulate matter (Williams, 1991). In excess of 80 percent of facilities also have scrubbers and/or fabric filters to control other emissions, and about half of all facilities have continuous emissions monitoring to insure that emissions do not exceed allowable levels.[6] Unfortunately, the success of air-control technologies has created an ash with a higher concentration of metals. Fly ash—or the ash captured from stack gases—makes up about 10 percent of all ash and commonly contains high concentrations of heavy metals. Trace amounts of furans and dioxins may also be contained in the fly-ash component. Fly ash and the remaining bottom ash commonly are mixed together before disposal.

Although the U.S. EPA recently ruled that incinerator ash is non-hazardous (see next section), the environmental consequences of ash disposal remain controversial. In most cases a mixture of fly ash and bottom ash passes the EPA's EP (extraction procedure) test for toxicity, while fly ash alone often fails (U.S. Conference of Mayors, 1990).[7] A primary issue is, therefore, whether operators should be allowed to mix and co-dispose fly and bottom ash. To avoid potential environmental damages, some suggest that fly ash should be collected separately and treated as a hazardous waste. Others questioned the validity of the EP test used to measure toxicity, which deals primarily with the leachability of metals and selected organic compounds. In some cases test results on identical samples have shown poor reproducibility.[8] U.S. EPA's current toxicity test, the TCLP (toxic characteristic leaching procedure), in recent field applications has shown that "levels of heavy metals present in MWC [municipal waste combustor] ash leachate from monofills are close to the significantly more restrictive drinking water standards and far lower than the TCLP toxicity criteria" (Integrated Waste Services Association, 1992a). Nonetheless, WTE industry representatives assert that both toxicity tests "greatly exaggerate the potential for heavy metals leaching from MWC ash" (Integrated Waste Services Association, 1992b).

Controversy also exists about using ash as a resource in the production of various products. Ash has been mentioned and/or used as a resource in, for example, the production of roadbase materials, asphalt, cover for landfills, offshore reefs, erosion control, and concrete-like blocks. In fact, several

European countries have used ash as a resource for many years. While the technical obstacles to using ash in these and other products are being overcome, some environmentalists argue that these uses are unacceptable. In particular, they assert that once ash is out of a controlled environment the heavy metals and other contaminants may eventually be found in unacceptable uses and locations. From their perspective, ash disposal is less environmentally threatening than the use of ash as a resource.

Surveys show that the public shares in the concern about ash disposal. A recent poll by the National Solid Wastes Management Association found that about half of all respondents had a concern that incinerator ash poses an environmental threat.[9]

Despite scientists' general finding that atmospheric emissions from WTE pose relatively minor health and environmental risks, public perceptions have often differed. Although public surveys by the National Solid Wastes Management Association and others show that the public is less worried about air emissions from incinerators today than it was a few years ago, many individuals view those emissions as an environmental threat. To some extent, this discrepancy can be explained by a lack of information and the public's perception of risk. Although confidence in WTE technologies can increase with experience, risks—of this and other solid waste management alternatives—can never be reduced to zero. The controversy is increased by "qualifying" statements in reports that are generally supportive of WTE. For example, the United States Conference of Mayors (1990) reports that

The major finding of these evaluations is the conclusion that inclusive of ash residue management, properly designed, operated, and maintained MSW incineration facilities equipped with modern pollution control devices are confidently expected to yield risks from all pathways which can be held below levels normally of regulatory concern in the United States for protection of human health (p. 2). Based upon the evaluations of this comprehensive review by leading experts, MSW incineration could easily serve as a key foundation (important component) for environmentally sound MSW management (p. 11).

The report states further that "Unless these technologies are properly maintained and operated, incineration of MSW may, in some cases, present unacceptable high risks to humans and/or the environment" (p. 8). They further conclude that "Diligence will be necessary to ensure that incineration of MSW presents risks normally below those of regulatory concern. . . ." (p. 10). Possibly most important in the controversy about health and environmental risks are (1) a fundamental mistrust of information about WTE, no matter the source, and (2) a concern that health and environmental risks, however small, will be borne inequitably.

2.2.3 Environmental and Health Risks of Alternative Management Technologies

When a community assesses the potential environmental and health consequences of WTE, it cannot do so in isolation. If WTE is not selected, another technology or technologies—e.g., landfilling, recycling, composting, and source reduction—must be selected, and the environmental and health risks associated with the alternative(s) must be compared to the risks associated with WTE. (This assumes, of course, that the community does not simply export its waste to another state or community, an option that includes its own uncertainties. See next section.)

While a detailed discussion of the health and environmental consequences of these alternatives is beyond the scope of this chapter, a couple of general observations are warranted. First, there is general agreement that the health and environmental risks associated with landfills are becoming less severe as new and more restrictive construction and operation rules are put into effect. The adoption of new liner systems, better groundwater monitoring systems, and increased knowledge about where landfills can be sited with minimal environmental risks should make landfilling more reliable and less risky.

Second, while the public generally prefers composting and recycling to landfilling and incineration on environmental grounds, the scientific evidence in support of that argument is in some cases lacking. For example, a recent study by the New Jersey State Advisory Council on Solid Waste Management (1992) found that composting may not be as safe as once thought because the compost often contains heavy metals and toxic materials. Raloff (1993) reports that "no proven means exists for reliably removing all hazardous materials from clean compostables once they have been mixed" (p. 56). Raloff also reports that contaminants such as asbestos can range from a trace to as high as 1 percent of compost material. To some extent, composting is similar to incineration in that the process increases the degree to which heavy metals and toxics are "bio-available" (Raloff, 1993).

In another recent study by Chilton and Lis (1992), the environmental consequences of recycling are questioned. They report that recycling processes, such as those that include de-inking and bleaching, produce pollutants and consume energy and other materials. In a review of the environmental consequences of plastics recycling, Curlee (1986) concludes that air and solid waste pollutants can occur and in some cases have limited the viability of recycling processes. Kreith (1992b) concludes that

Recycling may not be as beneficial and environmentally benign as the public reaction suggests. There is air and water pollution from the pick-up and transportation of the waste material to a storage site, from sorting and shipping the material to a manufacturer who can use it, and during the final manufacturing process that converts the material to another useful product (p. 2).

Visalli (1989) compared the similarities of environmental impacts from the four principal methods of managing MSW—landfilling, WTE, composting, and recycling. Visalli concluded that "It should be clear that all methods of processing solid waste result in process emissions and effluents, and in ash or sludge residues, that have potentially hazardous compounds. In many cases, the compounds are quite similar. There are, of course, potential dissimilarities.... Nonetheless, all the processes have the potential to impact public health and the environment adversely" (p. 12). Visalli goes on to conclude that "The lack of this knowledge, and the inability to compare the risks associated with the various methods of managing solid waste, is a serious problem. Local decisions regarding integrated waste management systems are being hindered or influenced by a biased perception of the environmental impacts from the four major methods of managing solid waste" (p. 14).

Numerous polls have shown that the vast majority of the public prefers recycling and composting, and most people state that they are willing to pay more for recycling than for landfilling or incineration. A Gallup Poll in 1989 found that 72 percent of those who recycled at that time did so because of environmental concerns. A more recent survey found that 86 percent of respondents strongly agree or somewhat agree that a community should first establish a strong recycling program before thinking about WTE.[10] While few would argue with the widely held belief that recycling and composting programs offer potential environmental and health benefits, it is interesting that recycling and composting have not been subjected to the scientific scrutiny given to landfilling and, in particular, waste-to-energy.

2.3 LEGISLATIVE AND REGULATORY UNCERTAINTIES

Any community that is considering a WTE project must recognize that many of the benefits as well as the risks of WTE are derived from federal and state legislation and regulations. Although regulations have been a concern for waste managers for decades, in recent years, the uncertainties have increased enormously. Not only do regulations now touch on more aspects of a WTE project—e.g., environmental controls, the price of energy produced, financing options, and the mandated use of particular technologies or approaches—the sources of those regulations are now themselves uncertain. In the past decade, in particular, there has been a marked shift toward more state and federal control of municipal waste regulations and less control by local governments. Local governments are now presented with a choice of options to manage their MSW; however, each option carries its own regulatory uncertainties, which are a function of interpretations of current regulations as well as the promise that new legislation and regulations will soon be put in place to "muddy the waters" even more.

As an aside, the move to more state and federal control of MSW regulation is warranted in many respects. Five arguments are particularly relevant. First, any environmental or health risks associated with MSW management are likely to cut across local jurisdictions, which suggests a need at the state and/or federal levels to internalize or otherwise respond to those environmental externalities. Second, if complicated and costly regulations need to be developed or if government assistance is needed to respond to environmental or technology problems, needless duplication can be avoided if the state and/or federal governments take responsibility. Third, widely varying rules and approaches to managing MSW from county to county (and, in some cases, from state to state) can impose large costs on suppliers (and ultimately consumers) of goods who must respond to numerous rules about, for example, packaging. A set of consistent regional and, preferably, national rules concerning product design and acceptability can lead to significant cost reductions for producers and price reductions for consumers of household goods that eventually enter the municipal waste stream. Fourth, the quantity, quality, and, at least in theory, credibility of information about MSW and management options can be improved by more state and federal involvement. As management options multiply and technology, environmental, and financial questions become more complex, federal and state governments must be called upon increasingly to provide information and decision methodologies. Recent calls for an effective and credible clearinghouse for information on MSW management are a reaction to this need. Finally, as waste facilities and programs become larger and cross state boundaries, the federal government must implement and enforce rules of trade as part of its oversight of interstate commerce.[11] The current debate over allowing state restrictions on interstate shipments of MSW is a case where federal involvement will be required to, at a minimum, referee battles among the various states.

Despite the rationality of increased state and federal involvement, solid waste management will remain the purview of local governments for the delivery of services. The local decision maker must, however, acknowledge and adjust to the fact that the rules of the game are increasingly out of his or her control. The following subsections present an overview of recent legislative and regulatory actions in the areas of environmental and health controls, financial initiatives, and other measures such as stated goals and preferences for particular management approaches. While some risks to the community have been lessened by recent actions, there are a host of issues yet to be decided that will greatly influence the overall viability of WTE and other MSW management options.

2.3.1 Environmental and Health Regulations

At the federal level there are two main pieces of legislation that mandate regulations concerning WTE atmospheric emissions and ash management—the Clean Air Act of 1970 (CAA) and the Resource Conservation and Recovery Act of 1980 (RCRA). In December 1989 the U.S. EPA issued proposed rules for MWCs in response to the original CAA. Those rules were finalized in February 1991.[12] For example, the rules, commonly referred to as the New Source Performance Standards (NSPS), mandated that new WTE facilities (i.e., where construction began after December 1989) with capacities of more than 250 tons of MSW per day must reduce emissions of furans, dioxins, and heavy metals (with the exception of mercury) by more than 99 percent, and sulfur dioxide and hydrogen chloride by 90 to 95 percent. In addition, organic emissions must be reduced by 95 percent, and acid-gas emissions by about 94 percent. These percentages are calculated in relation to uncontrolled emissions. The rules also require reductions in nitrogen-oxide emissions of about 45 percent and require continuous monitoring of several emissions. In terms of cost impacts, the U.S. EPA estimates that the annualized cost per unit of MSW combusted will be about $11 per ton. Cost increases for the typical plant are estimated to range from $10 to $19 per ton of MSW combusted. Although tipping fees are often not reflective of actual cost, Government Advisory Associates (1991) estimates that the average tipping fee for all existing U.S. WTE facilities in 1990 was $45.34 per ton, with a range of $3 to $270 per ton.

The Clean Air Act Amendments (CAAA), which became law on November 15, 1990, require that the U.S. EPA revise its recent rules on air emissions. The new guidelines must apply to all size categories of municipal waste combustors and reflect Maximum Achievable Control Technology (MACT), which is even more restrictive than the Best Demonstrated Technology (BDT) standards used by the U.S. EPA in its 1991 rule. For new MWCs, MACT can be no less stringent than the best performing similar units within that category. For existing facilities, MACT can be no less stringent than the best performing 12 percent of existing sources within that category.

The amendments also require that the U.S. EPA issue limitations for emissions of lead, cadmium, mercury, and dioxins. In addition, the amendments require operator training and certification for all WTE operators. Although the CAAA mandate that the U.S. EPA propose standards for new and existing units with capacities in excess of 250 tons per day by November 15, 1991, and units with capacities below 250 tons per day by November 1992, it is unlikely that any new rules will be proposed before the end of 1993. The additional costs of meeting these more restrictive environmental controls are uncertain at this time.

The Resource Conservation and Recovery Act (RCRA) is the main piece of federal legislation dealing with landfill disposal. Subtitle D of RCRA deals with non-hazardous waste and Subtitle C deals primarily with hazardous waste disposal. As mentioned in the previous subsection, there is much controversy about the toxicity of incinerator ash and whether ash should be classified as a hazardous waste under Subtitle C of RCRA, a non-hazardous waste under Subtitle D of RCRA, or as a special waste. Incinerator ash currently falls under Subtitle D as a "special waste," which requires special handling regardless of the test results concerning toxicity. (See previous subsection.) Prior to September 1992 the U.S. EPA had not promulgated any specific rules on how ash is to be managed. As a short-term measure, Congress included a provision in the 1990 Clean Air Act Amendments to exempt ash from regulation as a hazardous waste for two years, with the expectation that a final decision about ash management would be included in a reauthorization of RCRA. Unfortunately, during the past three sessions of Congress, RCRA reauthorization has fallen into a political wasteland, and it is uncertain when a final federal decision about ash management will be made.

In the absence of sufficient federal guidance on ash disposal, states have taken the lead in developing requirements and rules. Williams (1991) reports that

Michigan, for example, has legislated incinerator ash as a "special" waste that must be disposed of in dedicated landfills, while New York and Massachusetts regulate waste-to-energy ash as a "special" waste. In Pennsylvania, New Jersey and Rhode Island, ash is tested to determine appropriate disposal, and still other states are requiring testing of ash to establish a database on the effects of recycling, rather than to determine disposal (p. 252).

In May 1992 Minnesota banned the disposal of ash in municipal landfills and required specially lined monofills with the specific type of liner (five separate liner requirements are mentioned) depending on measured pollution levels of incoming ash.[13] While many states require special handling of ash, the most common practice is to landfill ash in specially designed monofills in RCRA Subtitle D landfills. Varying regulations and perceptions about ash from state to state have led to many court challenges with varying outcomes.

A decision about ash disposal at the federal level is of no small consequence to current WTE operators or to any community contemplating a WTE project. For every 1 ton of MSW combusted, about 0.25 tons of ash is produced. And for those states that currently do not require special handling and disposal of ash, disposal costs could go up by an order of magnitude if ash is classified as a hazardous waste under Subtitle C of RCRA. For example, the city of Chicago recently reported in court documents that if ash is judged to be hazardous, its cost of ash disposal would escalate from $23 to $123 per ton.[14]

The U.S. EPA's position on ash management has been clarified greatly by a September 18, 1992, memo to all U.S. EPA regional administrators from the former U.S. EPA administrator William Reilly. In that memo Reilly states that incinerator ash is excluded from regulation as a hazardous waste pursuant to Section 3001(i) of RCRA. As a result of Reilly's memo, the current federal position is that ash can be disposed of in MSW landfills along with non-combusted MSW. This position can, of course, be changed by the current U.S. EPA administrator or by Congress when it finally considers ash management as part of RCRA reauthorization or as part of some other measure.

Further complicating the issue is the Supreme Court's impending decision to review a U.S. appeals court decision concerning a suit brought by the Environmental Defense Fund (EDF). In that suit, EDF filed suit against the city of Chicago and alleged that Chicago's incinerator violated RCRA because its ash was not managed as a hazardous waste. While a federal district court rejected the EDF argument, a U.S. appeals court reversed the decision and the Supreme Court was asked to consider the case. The high court instructed the 7th Circuit Court to reconsider the case in light of the U.S. EPA's September 1992 guidance on incinerator ash management. However, the 7th Circuit Court in January 1993 reaffirmed its November 1991 ruling that ash is subject to hazardous waste regulations. The issue will now return to the Supreme Court for final disposition.

2.3.2 Regulations that Directly Influence Financial Viability

While RCRA and CAA address environmental questions and thus indirectly influence the cost of WTE projects, other federal legislation influences the economic viability of WTE more directly. Of particular importance are the Public Utility Regulatory Policies Act (PURPA) of 1978 and the Tax Reform Act of 1986 (TRA86).

One of the primary purposes of PURPA is to promote the development of renewable resources of energy production by providing economic incentives. WTE facilities are eligible for certification as qualifying facilities under PURPA if the facility's size does not exceed 80 megawatts (MW) of electricity-generating capacity. (Note that most existing WTE facilities produce electricity and all facilities in the planning and construction will produce electricity solely or co-generate electricity with steam.) If a WTE facility qualifies under PURPA, the local utility *must* purchase electricity generated by the facility at a price equal to the "avoided cost" of the utility.

There is little doubt that PURPA has been instrumental in promoting WTE and other renewable-energy technologies. However, there is also little doubt that PURPA and its implementation have been a source of uncertainty for communities considering a WTE facility. This uncertainty arises from two sources. First, and the lesser of the two, is uncertainty about the continuation of the 80 MW power cap. The U.S. Department of Energy and other organizations have encouraged that this cap be lifted to remove barriers to larger and possibly more efficient WTE projects (U.S. DOE, 1991b). The removal of these caps is important for large facilities (greater than 80 MW) since electricity sales generate about one-third of a typical WTE facility's revenues (Kiser, 1991a).

The second and more important uncertainty has to do with the price utilities are required to pay WTE operators. "Avoided cost" as defined by the Federal Energy Regulatory Commission has two components—energy and capacity. The energy component reflects the cost of fuel the utility would otherwise have to purchase if it were not obtaining power from the WTE facility. The capacity component is more complicated, but basically reflects the cost of capacity requirements that the utility would have to purchase in the absence of power from the WTE facility. For the WTE facility to obtain a capacity component to its electricity price, it must be shown that the purchasing utility will need to add additional generating capacity during the life of the WTE facility. If the need for this additional generating capacity cannot be demonstrated, the WTE facility will receive a payment based solely on the avoided cost of energy. In some cases, WTE projects have ended up receiving a much lower price for their electricity than the developers believed most likely at each project's inception. Government Advisory Associates (1991) reports that WTE facilities received an average 5.59 cents per kilowatt hour (kWh) in 1990, with a range of 1.49 to 12.70 cents per kWh. Note that electricity prices vary significantly by region, with the Northeast being highest at 6.87 cents per kWh and the South being lowest at 3.49 cents per kWh.[15] A further complication with PURPA has to do with its requirement for contract durations. Long-term contracts are not required. The contract's length results from the negotiation process. Thus, PURPA "opens the door" for negotiations but does not ensure a particular electricity price over a long period of time.

Acknowledging electricity-pricing uncertainties, several states have established additional economic incentives for WTE facilities. For example, Illinois and Connecticut require the electricity rate to be equal to the average price of electricity paid by the units of government that benefit from the WTE facility. New Jersey requires rates based on full avoided cost. Oklahoma adds 1.5 cents per kWh to the utility's avoided cost in recognition of a preference for WTE. In addition, other non-price economic incentives have also been put in place. For example, Michigan has mandated that a certain quantity of its power be purchased from WTE facilities. Some states, such as Maine, force utilities to give PURPA facilities preferential treatment when making decisions about capacity additions.[16] Of course, what states give in terms of preferences for WTE facilities can also be taken away. To the extent that state incentives are retractable, WTE projects will face financial risks.

The Tax Reform Act of 1986 (TRA86) is discussed in detail in Chapter 5 of this work. WTE facilities were influenced primarily by the act's restrictions on the local government's ability to use tax-exempt financing for WTE facilities. Essentially, TRA86 made it more difficult to finance a WTE facility with tax-exempts if the private sector is in any way involved with the facility. Given that many facilities are owned, constructed, and/or operated by a private concern, tax-exempt financing is no longer possible for many projects. The restrictions on tax-exempts, of course, lead to higher financing costs, which result in higher facility costs.[17]

2.3.3 Other Regulatory Uncertainties

There are numerous other federal and state initiatives that may have a significant impact on the future viability of WTE. Those initiatives may make minor changes in the "playing field" in terms of WTE's competitiveness with other management options, or changes may be more severe. For example, the U.S. EPA included a provision in the draft New Source Performance Standards (NSPS) for municipal waste incinerators that would have required WTE facilities to separate at least 25 percent of all incoming waste for recycling. Although generally supported by environmentalists as an essential "shot-in-the-arm" for the fledgling recycling industry, the WTE industry was not in favor of the requirements. About 80 percent of existing WTE facilities recover ferrous metals and 25 percent collect aluminum. In addition, about 80 percent of all planned facilities are located in communities that have active recycling programs (Kiser, 1991b). Opponents to the 25 percent rule argued that recycling was already taking place, the 25 percent rule was an arbitrary number, and the rule would place an undue financial burden on many existing and planned facilities. With the encouragement of Vice President Quayle's Council on Economic Competitiveness, the U.S. EPA reversed its 25 percent recycling requirement before the final rule was published.

Other successful and unsuccessful attempts have been made to promote recycling. For example, numerous bills have been introduced in Congress to require, for example, that selected products contain a minimum recycled content or to require industries that manufacture selected goods to insure that a certain percentage of the industry's output is recycled. In fact, minimum content provisions and recycle credit systems have been included in various drafts of a reauthorized RCRA. Recycle credits would be given to companies that recover a portion of the waste they generate. Firms that do not meet their minimum recycle level would be forced to purchase credits from companies that receive excess credits as the result of exceeding their requirements. Market forces would determine the price at which credits would be traded.

Little has been done at the federal level to directly stimulate additional recycling. However, there are some exceptions. For example, the U.S. EPA has issued rules that give preference to selected recycled goods when the federal government makes procurement decisions. Other measures have been adopted by federal departments and agencies to promote recycling in one form or another.

While there remains great uncertainty about the federal government's future promotion or neutrality on recycling, there is little doubt that state governments are moving to promote recycling in various forms. The National Solid Wastes Management Association (NSWMA, 1991) reports that a total of 140 laws were passed in 38 states in 1990 to promote recycling. In fact, only 2 states did not pass a law dealing with recycling in either 1989 or 1990. In several states minimum content laws for newsprint are now in effect and have promoted the newsprint recycling market. Numerous states have also implemented voluntary or mandatory recycling and source-reduction goals of 25 to 50 percent.

Other potential changes in the "playing field" may result from, for example, federal approval of a state's right to restrict importation of MSW from other states for disposal. At the time of this writing, Congress is moving in the direction of allowing states such rights. Past moves by some states to restrict garbage importation have been set aside by federal courts on the grounds that such restrictions violate interstate commerce provisions of the U.S. Constitution. While the implications of allowing MSW import restrictions for WTE are not totally clear, it is likely that some populous northeastern states, which now export a significant portion of their MSW to landfills in other states, will be more inclined to adopt WTE.[18]

Other legislative moves are a direct threat to WTE. For example, the state of Rhode Island implemented legislation in July 1992 that bans WTE facilities. The state ban—the first of its kind in the United States—is made much more controversial by the fact that the Rhode Island Solid Waste Management Corporation (RISWMC) has been working for more than a decade on a comprehensive approach to waste management, which was to include at least two WTE facilities. In fact, agreements between the RISWMC and Ogden Projects, Inc., had resulted in plans to locate two WTE facilities—one in North Kingstown and another in Johnston. Both were in the advanced stages of planning at the time the ban was issued. To make matters worse, Rhode Island has only one major landfill, and the state has less than two years of licensed landfill capacity remaining. If built, the two WTE facilities would have managed about half of the state's total solid waste stream. In addition to banning WTE, the recent legislation calls for a 70 percent recycling goal, which far exceeds their current or likely future recycling level.

Without phenomenal success with their recycling programs, significant landfill expansion, and/or the construction of one or more WTE facilities, Rhode Island may be forced to export a large percentage of its waste stream in the near future—an ironic situation since Rhode Island has been the lone state to successfully ban the importation of solid waste. (They got around the interstate commerce restrictions because the state's only large landfill is owned by the state and was declared a public resource in a court case.)

In September 1992 Governor Sundlum formed a 12-person commission to study and make recommendations on the future of solid waste management in his state. The commission could recommend that the ban be reversed or other measures could be prescribed. In response to the ban, Ogden filed a suit in November 1992 against Rhode Island for damages. Ogden claimed damages of more than $50 million and asked the U.S. District Court to overturn the recent legislation banning WTE. The Rhode Island situation is crucial for the future of WTE in the United States. If Rhode Island is successful in maintaining its ban on WTE—i.e., politically, in the courts, and in terms of managing their solid waste—other states may follow.

At the federal level, a bill was introduced in January 1993 by representative towns of New York to set a moratorium on the construction or expansion of WTE facilities until 2000. The proposed bill would also classify incinerator ash as a hazardous waste and require it to be disposed of in double-lined monofills. The utilization of ash for any purpose would be prohibited.

A community contemplating a WTE facility must consider that the "playing field" will probably shift either in favor of or against WTE during the life of its facility. It must assess the financial and other risks imposed by potential shifts away from WTE and ultimately decide on how risk averse it wants to be when making a decision about a waste technology that may have its future costs and benefits altered greatly by legislative and regulatory initiatives that are often out of the local government's control.

2.4 UNCERTAINTIES ABOUT THE FUTURE OF ALTERNATIVES TO WTE

The controversy over WTE extends beyond uncertainties about potential environmental damages and risks posed by ever-changing regulations. There is also uncertainty about what alternatives to WTE will cost in future years and how much of the waste stream those alternatives can realistically be counted on to manage. More specifically, how much will landfill cost in relation to WTE? Will there be sufficient landfill capacity, no matter the cost? How much of the waste stream realistically can be recycled and composted and how much will recycling and composting cost as compared to landfilling and WTE?

Although tipping fees do not reflect the cost of operations in many cases, it is noteworthy that the average tipping fee for existing and planned U.S. WTE facilities was $50.99 per ton in 1990. Existing facilities averaged $45.34 per ton, while planned facilities averaged $64.14 per ton. On a regional basis, tipping fees for WTE were highest in the Northeast at $62.34 per ton and lowest in the South at $37.24 per ton (Government Advisory Associates, 1991). To add further perspective, consider that the cost of MSW management is a growing but relatively small portion of most municipal budgets. A survey by the Office of Technology Assessment (1989) found that MSW budgets average only about 5 percent of total municipal budgets, with a range of 0.1 to 19.2 percent. Information from the Bureau of the Census places MSW expenditures at less than 10 percent of municipal budgets. On a per capita basis, MSW expenditures average about $60 and range between $6 and $130. The average family spends only about 1 percent of its total income on MSW management.

Despite the relatively low contribution of MSW management to municipal budgets, concern has been raised about the risks associated with financing capital-intensive projects, such as WTE facilities. The average planned WTE facility had capital costs of $126.1 million in 1990, up from $90.6 million in 1988 (in 1982 dollars). Existing facilities had capital costs of only $53.8 million in 1990, up from $34.7 million in 1988 (Government Advisory Associates, 1988 and 1990). For many communities, a WTE project is the largest capital investment their local governments have ever undertaken. Local financing of a large WTE facility can potentially alter a community's credit rating, which not only raises the interest cost for the WTE project but also hinders the community's ability to borrow for future purposes unrelated to MSW management.[19] The financial risks associated with local financing of WTE facilities are explored in detail in Chapter 5 of this work.

2.4.1 Landfilling

A great deal has been written in recent years about reductions in landfill numbers and, to a lesser extent, reductions in landfill capacities. Glenn (1992b) reports that the number of U.S. landfills decreased from just under 8,000 in 1988 to only 5,812 by the end of 1991, a 27 percent reduction; and the U.S. EPA projects that only 4,000 facilities will be operational by the end of 1992 (Repa and Sheets, 1992). While these closures seem ominous, they are but a continuation of a trend that dates back to the 1970s. For example, Repa and Sheets report that during the 1970s, 70 percent of all U.S. landfills (some 14,000 facilities) closed. Further, the lower number of landfills does not mean necessarily that capacity has dropped, because smaller landfills are often replaced by larger and more efficient facilities. In fact, the U.S. EPA reports that the percentage of MSW managed by landfilling increased steadily from 1960 when 62.5 percent was landfilled to 1985 when landfilling accounted for 82.9 percent of all MSW.[20] (The landfill percentage did decrease to 66.6 percent by 1990, due to increases in recycling and WTE.)[21] Repa and Sheets report that available data suggest that new landfills have larger capacities than landfills being closed, which may be providing a net increase in capacity.

Selected states do appear, however, to be headed for a crunch in landfill capacity, presumably due in large part to public opposition to siting new facilities. Repa and Sheets report that based on 1991 data, 10 states probably have less than 5 years of remaining capacity, and 18 states probably have less than 10 years of capacity. During the past 5 years, 5 states have reported an increase in landfill capacity, 8 states have reported a decrease, and the remaining states have observed little change in capacity.

The rapid closure of landfills is due primarily to stricter environmental regulations, and it is likely that recently published RCRA, Subtitle D, landfill rules will push the industry toward larger regional landfills to take advantage of economies of scale. In issuing those rules, the U.S. EPA estimated that the cost per ton of landfilling under the new rules would be about $48 per ton; or, according to the U.S. EPA's estimate, about $2 higher than the current average cost for MSW landfill disposal (40 CFR 257, 258). Note that Glenn (1992b) estimates that the average U.S. landfill tipping fee (not necessarily reflective of cost) in 1991 was $26.50 per ton, with a range of $0 to $200. In another survey by Aquino (1991), tipping fees were found to vary widely from region to region in 1990. For example, the Northeast, which has already implemented many of the environmental safeguards required in the new rules, was highest at $64.76 per ton, with the West Central and South Central areas being lowest at only $8.50 and $11.28 per ton, respectively. The impacts of the new landfill rule may be primarily a function of where you live and the degree to which environmental standards have already been met.

Further note that some analysts speculate that landfill cost escalations and capacity reductions have been overblown. For example, Bailey (1991b) argues that, overall, the supply of landfill space exceeds demand, which should send landfill prices down in some areas and keep them from rising very much in others. Bailey further argues that landfill costs rarely exceed $30 per ton and that recent landfill price jumps are due in large part to excessive rents—i.e., profits—on the parts of major waste companies. Supposedly, landfill prices will decrease as the market adjusts to the imbalance between landfill supply and demand.

With respect to a particular area's landfill capacity, the question is one of siting rather than an inherent inability for landfilling to handle MSW. Aside from state mandates to reduce landfilling and other incentives of the sort, a community could adopt landfilling as its sole method of managing municipal waste. And with the implementation of the new RCRA landfill rules, the environmental risks associated with landfilling will be reduced.

2.4.2 Recycling and Composting

As mentioned earlier in this chapter, the public seems to prefer recycling and composting over either landfilling or WTE. And, in fact, recycling and composting have been adopted at a rapid rate in recent years. The U.S. EPA

(1992a) reports that the percentage of MSW managed by recycling increased from 9.6 percent in 1980 to 14.9 percent in 1990. Composting increased from 0 percent in 1980 to 2.1 percent in 1990. Three states (Washington, Minnesota, and New Jersey) report that at least 30 percent of their MSW is managed by recycling, and numerous states have established recycling goals of 25 percent or greater (Glenn, 1992b).

Curbside collection programs have experienced tremendous growth. While only 1,050 programs existed in 1988, more than 3,900 programs were in place in 1992 serving more than 65 million people in the United States (Glenn, 1992b; Council for Solid Waste Solutions, 1991). Tremendous growth has also been seen in the number of material recovery facilities (MRFs)—facilities where commingled recyclables, at least part of which come from the residential sector, are sorted and processed for market. MRFs increased in number from 47 facilities in 1990 to 126 facilities in 1991, and another 18 facilities were under construction at that time (Glenn, 1991).

There has been much speculation that many communities that were considering or actively planning a WTE facility delayed or canceled those plans because of uncertainty about the potential role that recycling could play in their communities.[22] Communities often question whether recycling can manage a large percentage of their waste stream and significantly extend the lives of their current landfills. If a WTE facility is still in consideration, they question how an appropriate facility size can be determined without first determining the limits of recycling. They question whether a recycling program will remove materials from the waste stream that will alter the Btu value of the remaining MSW and thus alter the technical and economic viability of WTE. They also question whether recycling will be a lower cost option than WTE—both in the sense of comparing direct "out-of-pocket" costs and in terms of the avoidance of potential environmental damages (see Chapter 6 for further details). While the answers to these questions are not clear-cut at this time because of limited information and because the answers may depend on the conditions of the particular community, very few community leaders face opposition when proposing a recycling program. Recycling programs have therefore increased dramatically in number.

Although recycling can, and does, play a major role in the management of MSW, some analysts have recently raised questions about the percentage of the total waste stream that can realistically be recycled. Kreith (1992b), for example, believes that a recycling rate of 25 percent may be difficult and costly to reach in many communities, especially in sparsely populated areas. Certainly, some recycling programs face severe obstacles if their goals are to reach a 40 to 50 percent recycling rate.[23] The U.S. EPA (1992a) projects that under optimistic conditions recycling will not exceed 30 percent by 1995 and not exceed 35 percent by 2000.

While the current data about recycling costs are of questionable quality, the information that is available suggests that for most communities recycling costs are higher than the current or anticipated future costs of landfilling or WTE. Glenn (1992d) reports that curbside recycling programs in, for example, Austin, Texas, and Philadelphia, Pennsylvania, cost about $75 and $160 per ton, respectively. Both of these numbers exceed the current or projected cost of landfilling or WTE. The Office of Technology Assessment (1989) draws similar conclusions about the cost of curbside recycling programs. Its survey found the cost of curbside recycling programs ranged from $26 to $110 per ton, with an average of $62 per ton. Recycling costs were found to be particularly sensitive to the engineering efficiency of the collection process, the level of participation by residents, and the prices obtained for materials collected. The National Solid Wastes Management Association (1992) estimates that it costs an average $50.30 per ton to process recyclables at a materials recovery facility, and that sales of recovered materials do not cover the cost of processing. However, proponents of recycling argue that when comparing recycling with other options, it is not fair to compare the total cost of collecting and processing recyclables with only the cost of landfilling or WTE because in most cases the net cost of processing recyclables is less than landfilling or WTE. Nonetheless, proponents of recycling acknowledge that the cost of collecting recyclables is expensive relative to collection for landfilling or WTE.

Despite its potentially higher cost, many communities have decided that recycling is the most preferable means of managing MSW because of its presumed lower environmental damages and because of the severe difficulties in siting either a new landfill or WTE facility. However, those communities still must deal with the question of how much of the waste stream can, in fact, be recycled and whether a "successful" recycling program will eliminate their need for new or expanded landfill capacity and/or a WTE facility.

As with other uncertainties that community leaders face when making decisions about MSW, the economic viability of recycling programs is largely outside of their control. Markets for many recycled materials are risky and prices for recovered materials are currently depressed because of insufficient demand and stiff competition from virgin materials. Information about the costs of alternative approaches to recycling and the cost and benefits of expanding the program to collect additional materials and products is less than complete.[24] In addition, uncertainty exists about the degree to which individuals in a community will participate in voluntary or mandatory programs and the effectiveness of programs to boost participation. Nonetheless, many community leaders have obligated themselves to examining the potential that recycling offers. This obligation has, in turn, made any decision about WTE more uncertain.

2.5 UNCERTAINTIES ABOUT WTE TECHNOLOGIES

If a community decides to adopt WTE, it must first select among various available technologies and assess the technological uncertainties associated with each. This subsection presents a brief overview of the major categories of WTE technologies and the technical problems adopters of those technologies may face.

At the present time, there are three main types of municipal waste combustors used to burn MSW—mass-burn systems, modular systems, and refuse-derived fuel (RDF) systems. Mass-burn facilities—currently, the most popular—are large facilities that are designed to burn unprocessed, mixed MSW. The design capacity of operational mass-burn facilities in the United States in 1990 averaged about 912 tons per day, with mass-burn facilities in the planning phases averaging more than 1,150 tons per day. The largest mass-burn facilities have capacities of about 3,000 tons per day. Modular systems are much smaller, factory-fabricated plants also designed to burn unprocessed, mixed MSW. In 1990 the design capacity of the average operational modular unit was 133 tons per day, while modular facilities in the planning phases averaged 242 tons per day. RDF systems are a class of facilities that use mechanical means to separate the combustible and noncombustible fractions of MSW and process the combustible fraction into a more homogeneous fuel. RDF is then used in dedicated boilers to produce steam or electricity or used as a supplement in co-fired boilers along with either coal or oil. The design capacity of existing RDF facilities averaged about 1,003 tons per day in 1990. RDF facilities in the planning stages averaged 1,333 tons per day (Government Advisory Associates, 1991).

Other existing and developmental technologies have been used in several demonstration facilities but have failed to penetrate the market to any significant extent. For example, pyrolysis processes, in which MSW is chemically decomposed by heat in the absence of oxygen, have been attempted with little success. Pyrolysis produces combustible gases and liquid tar that could potentially be marketed but also produces a solid residue that must be managed. Other developmental technologies, such as fluidized bed combustion, burn MSW in a liquid suspension of intensely hot particles of sand. Although fluidized bed combustion offers potentially attractive emission controls, its cost and various technical problems have limited its use. Anaerobic digestion is also in the developmental stages. This process uses anaerobic microorganisms to decompose the organic fraction of waste to produce combustible gas.[25]

2.5.1 Mass-Burn Facilities

Mass-burn facilities are designed to burn heterogeneous MSW in a single combustion chamber under conditions of excess air—i.e., more air is provided than would be needed if the waste were burned uniformly. Most mass-burn facilities burn MSW on a sloping, moving grate that is vibrated or otherwise moved to agitate the waste and mix it with air. Other systems burn the waste in a rotating kiln. Some facilities have front-end materials separation for recycling, although many only recover ferrous waste from the ash after combustion is complete.

With respect to energy recovery, older mass-burn facilities use refractory furnaces, which have a temperature-resistant coating that decreases the transfer of heat during the combustion process. In these facilities, energy is recovered by a boiler that is downstream from the combustion chamber. The more modern systems use a water-wall design to capture heat in the combustion chamber in addition to downstream boilers. In this design, the walls of the furnace consist of closely spaced tubes through which water circulates. The water cools the furnace walls and absorbs thermal energy to produce steam for direct use or electricity production.

As compared to the now obsolete refractory furnace, water-wall facilities do a much better job of energy recovery. Although early water-wall designs had serious corrosion problems, modern facilities use various tube linings to reduce corrosion to a manageable level. The corrosion problem is worsened by the combustion of chlorine-containing materials, such as PVC plastics. System availability and fouling of heat transfer surfaces also pose potential problems. System availability does not usually exceed 80 to 85 percent because of the need to clean out the grates that become clogged with partially burned or non-combustible materials.[26] Fouling results from the deposition of slag and fly ash on heat transfer surfaces and requires periodic maintenance.

2.5.2 Modular Systems

Modular systems are similar to mass-burn facilities in that they are designed to burn unprocessed, mixed MSW. They differ, however, in terms of size and combustion design. Modular systems, which are usually factory manufactured and transported by truck to their needed location, use two combustion chambers instead of one. Their relatively small size and transportability make them attractive to small communities or for specialized purposes. The primary chamber is operated in a slightly oxygen-deficient environment, which serves to partially burn the waste and vaporize much of the remaining input. The secondary chamber is operated in an excess-air environment to fully burn the gases not combusted in the primary chamber. As compared to mass-burn systems, modular systems do not burn MSW as completely, and, therefore, ash quantities are higher. Energy recovery is also compromised.[27]

2.5.3 RDF Systems

The first generation of RDF facilities experienced several mechanical problems and obtained a reputation of questionable reliability. The latest technologies have overcome many of these problems and are being considered by many communities. RDF facilities use mechanical methods to shred incoming MSW, separate the ferrous and other non-combustible materials, and produce a combustible fraction suitable as a fuel in a dedicated furnace or used as a supplemental fuel in conventional boiler systems designed to burn oil, coal, wood, or biomass. RDF falls into one of three categories: coarse RDF, fluff RDF, and densified RDF. Densified RDF refers to the combustible portion of MSW that has been extruded into pellets to reduce the cost of transportation and storage. Coarse and fluff RDF refer to the heavy and lighter fractions, respectively, when densification is not used.

One of the most attractive aspects of RDF is its potential use as a supplemental fuel in conventional boilers. However, at this point in time many potential demanders of RDF as a supplemental fuel have been reluctant to burn RDF in conventional steam- and electricity-generating facilities. Diaz, Savage, and Golueke (1982) cite five main reasons for this aversion: "(1) the varied particle size and composition of most refuse-derived fuels; (2) the presence of materials (i.e., 'contaminants') that are characterized by unsatisfactory combustion properties; (3) high moisture content; (4) relatively high ash content; and (5) a mediocre heating value as compared to conventional fuels" (p. 36).

2.5.4 Environmental Controls

As discussed in section 2.3.1, modern WTE facilities are currently required to use best available control technologies (BACT) to control various air emissions. Fabric filters or electrostatic precipitators are used for the removal of particulate matter and scrubbers are typically used to remove acid gases. Other state-of-the-art control technologies are also often used for the control of nitrogen-oxide emissions.

The recently passed Clean Air Act Amendments of 1990 will require a shift to maximum achievable control technology—a step up from BACT—and require controls on emissions not regulated in the current U.S. EPA rules—i.e., mercury, cadmium, and lead. To be sure, the CAAA will result in the wider use of air pollution control systems and subsequent lower emission levels. Retrofits of operational and currently planned facilities are likely to be required with potentially significant impacts on total facility costs.[28]

As is the case with recycling and, to a lesser extent, landfilling, WTE technology innovation is proceeding at a rapid rate in response to stricter environmental regulations and increasingly competitive markets for waste management systems. The community that is considering a WTE project must assess the reliability of the currently available WTE technologies and their abilities to meet ever stricter environmental mandates. The reactions of communities considering WTE facilities to these types of technical uncertainties is explored in more detail in the case-study portion of this work (Chapter 6).

2.6 POTENTIAL FAILURES IN THE DECISION-MAKING PROCESS

Advocates of a WTE facility at the community level will likely acknowledge that the most severe threat to a WTE project is a fundamental breakdown in the local decision-making process, irrespective of information on potential environmental damages, regulatory and financial risks, and technology uncertainties. Cursory evidence suggests that advocates of WTE generally have not reached out to community leaders in the early stages of the decision process. And once opposition is mounted, as it is in almost all cases, WTE advocates generally react strongly to that opposition. The debate about WTE often, therefore, shifts from an assessment of the facts and options to an all-out war among sides that have staked their positions more on ideology than on an unbiased assessment of the pros and cons of the various alternatives. WTE opponents may view WTE advocates as symbols of big business, financial greed, and everything that is "wrong" with our systems for environmental control. WTE proponents often view opposition groups as fanatical environmentalists with little ability to grasp the "reality of the situation."

Kreith (1992b) writes that "One of the most important reasons for this conflict is a lack of confidence by the public in the safety and reliability of some waste management technologies" (p. 3). Possibly more important is the public's general lack of trust in certain sources of information, particular pieces of information, and the manner in which decisions are made. Evidence (see Chapter 6) suggests that the public's perception of conflicting information and the subsequent politicization of WTE in the United States has caused WTE to be rejected in many communities; and in those communities that have actively planned a facility, the decision to abandon or proceed with that project often is based more on the minimization of political damage and less on an unbiased assessment of the relative merits of alternative MSW management approaches.

NOTES

1. Household hazardous wastes typically make up about 1 percent of the municipal waste stream, or about 15 pounds per household per year. These hazardous wastes are difficult to manage because of their small percentages, the need for a sophisticated collection system, and the potential liabilities that are borne by collectors and processors. While curbside collection is not considered a viable option, several states have experimented with household hazardous waste "collection days" during which individuals can bring their hazardous wastes to a collection center for

disposal. Unfortunately, these programs have typically had small participation rates of between 2 and 5 percent. See Woods (1991a) for additional details.

2. See, for example, Denison and Silbergeld (1988).

3. See, for example, United States Conference of Mayors (1990).

4. See, for example, Gutfeld (1992).

5. For more information on the relationship between plastics incineration and emissions of furans and dioxins, see, for example, Curlee (1986 and 1989), Magee (1988), and New York State Energy Research and Development Authority (1987), and United States Conference of Mayors (1990).

6. See Kiser (1992b) for additional information on current environmental controls. See, for example, Farber (1992) for additional information about continuous emissions monitoring at WTE facilities.

7. For more information on the toxicity characteristics of fly and bottom ash, see, for example, Cook (1989) and Denison and Silbergeld (1988).

8. See, for example, United States Conference of Mayors (1990).

9. For more information on the environmental risks associated with ash disposal, see, for example, Cook (1989), Denison and Silbergeld (1988), Kreith (1992a), United States Conference of Mayors (1990), Williams (1991), and Woods (1991b).

10. See Integrated Waste Services Association (1992b) for additional details.

11. See Curlee (1987) for a further discussion of the roles of local, state, and federal governments in the management of MSW.

12. The proposed rules are reported in the *Federal Register*, "Emission Guidelines: Municipal Waste Combustors," Vol. 54, No. 243, pp. 52209–52304. Final rules are reported in *Federal Register*, "Standards of Performance for New Stationary Sources: Municipal Waste Combustors," Vol. 56, No. 28, pp. 5488–5527. For a summary of the provisions of the new rules, see, for example, Williams (1991, Chapter 8) or *Waste Age* (March 1991). Different requirements were established for existing plants.

13. See *Solid Waste Report*, 1992b, Vol. 23, No. 20, p. 198, May 18.

14. See *Solid Waste Report*, 1992c, Vol. 92, No. 23, p. 219, June 11.

15. For comparison purposes, the Energy Information Administration (1986) reports that more than 40 percent of all coal-fired power plants in the United States had average generating costs in the 2.0 to 2.9 cents per kWh range in 1986. Costs for gas turbine facilities, often used for peaking, were about 4.86 cents per kWh in 1986.

16. See Migden (1990) for an excellent overview of various state-level economic incentives to promote the adoption of WTE.

17. Hilgendorff (1989) argues that the TRA86 hastened local decision makers' plans to adopt WTE just prior to the law's implementation in order to take advantage of soon-to-expire federal tax exemptions. TRA86 also slowed some projects subsequent to its passage, according to Hilgendorff. Chapter 5 of this work presents a detailed analysis of the effects of TRA86 on WTE project cancellation in the late 1980s.

18. Interstate transport of MSW topped one million tons in 1989 and 1990 in New York, New Jersey, Illinois, Missouri, and Pennsylvania. An additional 11 states exported between 100,000 and 999,999 tons (*Solid Waste Report*, 1992d).

19. See, for example, Hilgendorff (1989) and Sundberg (1988) for additional details about financing WTE facilities.

20. See U.S. Environmental Protection Agency (1992a) for detailed statistics on the historical, current, and projected use of alternative MSW management practices.

21. Data on landfill numbers and capacities are somewhat lacking at this time. For example, Repa and Sheets (1992) summarize available estimates from different sources and find a wide range of estimates. Quoting from Repa and Sheets,

A U.S. Government Accounting Office (GAO) survey done two years after EPA's work showed 7,575 MSW landfills existing in 1988—1,500 more landfills than EPA estimated two years earlier. Other surveys conducted during 1990 and 1991 showed totals ranging from 5,368 to 7,378. These inconsistencies can be attributed only partly to landfill closures and openings. Over the survey period, some states revised their definition of landfill to exclude "open dumps," others were revising their landfill permit process and could only guess at the number of MSW landfills within the state, and a few had no formal accounting process. The reported number of MSW landfills in the United States in 1990–1991 ranged from 4,462 to 10,467, when the extremes are totaled (p.22).

22. This question was explored as part of our case studies. See Chapter 6.

23. Recycling of some materials, such as plastics, faces significant technical and cost hurdles. Although the recycling rate for plastic bottles reached 14 percent in 1991, an increase of 56 percent from the previous year (Society of the Plastics Industry, Inc., 1992), total plastics recycling was less than 3 percent. Recent trends— such as increased competition from virgin materials and the pullout of some large corporations from the recycling business—have lowered expectations for plastics recycling and have put in question the plastic industry's 25 percent recycling goal (see, for example, Meade, 1992). A recent study by Curlee and Das (1991) found that a plastics recycling rate in excess of about 14 percent will be difficult to achieve if industry continues to target clean, segregated wastes, such as soda bottles and milk jugs. Significant improvements in the technologies and approaches to collect and recycle commingled and more contaminated plastics could result in plastics recycling rates in excess of 50 percent. The U.S. EPA (1992a) projects that under optimistic conditions plastics recycling will not exceed 7 percent by 1995 and not exceed 12 percent by 2000.

24. Meade (1992) estimates, for example, that plastics may make up only 5 percent of the weight of recyclables collected in a curbside program but may contribute as much as 30 percent of the total cost of collection. Communities face a complicated set of questions when evaluating the costs and benefits of including additional materials and products in a recycling program.

25. Overviews of the various existing and developmental WTE technologies are given in several reports. See, for example, Brickner (1987), Diaz, Savage, and Golueke (1982), Kolb and Wilkes (1988), Office of Technology Assessment (1989), Robinson (1986), and Williams (1991).

26. See, for example, Diaz, Savage, and Golueke (1982, p. 4).

27. See, for example, Office of Technology Assessment (1989) and U.S. EPA (1987).

28. See, for example, Frillici and Schwarz (1991) for a detailed discussion of current air emission controls and the changes that are likely to be mandated as a result of the 1990 CAAA.

Chapter 3

An Overview of Waste-to-Energy in the United States

3.1 INTRODUCTION

The focus of the previous chapter was on issues that make waste-to-energy a controversial MSW management alternative, especially at the level of the local community. This chapter discusses several issues that are more national in scope. In particular, this chapter presents (1) a brief history of the adoption of WTE in the United States and an overview of the WTE facilities in operation and in the planning phases, (2) an overview of the structure of the WTE industry in the United States, (3) a brief discussion of the quantity and composition of MSW in the United States, and (4) projections of the total U.S. production of energy from MSW combustion during the coming years and decades.

3.2 THE ADOPTION OF WTE IN THE UNITED STATES

3.2.1 A Brief History

In 1960 WTE capacity was essentially zero in the United States, and by 1975 only about 0.5 percent of all MSW was combusted with heat recovery. The 1980s saw a rapid increase in WTE construction, and by 1990 more than 15 percent of all U.S. MSW was burned to retrieve its heat value (U.S. Environmental Protection Agency, 1992a).

WTE has been used even more in Europe and Japan. Although it is difficult to compare the numbers from those countries with the United States because of different definitions of what constitutes the municipal waste stream and other differences in methodologies, it is generally agreed that Sweden, Denmark, Switzerland, and Japan incinerate more than 50 percent of their MSW. Some of these countries may, in fact, approach a 70 percent WTE rate. In addition, countries such as France and the Netherlands combust in the range of 30 to 40 percent of their MSW.[1]

The idea of using garbage as a fuel is, however, far from new. In fact, WTE was first used in 1896 in Hamburg, Germany, and was adopted in New York City only two years later. Although the primary purpose of these first facilities was waste volume reduction, some energy in the form of steam was recovered for internal uses. The first WTE facility to produce electricity started operations in 1903, also in New York City. However, the conversion of garbage to electricity was not an immediate hit. Incineration, primarily without any form of heat recovery, continued to grow throughout the first half of the twentieth century, mostly in densely populated areas. By 1969, 364 incinerators had been constructed, with 43 facilities having some type of limited, in-house, energy retrieval and use.

During the 1960s, several U.S. companies improved on modular incinerator technologies to overcome some of the operational problems experienced with earlier systems. At the same time several European companies were experimenting with more efficient ways to recover energy, and in 1957 the first waterwall facility was built in Switzerland. Waterwall systems did not appear in the United States until 1967 when a system developed by a U.S. company was constructed in Norfolk, Virginia. That same year, two German companies were also successful in marketing waterwall facilities in the United States.

A major shock came to the incineration industry in 1970 with the enactment of the Clean Air Act (CAA). The CAA, in essence, banned the uncontrolled burning of MSW and placed restrictions on particulate emissions that posed problems for many older facilities. About 50 percent of existing incinerators were closed following the enactment of the CAA, primarily because required retrofits were too expensive. Although the construction of incinerators with and without heat recovery continued in the early 1970s, adoption was no doubt slowed by the CAA and by relatively cheap energy prices.

The oil price shock of 1973 and, more importantly, the passage of the Public Utility Regulatory Policies Act (PURPA) in 1978 jump-started the U.S. WTE industry. As discussed in the previous chapter, PURPA required utilities to purchase electricity from WTE and renewable-energy facilities at a price equal to the utility's avoided cost. This economic incentive, in addition to the momentum that had built up for WTE during the 1970s due to the "energy crisis," resulted in the rapid adoption of WTE facilities in the 1980s.[2]

3.2.2 The Current Status of WTE in the United States

As of 1990 there were 202 WTE facilities either operational, under construction, in shakedown, or in the advanced stages of planning.[3] Advanced-planned facilities numbered 62, with the remaining 140 facilities categorized as "existing sites" according to the Government Advisory Associates (GAA, 1991) data base. Of the existing facilities, GAA reports that 36.4 percent are in the South, 28.6 percent in the Northeast, 23.6 percent in the north-central region, and 11.4 percent in the West. The distribution of planned facilities is, however, quite different, with 53.2 percent in the Northeast, 21.0 percent in the South, 16.1 percent in the northcentral region, and 9.4 percent in the West. Existing facilities are located in 38 states, with New York, Minnesota, and Florida having the most facilities at 12, 14, and 14, respectively. The 62 projects in the advanced-planned stage are located in 24 states, with New Jersey, New York, and Pennsylvania having the most at 10, 8, and 8, respectively. Of all the operational facilities, 2 began operations in the 1960s, 12 began in the 1970s, and 114 began in the 1980s.

GAA reports that the largest percentage of existing facilities are of the mass-burning type—i.e., 53 percent. Modular units and all RDF processes account for about 27 and 21 percent, respectively. A major shift has occurred with planned facilities in that almost 60 percent are of the waterwall, mass-burn type. Rotary combustor, mass-burn units account for 19.4 percent of planned units, and modular units account for only 6.5 percent. Only about 13 percent of advanced-planned facilities will produce RDF (GAA, 1991).

With respect to the types of energy produced, existing facilities are about evenly split between electricity only (37.1 percent) and steam only (32.9 percent). About 21 percent of existing facilities co-generate steam and electricity, and 8.6 percent produce RDF that is burned off-site. Planned facilities will rely more exclusively on sales of electricity, with 77.4 percent of advanced-planned facilities producing electricity only. Only 4.8 percent of these planned units will produce steam exclusively, 14.5 percent will co-generate steam and electricity, and only 3.2 percent will produce RDF for off-site purposes. Of those existing facilities that produce electricity, 32.5 percent have gross power ratings below 10 megawatts (MW). About 29 percent have ratings between 10 and 25 MW, about 19 percent between 25 and 50 MW, and 20 percent over 50 MW. Of the advanced-planned units, only 14.3 percent will have ratings below 10 MW. Some 30.4 percent will be in the 10 to 25 MW range, 35.7 percent between 25 and 50 MW, and about 20 percent over 50 MW.[4] Total power output at existing WTE facilities was almost 2,617 MW in 1990. Another 1,945 MW were in the advanced-planning stage at that time.

Prices paid for electricity from WTE plants in 1990 varied significantly from region to region. While the national average for all advanced-planned and existing facilities was 5.59 cents per kilowatt hour (kWh), facilities in the Northeast were paid an average 6.86 cents per kWh, and southern facilities were paid only 3.49 cents per kWh. At the national level, existing facilities fetched 5.62 cents per kWh, while planned facilities were to be paid a slightly lower 5.53 cents per kWh.

In terms of facility design capacity, planned units are significantly larger than existing units. The design capacity of existing units in 1990 averaged about 656 tons per day (tpd), whereas planned units averaged more than 1,100 tpd (GAA, 1991). Existing mass-burn units averaged 913 tpd, modular units averaged 133 tpd, and RDF facilities averaged 1,003 tpd. Advanced-planned units were larger for all types of facilities. Mass-burn facilities in advanced stages of planning averaged 1,150 tpd, modular units were at 242 tpd, and RDF facilities averaged 1,332 tpd. Total existing capacity in 1990 was 91,810 tpd, while planned capacity was at 68,255 tpd. Mass-burn technologies account for a vast majority of existing and even a larger percentage of advanced-planned capacity. (Note that the actual capacity of WTE facilities is about 80 percent of design capacity because of down-time for maintenance and repairs.)

For existing and planned WTE facilities as a whole, ash production is projected to be about 23 percent of the weight of unprocessed MSW. For the nation as a whole, about 61 percent of that ash is or will be sent to an ash monofill—i.e., a landfill that accepts WTE ash exclusively. The remaining 39 percent of ash is or will be sent with MSW to regular MSW Subtitle D landfills. When broken down between existing and planned facilities, only about 53 percent of ash from existing facilities is sent to a monofill, whereas a projected 82 percent of ash from advanced-planned facilities will be disposed of in monofills. Differences also exist from region to region. For example, about 78 percent of ash from facilities located in the Northeast is or will be sent to a monofill, while only 40 percent of ash from southern facilities will be sent to a dedicated ashfill. Ash disposal fees averaged $31.78 per ton for all facilities constructed or advanced planned, with a range of fees from $2.78 to $133 per ton. On a regional basis, the Northeast pays the most for ash disposal at about $50 per ton, while the South pays the least at a little more than $19.50 per ton.

A marked change has also occurred with respect to the type of pollution control equipment used. For example, existing mass-burn facilities in 1990 employed dry scrubbers in about 55 percent of facilities, 48 percent had baghouses, and less than 6 percent had systems to control nitrogen oxides. (The percentages for existing modular systems were 16, 16, and 2 percent, respectively.) However, 96 percent of facilities in the advanced-planning stages will use dry scrubbers, 88 percent will use baghouses, and 47 percent will have systems to reduce nitrogen oxides. (The percentages for planned modular systems are 80, 80, and 0 percent, respectively.)

Curbside recycling has been quite prevalent in communities that have constructed or planned a WTE facility. More than 53 percent of all areas that have existing facilities also have a curbside recycling program, while some 71 percent of communities planning a facility in 1990 had such programs. With respect to recovery of materials for recycling at WTE facilities, only 24 percent of facilities in the advanced-planning stage had intentions of recovering materials prior to combustion. However, ferrous metals are to be recovered after combustion in 100 percent of planned facilities. More than 42 percent of existing facilities have some kind of pre-combustion recovery of recyclables, and 95 percent of those facilities recover ferrous materials post-combustion (GAA, 1991).[5]

Finally, tipping fees charged by WTE facilities also vary from region to region and among technology types. The average tipping fee for all U.S. WTE facilities in 1990 was $51 per ton, with a range of $3 to $270 per ton. On a regional basis, the Northeast had the highest fees at more than $62 per ton, while the South had the lowest at about $37 per ton. The northcentral and western regions averaged $46 and $56 per ton, respectively. Mass-burn facilities tend to have the highest tipping fees, averaging $56 per ton, followed by modular units at $51 and RDF processes at $41 per ton, respectively. When broken down into existing and planned facilities, the data show that existing facilities have an average tipping fee of about $45 per ton, while planned facilities average more than $64 per ton.

3.3 WTE INDUSTRY STRUCTURE IN THE UNITED STATES

The WTE industry in the United States has become increasingly concentrated during the past decade. As of the early 1980s, numerous U.S. companies were in the business of developing, constructing, and operating WTE facilities in the United States. By 1990 the number had dropped greatly, and the industry is now comprised of less than 10 full-service WTE companies. As of 1990 the major full-service companies included:

ABB Resource Recovery Systems, Windsor, Connecticut

American Ref-Fuel Company, Houston, Texas

Combustion Engineering, Stamford, Connecticut

Foster Wheeler Power Systems, Inc., Clinton, New Jersey

Montenay Power Corporation, Mineola, New York

Ogden Martin Systems, Inc., Fairfield, New Jersey

Reading Energy Company, Philadelphia, Pennsylvania

Westinghouse Electric Corporation, Pittsburgh, Pennsylvania, and

Wheelabrator Technologies, Inc., Hampton, New Hampshire (GAA, 1991)

A 1989 study by Kidder, Peabody, Inc. (Sweetnam, 1989) found that in terms of total WTE capacity, Ogden Martin and Wheelabrator were the largest firms in the industry—accounting for 19 and 17 percent, respectively, of the total market (based on tons-per-day capacity awards through May 1989). The next 2 largest firms were Combustion Engineering (8 percent) and American Ref-Fuel (7 percent). The 4-firm concentration ratio for the domestic WTE industry was therefore 51 percent,[6] which is relatively low compared to other similar industries. For example, manufacturers of turbines and generator sets have a 4-firm concentration ratio of about 90 percent, and many industrial manufactures are in excess of 50 percent.[7] The Kidder, Peabody study found that 20 companies had been awarded two or more contracts to build WTE facilities, although many of these were awarded in the late 1970s and early 1980s. In fact, of the 194 project awards in the Kidder, Peabody study, only 27 percent occurred prior to 1984. Kidder, Peabody also found that many firms had built only one or two facilities and then had exited from the industry. They report that the facilities built by these miscellaneous vendors have had mixed operating records. While many have been successful, some have had serious operating problems.

An examination of those facilities that were in either the advanced stages of planning or construction as of 1990 shows that the WTE industry is continuing to become more concentrated. Table 3.1 provides details. In terms of total tons-per-day design capacity, Wheelabrator and Ogden continue to be the largest firms. Westinghouse and American Ref-Fuel trail closely to give a 4-firm concentration ratio of about 65 percent. Only 4 additional firms contributed more than 2 percent of the WTE capacity being planned or constructed. A total of at least 23 different firms were active in WTE planning and/or construction in 1990.

The major WTE industry players are typically wholly or partially owned subsidiaries of large vertically integrated firms with significant experience in the engineering and construction of power and process facilities. Some also have vertical links to the large waste management firms. For example, American Ref-Fuel is a joint venture of Air Products and Chemicals, Inc. (an international supplier of industrial gases and air-separations process equipment) and Browning-Ferris Industries (the second largest waste management firm in the United States). Many of these firms made a major push in the WTE area in the late 1970s and early 1980s as their more traditional markets experienced slow or negative growth. Additional incentives to enter the growing WTE market included (1) U.S. landfill closures, (2) the continued growth in MSW volumes, and (3) the significant growth in WTE capacity and technology innovation that was occurring in Europe and Japan during the 1970s and 1980s. Some U.S. vendors obtained exclusive rights to European technologies, which many considered to be superior to U.S.–developed systems. Finally, market entry was encouraged by public policies that supported renewable energy production and by what appeared to be ever-increasing energy prices.

The more recent movement toward larger firms and a more concentrated industry is consistent with altered market conditions. Recent project cancellations and a general public mistrust of WTE have increased the competitive pressures on all vendors. Of equal importance, however, are more severe barriers to market entry that result from several trends. First, the

Table 3.1 Vendors of WTE Facilities in the United States: 1990 (in total tpd design capacity being constructed or in the advanced stages of planning)			
Company Operating as Vendor	Number of Projects	TPD Design Capacity	% of Total
Wheelabrator	6	11,750	17.5
Ogden Projects	10	11,340	16.9
Westinghouse	9	10,743	16.0
American Ref-Fuel	6	9,877	14.7
ABB Resource Recovery[1]	3	5,250	7.8
Foster Wheeler	5	4,795	7.1
Thermo Electron Energy Systems	1	2,100	3.1
Montenay Power Corporation	2	1,400	2.1
Reading Energy Company	1	1,200	1.8
Newest	1	1,000	1.5
Babcox and Wilcox	1	990	1.5
Blount Energy Systems	1	710	1.1
United Biofuels	1	700	1.0
Reuter	1	660	1.0
Intercon	1	560	0.8
Lawson Fisher	1	560	0.8
Waste Service Technologies	1	550	0.8
Enerco	2	510	0.8
Riley/Takuma	1	500	0.7
Laurent Bouillet	1	450	0.7
Consumat	1	330	0.5
American Energy Corporation	1	200	0.3
Technochem Environmental Services	1	70	0.1
Not Identified	2	1,020	1.5
Totals	60	67,265	100

Source: derived from GAA, 1991.
[1] Ogden Martin acquired ABB in early 1993.

long lead times now required to negotiate a contract, obtain funding, site the facility, obtain permits, establish a buyer for energy outputs, and so forth limit WTE projects to large firms that can wait many years for payoffs. Second, the perceived technical, environmental, and financial risks associated with WTE encourage communities to go with only established, big-name corporations. Third, the increasing complexity of meeting environmental and other regulations requires greater and greater expertise, which can usually be provided least expensively by larger firms. Fourth, many communities now require integrated MSW management systems, including waste collection, recycling and composting programs, and ash disposal, in addition to the construction and operation of the WTE facility. To offer these various services, some companies have expanded vertically.

Additional changes in the domestic WTE industry may occur as a result of the U.S. entry of a major European competitor. Electricite de France's subsidiary Traitement Industriel Des Residus Urbains (TIRU) recently got voter approval and is finalizing permits for a 240 tpd/7 MW facility in Shirley, Massachusetts. The project, which will include centers for recycling and household hazardous waste collection, employed sophisticated methods to inform the public and gain their support.[8] Some domestic WTE firms have been criticized for being overly reactive to opposition groups, rather than being proactive to elicit input and cooperation from the public in the early stages of project development.[9]

3.4 THE POTENTIAL FOR ENERGY PRODUCTION FROM MSW COMBUSTION

One of the main arguments that has been used in support of WTE technologies is the displacement of conventional forms of energy. This section presents estimates and projections of energy production from WTE for recent years and the coming decades under various assumptions. Those numbers are then compared to total current and projected U.S. energy consumption.

3.4.1 General Approach

Information from a variety of sources is used in a four-step approach to project energy from WTE over the time period 1990 to 2015. In the first step, the total quantity of MSW is projected. The current and future heat value of a typical pound of MSW is assessed in the second step. The third step addresses trends in total U.S. WTE capacity. The final step combines the results of the first three steps to formulate high, medium, and low projections of energy from WTE. Due to limitations on data and uncertainties at each step, projections presented here should not be interpreted necessarily as predictions, but rather as reference points and reasonable bounds.

3.4.2 Projected MSW Quantities

Projections of MSW quantities in the United States are complicated by the lack of a universally accepted definition of what constitutes MSW and limited data availability. The definition of MSW adopted here is consistent with that used by the U.S. EPA (1992a) and defined in Subtitle D of the Resource Conservation and Recovery Act (RCRA). MSW includes durable goods, non-durable goods, containers and packaging, food wastes, and yard trimmings from the residential, commercial, institutional, and industrial sectors. MSW does not include everything that might be landfilled in Subtitle D landfills, such as municipal sludge, non-hazardous industrial wastes, shredder residue from automobile recycling operations, and construction and demolition wastes. While MSW is defined to include some miscellaneous wastes from the industrial sector, such as lunchroom wastes, office paper, and corrugated boxes, MSW does not include non-hazardous industrial waste that results directly from the manufacturing process. In some cases, these omitted and "gray area" waste streams are managed with MSW in the same facilities and can cause confusion when comparing estimates of the size of the MSW stream from city to city.

According to the U.S. EPA, about 196 million tons of MSW were produced in 1990 in the United States, and the U.S. EPA projects that about 222 million tons will be produced in the year 2000.[10] For comparison purposes, the Office of Technology Assessment (1989) estimates that "at least 250 million tons of hazardous waste are generated annually and the amount of non-hazardous industrial solid waste is even greater" (p. 73).

The only publicly available historical data on MSW quantity and composition are from Franklin Associates, which has provided a series of reports for the U.S. EPA. The most recent report (U.S. EPA, 1992a) provides historical and projected MSW quantity and composition numbers for the period 1960 to 2000. Franklin uses a materials-flow approach to make estimates and projections. In other words, they trace the flow of materials from production to consumption to disposal. The approach does not rely on data collected at the point of generation.

From a conceptual perspective, the generation of MSW is primarily a function of gross national product (GNP) and population; empirical analysis shows this to be true. MSW quantity data were taken from Franklin Associates' most recent update (U.S. EPA, 1992a) and regressed against real GNP, population, and other potential explanatory variables, e.g., per capita GNP. Regression results show extremely high R-squared numbers—in excess of 0.99 when MSW is regressed against real GNP. The addition of population or per capita GNP does not add to the fit of the regression, and multicollinearity leads to a non-intuitive negative sign on population and results in the explanatory variables being insignificant. MSW quantity was therefore estimated as a simple function of real GNP.

One approach to projecting MSW quantity is to assume that the historical relationship between real GNP and MSW quantity will not change over the projection time frame and base quantity projections on assumed future real GNP growth. A real GNP growth figure of about 2 percent per year is consistent with many projections. However, MSW quantity projections based on this simple approach are not acceptable because of structural changes that are occurring and likely to occur in future years. More specifically, as of 1992 at least 22 states had passed laws mandating that their municipal waste streams be reduced by 25 percent or more by no later than the year 2000 (tabulated from tables in Glenn, 1992b). While there is wide agreement that many of these goals are not defined well and are unlikely to be met by their target times, there is general agreement that some structural changes will occur to alter the basic relationship between GNP and MSW quantity.

3.4.2.1 Base-Case MSW Quantity. To reflect anticipated successes in reducing the quantity of MSW, the following simple approach is adopted for the base-case MSW quantity projections. For each year in the projection time frame (1991 to 2015), the quantity of MSW is reduced by 0.5 percent per year below the quantity level projected in the absence of efforts to promote source reduction—or, in other words, in the absence of any changes in the historical relationship between real GNP and MSW quantity. For example, the quantity of MSW produced in 2015 is projected to be 12.5 percent less than its projected value with no source-reduction efforts.

Under the assumed base-case conditions, the quantity of MSW in the United States is projected to grow from its estimated 1990 level of about 196 million tons to 218 million tons in 2000 and increase further to about 266 million tons in 2015.

3.4.2.2 Low-Case MSW Quantity. If source reduction efforts become a higher priority of federal and state governments and/or existing programs are more successful than experts currently believe they will be, the above base-case quantity projections will be too high. To reflect greater source reduction, it is assumed that MSW quantity is reduced by 1 percent per year below the quantity level projected under the assumption that the historical relationship between real GNP and MSW remains unchanged throughout the projection time frame (1991 to 2015). Under these assumptions, the U.S. MSW quantity is projected to be about 206 million tons in 2000 and increase to almost 228 million tons by 2015.

3.4.2.3 High-Case MSW Quantity. For the high-case scenario, it is assumed that real GNP increases by 2 percent per year over the projection time frame and MSW quantity continues to increase according to the historical relationship (1960 to 1990) between MSW quantity and real GNP.

Table 3.2 Historical and Projected MSW Quantity (in millions of tons)			
Year	Base Case	High Case	Low Case
1960	87.8	87.8	87.8
1965	103.4	103.4	103.4
1970	121.9	121.9	121.9
1975	128.1	128.1	128.1
1980	151.4	151.4	151.4
1985	164.4	164.4	164.4
1990	195.7	195.7	195.7
1995	203.9	209.1	198.6
2000	217.9	229.3	206.4
2005	232.8	251.7	213.9
2010	248.7	276.4	221.1
2015	265.7	303.6	227.7

Source of historical MSW quantities: U.S. EPA 1992a.

In other words, the high-case scenario assumes that source reduction efforts will not be successful. Whereas the base-case and low-case scenarios assume a 0.5 and 1.0 percent yearly reduction in MSW quantity, the high-case assumes no such reductions. Given the high-case assumptions, MSW is projected to increase to about 229 million tons by 2000 and increase further to almost 304 million tons by 2015. Table 3.2 and Figure 3.1 summarize historical and projected MSW quantity projections for all three scenarios.

For comparison purposes, note that Franklin Associates (U.S. EPA, 1992a) projects that U.S. MSW quantity will be about 208 and 222 million tons in 1995 and 2000, respectively.

3.4.2.4 *Per Capita MSW Quantity.* Table 3.3 and Figure 3.2 provide information on the per capita MSW quantity levels under the three scenarios. Note that in 1990, each person in the United States generated about 0.78 tons of MSW per year (or about 4.28 pounds per day). Under the base-case

Figure 3.1
Historical and Projected MSW Quantity (in millions of tons)

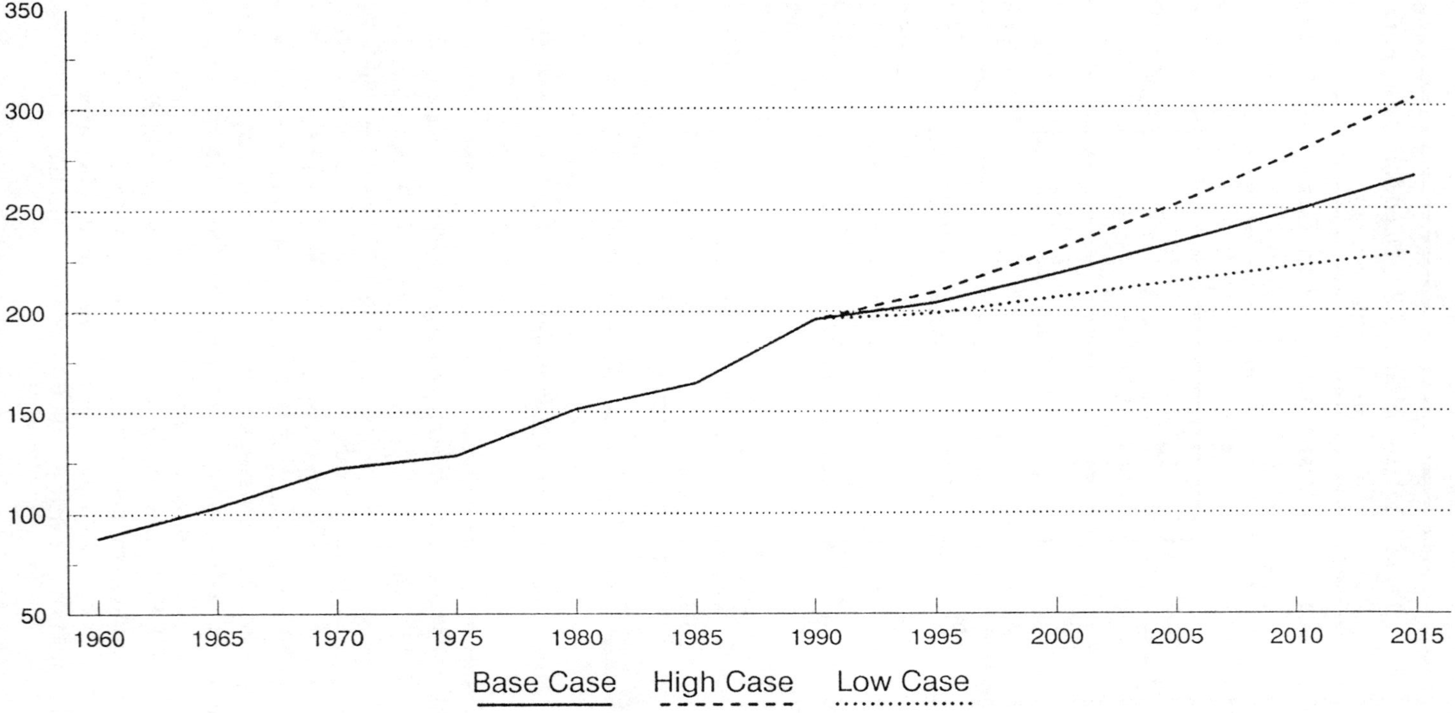

Base Case   High Case   Low Case

Table 3.3 Per Capita MSW Quantity (in tons)			
Year	Base Case	High Case	Low Case
1960	0.486	0.486	0.486
1965	0.532	0.532	0.532
1970	0.594	0.594	0.594
1975	0.593	0.593	0.593
1980	0.665	0.665	0.665
1985	0.687	0.687	0.687
1990	0.782	0.782	0.782
1995	0.784	0.804	0.764
2000	0.812	0.855	0.769
2005	0.845	0.913	0.776
2010	0.880	0.978	0.782
2015	0.919	1.051	0.788

assumptions, per capita levels are projected to increase to about 0.81 tons per year (4.45 pounds per day) and 0.92 tons per year (5.04 pounds per day) by 2000 and 2015, respectively. Hershkowitz (1987) and others have reported that MSW generation rates in European countries are much lower than in the United States. For example, Switzerland and the former West Germany produce only about 2.5 pounds per person per day, while Norway is as low as 1.7 pounds per capita. Exact comparisons are, however, difficult because MSW is defined to include different types of waste in different countries.

3.4.3 Projected Btu Value of MSW

The heat value of a typical pound of MSW obviously depends on its composition. The most recent Franklin Associates study (U.S. EPA, 1992a) presents estimated historical composition numbers for 1960 through 1990 and gives projected composition for the years 1995 and 2000. The estimated

Figure 3.2
Per Capita MSW Quantity (in tons)

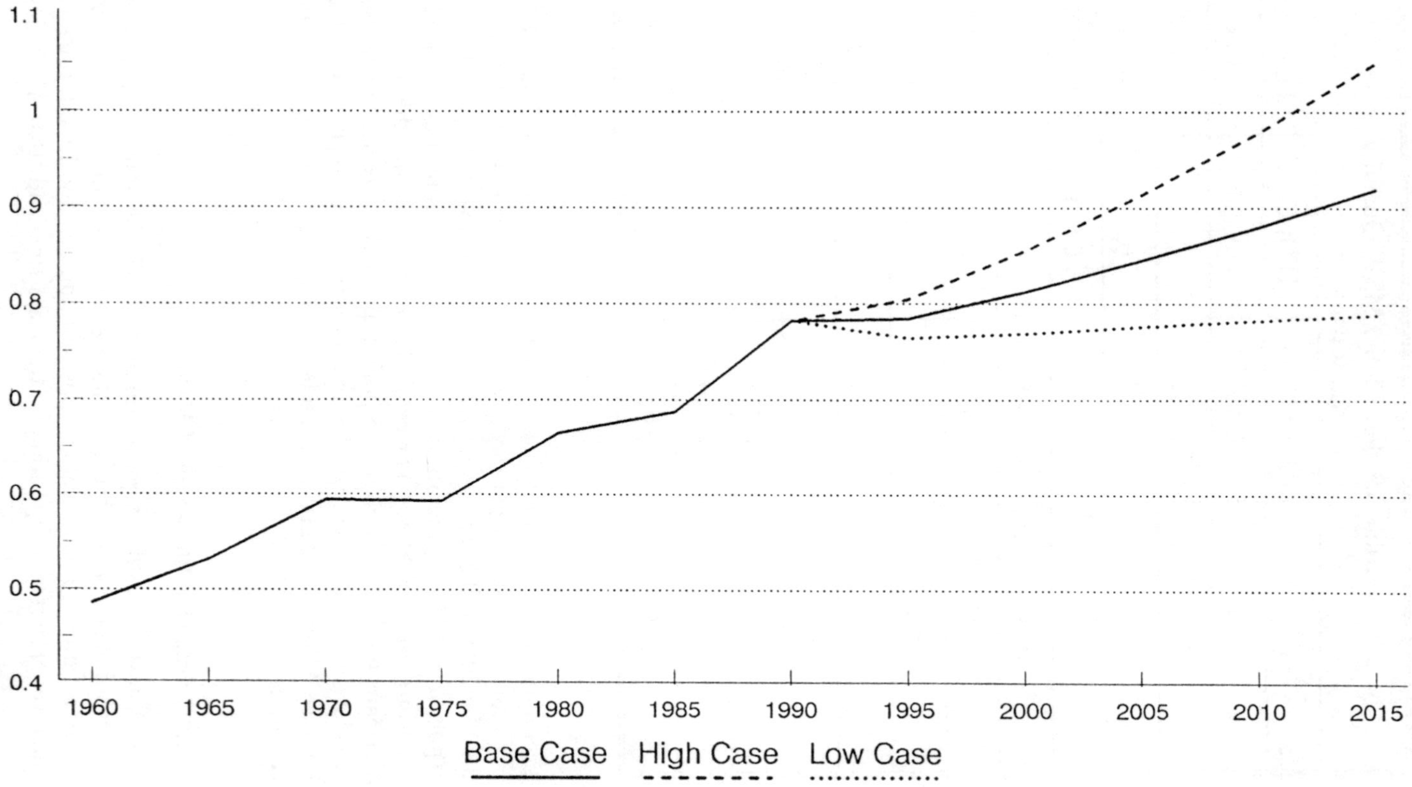

Base Case   High Case   Low Case

Btu values for each of the major MSW components are given in Office of
Technology Assessment (1989) and are adopted for this analysis.

Table 3.4 presents the historical and projected composition of MSW in
percentage terms for the time period 1960 to 2000 in five-year increments.
Table 3.5 presents the average estimated and projected heat value of a pound
of MSW over the same time period. Note that this time period is marked
by a rather sharp increase in plastics (from 0.5 percent in 1960 to 11.2
percent in 2000), a moderate increase in paper and paper board (from 34.1
percent in 1960 to 38.1 percent in 2000), and a large drop in food and
yard wastes.

The Btu value is estimated to have increased steadily since 1960 when it
was about 3,774 Btus per pound to 1990 when it was about 5,114 Btus
per pound. Note that the estimate for 1990 is very close to the average Btu
value reported by operators of existing and planned WTE facilities in the
United States. Government Advisory Associates (1991) reports an average
Btu value of 5,145 Btus per pound for all facilities in 1990. The Btu growth
is obviously coming from the increasing percentage of paper and, in particular, plastics. Plastics contributed only 70 Btus to the average pound of
refuse in 1960, while they contributed 1,162 Btus to an average pound of
MSW in 1990.

Table 3.6 and Figure 3.3 present our estimated and projected MSW Btu
values for the period 1960 to 2015. Our base-case projections for 2005,
2010, and 2015 reflect an assumed continuation of historical growth trends.
Under these assumptions, the Btu value of MSW will increase to about
5,980 Btus per pound in 2010 and to about 6,214 Btus per pound in 2015.

Future potential restrictions on the use of some packaging or on the
composition of packaging—e.g., a mandated shift away from plastics—may
alter the Btu value of MSW. Changes may also occur as many communities
ban yard waste from the MSW stream and recycling programs alter the mix
of MSW available for incineration. The effects of these changes are, however,
difficult to predict at this time.

To arrive at a low-case scenario, the base-case values are reduced, somewhat arbitrarily, by 10 percent for the entire projection time frame. The
high-case scenario assumes that the base-case numbers are increased by 10
percent. Additional work is warranted to evaluate the Btu impacts of various
voluntary and mandatory recycling and source-reduction programs that will
alter the composition of the waste available for energy production.[11]

3.4.4 Projected Fraction of MSW Managed by WTE

Projections of future energy from WTE are difficult to make because of
the great uncertainty about the degree to which WTE will penetrate its
potential market. As mentioned earlier, WTE is relatively new. As of 1960

Table 3.4 Historical and Projected Composition of MSW: 1960-2000
(in percent by weight)

Material	YEAR								
	1960	1965	1970	1975	1980	1985	1990	1995	2000
Paper and Paper Board	34.1	36.8	36.3	33.6	36.6	37.4	37.5	38.1	38.1
Glass	7.6	8.4	10.4	10.5	10.0	8.0	6.7	6.5	6.1
Metals	12.0	10.7	11.6	11.2	9.7	8.6	8.3	7.9	7.7
Plastics	0.5	1.4	2.5	3.5	5.2	7.1	8.3	9.6	11.2
Rubber and Leather	2.3	2.5	2.6	3.0	2.9	2.3	2.4	2.8	2.9
Textiles	1.9	1.8	1.6	1.7	1.7	1.7	2.9	2.9	3.0
Wood	3.4	3.4	3.3	3.4	3.3	5.0	6.3	6.5	7.2
Food Waste	13.9	12.3	10.5	10.5	8.8	8.0	6.7	6.3	5.9
Yard Waste	22.8	20.9	19.0	19.7	18.4	18.2	17.9	16.2	14.8
Other Organics	0.1	0.3	0.7	1.3	1.9	2.1	1.6	1.7	1.6
Other Inorganics	1.5	1.5	1.5	1.6	1.5	1.5	1.5	1.4	1.4
TOTAL*	100	100	100	100	100	100	100	100	100

Source: U.S. EPA, 1992a.
*   May not sum because of rounding

Table 3.5 Historical and Projected MSW Btu Value: 1960-2000
(in Btus per pound of MSW)

Material	Estimated Btus/pound of Material	Year								
		1960	1965	1970	1975	1980	1985	1990	1995	2000
Paper and Paper Board	6500	2216.5	2392.0	2359.5	2184.0	2379.0	2431.0	2437.5	2476.5	2476.5
Glass	0	0.0	0.0	0.0	0.0	0.0	0.0	0.0	0.0	0.0
Metals	0	0.0	0.0	0.0	0.0	0.0	0.0	0.0	0.0	0.0
Plastics	14000	70.0	196.0	350.0	490.0	728.0	994.0	1162.0	1344.0	1568.0
Rubber and Leather	9500	218.5	237.5	247.0	285.0	275.5	218.5	228.0	266.0	275.5
Textiles	6800	129.2	122.4	108.8	115.6	115.6	115.6	197.2	197.2	204.0
Wood	6500	221.0	221.0	214.5	221.0	214.5	325.0	409.0	422.5	468.0
Food Waste	2000	278.0	246.0	210.0	210.0	176.0	160.0	134.0	126.0	118.0
Yard Waste	2800	638.4	585.2	532.0	551.6	515.2	509.6	501.2	453.6	414.4
Other Organics	2800	2.8	8.4	19.6	36.4	53.2	58.8	44.8	47.6	44.8
Other Inorganics	0	0.0	0.0	0.0	0.0	0.0	0.0	0.0	0.0	0.0
TOTAL*		3774.4	4008.5	4041.4	4093.6	4457.0	4812.5	5114.2	5333.4	5569.2

* Source of material Btu estimates: Office of Technology Assessment (1989).

Table 3.6 Historical and Projected Heat Value of MSW: 1960-2015 (in Btus per pound)			
Year	Base Case	High Case	Low Case
1960	3774.4	3774.4	3774.4
1965	4008.5	4008.5	4008.5
1970	4041.4	4041.4	4041.4
1975	4093.6	4093.6	4093.6
1980	4457.0	4457.0	4457.0
1985	4812.5	4812.5	4812.5
1990	5114.2	5114.2	5114.2
1995	5333.4	5866.7	4800.1
2000	5569.2	6126.1	5012.3
2005	5746.4	6321.0	5171.8
2010	5980.1	6578.1	5382.1
2015	6213.7	6835.1	5592.3

there was essentially no WTE capacity in the United States, and as recently as 1985 only 4.6 percent of MSW was managed by WTE. About 15.2 percent was burned with heat recovery in 1990 according to Franklin Associates and U.S. EPA.

Industry experts are hesitant to speculate about future WTE capacity additions. For example, Steven Levy at the U.S. EPA (who maintains a data base on all planned and operational WTE facilities) estimates that WTE will account for about 17.5 percent of MSW in 1992, up from 16.9 percent in 1991. (Kiser [1992b] concurs with the U.S. EPA estimates.) Levy will not venture a guess beyond 1992, however. In their 1992 document, Franklin Associates (U.S. EPA, 1992a) projects that WTE will account for only 17 percent of MSW by 1995 and increase to 20.8 percent by 2000. The most recent Franklin projections are down from those reported in their 1990 document (U.S. EPA, 1990b)—i.e., 22.8 percent for 1995 and 25.5 percent for 2000. Curlee (1991) projects in his base case that WTE will account for 30 percent of MSW by 1995, 40 percent by 2000, 50 percent by 2005, and 55 percent by 2010. The author acknowledges, however, that at this

Figure 3.3
Historical and Projected Heat Value of MSW: 1960-2015 (in Btus per pound)

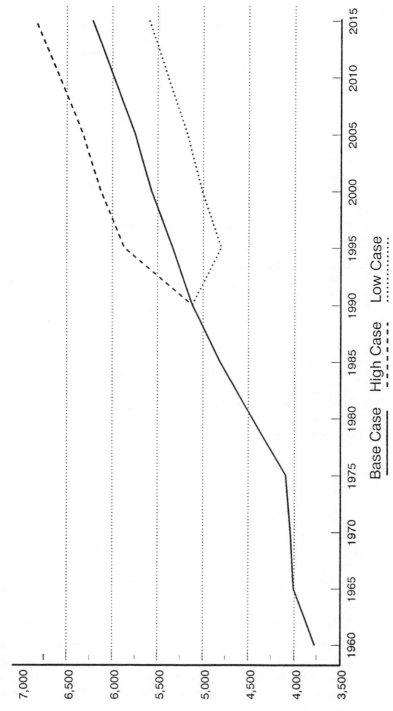

Base Case   High Case   Low Case

Table 3.7 The Percentage of MSW Combusted with Heat Recovery			
Year	Base Case	High Case	Low Case
1960	0.0	0.0	0.0
1965	0.2	0.2	0.2
1970	0.3	0.3	0.3
1975	0.5	0.5	0.5
1980	1.8	1.8	1.8
1985	4.6	4.6	4.6
1990	15.2	15.2	15.2
1995	20.0	18.0	25.0
2000	25.0	22.0	30.0
2005	30.0	25.0	40.0
2010	40.0	30.0	50.0
2015	50.0	40.0	60.0

Source of historical information: U.S. EPA 1992a.

time these projections are too high, especially given the recent cancellations of WTE projects.

Table 3.7 and Figure 3.4 present this study's assumed percentages of MSW that will be managed by WTE over the projection time frame. In the base case, WTE is projected to increase from 15.2 percent in 1990 to 30 percent in 2005 and to 50 percent by 2015. In the high case, WTE increases to 40 percent by 2005 and to 60 percent by 2015. In the low case, WTE increases to 25 percent by 2005 and to 40 percent by 2015.

3.4.5 Estimated and Projected Energy from MSW Combustion

Table 3.8 and Figure 3.5 combine information from Tables 3.2, 3.6, and 3.7 to estimate and project energy from the combustion of MSW over the time period 1960 to 2015. Energy from MSW combustion is estimated to have increased from less than 0.01 quadrillion Btus (quads) in 1970 to 0.02

Figure 3.4
The Percentage of MSW Combusted with Heat Recovery

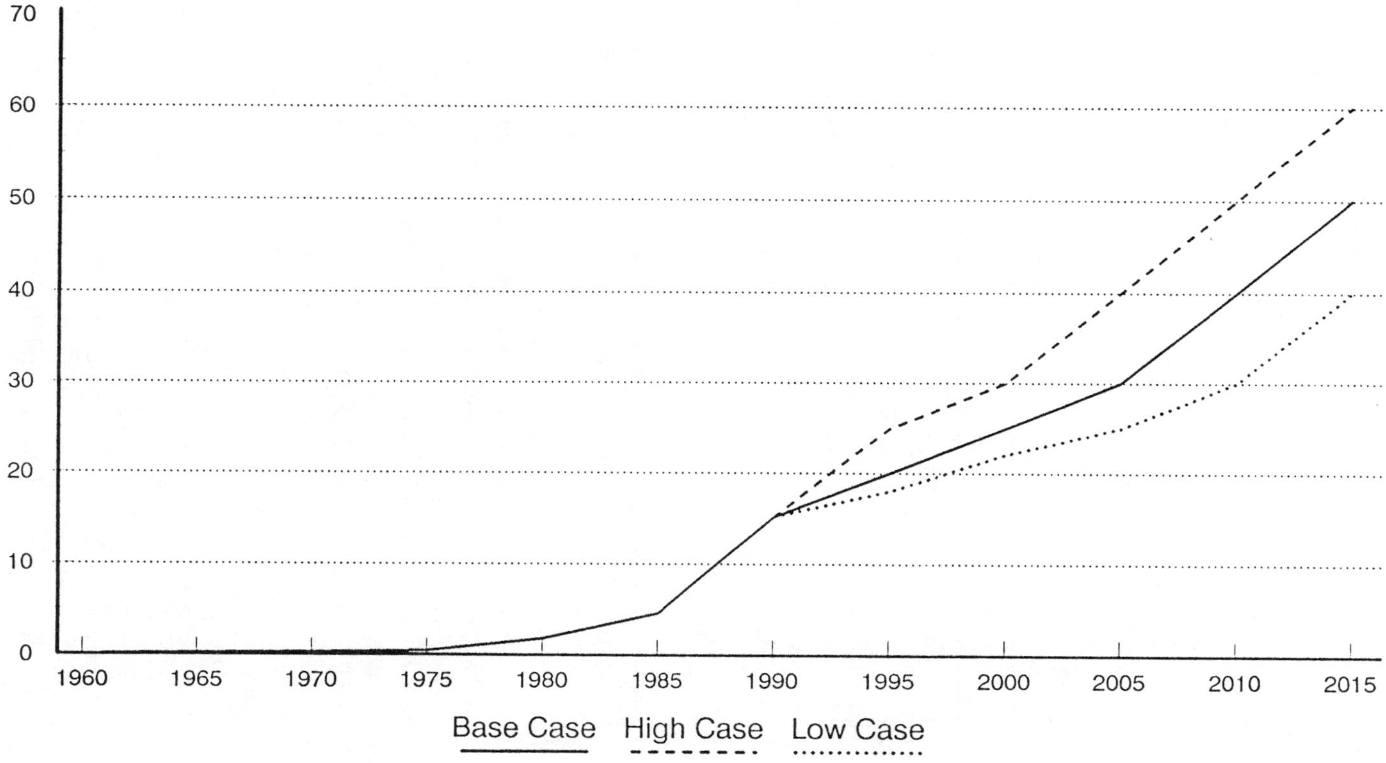

Base Case ——— High Case – – – – Low Case ....

Table 3.8 Estimated and Projected Energy from MSW Combustion (in 10^{15} Btus or Quads)			
Year	Base Case	High Case	Low Case
1960	0	0	0
1965	0.002	0.002	0.002
1970	0.003	0.003	0.003
1975	0.005	0.005	0.005
1980	0.024	0.024	0.024
1985	0.073	0.073	0.073
1990	0.304	0.304	0.304
1995	0.435	0.613	0.343
2000	0.607	0.842	0.455
2005	0.803	1.273	0.553
2010	1.190	1.818	0.714
2015	1.651	2.490	1.019

quads in 1980 to 0.30 quads in 1990. Under our base-case assumptions, WTE will produce about 0.60 quads by 2000 and increase to about 1.65 quads by 2015. Energy from WTE increases to 0.46 and 1.02 quads for 2000 and 2015, respectively, under our low-case assumptions. If our high-case assumptions hold true, WTE will produce about 0.84 quads in 2000 and increase to 2.49 quads by 2015.

Table 3.9 compares our projections to those of other studies. Leading Edge Reports has projected that total WTE capacity will be 250,000 tpd by 2000. If we assume that 90 percent of that capacity is utilized and we assume our base-case assumption of 5,569.2 Btus per pound of MSW, about 0.91 quads will be produced in 2000. The U.S. Department of Energy's *National Energy Strategy* projects that WTE will provide up to 2.1 quads by 2010 (U.S. Department of Energy, 1991a). Curlee's (1991) base-case projections place WTE at 0.95 quads in 2000, increasing to 1.58 quads by 2010, and increasing further to 1.97 quads by 2030. In two 1990 studies, the Solar Energy Research Institute (SERI, 1990) and Klass (1990) projected

Figure 3.5
Estimated and Projected Energy from MSW Combustion (in 10^{15} Btus or Quads)

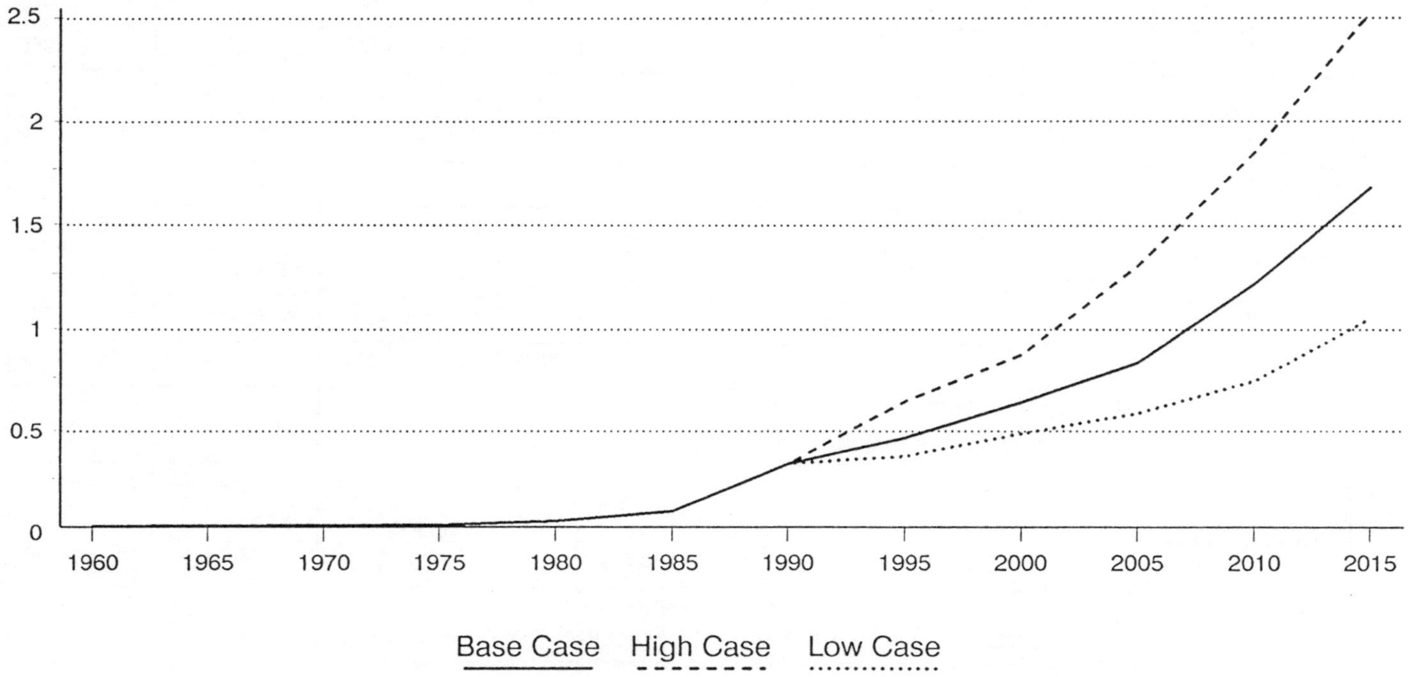

Base Case   High Case   Low Case
————   - - - - -   ....

Table 3.9 Comparisons with Other Projections of Energy from WTE
(in 10^{15} Btus or Quads)

Year	This Study			Curlee (1991)			Leading Edge Reports*	SERI (1990)			Klass (1990)	DOE (1991)
	Base Case	High Case	Low Case	Base Case	High Case	Low Case		Business as Usual	R&D Intensification Scenario	National Premiums Scenario		
1990	0.30	0.30	0.30	0.29	0.32	0.26		-	-	-		
1995	0.44	0.61	0.34	0.64	0.70	0.42		-	-	-		
2000	0.61	0.84	0.46	0.95	1.22	0.50	0.91	0.20	0.26	0.34	0.60	
2005	0.80	1.27	0.55	1.32	1.82	0.63		-	-	-		
2010	1.19	1.82	0.71	1.58	2.53	0.66		0.45	0.57	0.84		2.10
2015	1.65	2.49	1.02	1.71	2.87	0.72		-	-	-		
2020	-	-	-	1.81	3.17	0.75		0.66	0.89	1.00		
2025	-	-	-	1.89	3.50	0.79		-	-	-		
2030	-	-	-	1.97	3.84	0.82		0.87	1.20	1.17		

* Based on projected WTE capacity of 250,000 tpd in 2000. Projection assumes 90% capacity utilization and heat value of 5,569.2 Btus per pound.

WTE in the 0.2 to 0.6 quad range for 2000, increasing to between 0.45 to 0.84 quads by 2010, and increasing to between 0.87 to 1.17 quads by 2030.

To place these projections in perspective, consider that total U.S. energy consumption was about 83.4 quads in 1988 and is projected to increase to 97.4 quads in 2000 and to 108.4 quads in 2010 (Energy Information Administration, 1990). Thus, energy from WTE currently accounts for about 0.4 percent of all U.S. energy consumption. In our base-case, energy from WTE is projected to account for 0.6 percent of U.S. consumption by 2000 and increase to 1.1 percent by 2010. In our low-case, WTE will account for 0.5 and 0.7 percent in 2000 and 2010, respectively. If our high-case scenario is correct, WTE will represent about 0.9 percent of U.S. consumption in 2000 and increase to 1.7 percent by 2010. Thus, WTE is not expected to displace a large percentage of conventional energy forms used in the United States. However, when viewed in an absolute sense, the numbers are not small. For further perspective, consider that the Energy Information Administration (EIA) (1991) estimates that U.S. electric utilities consumed about 1.25 quads of petroleum, 2.87 quads of natural gas, and 2.91 quads of hydroelectric power in 1990. The EIA estimates that other energy forms— including wood, geothermal, wind, photovoltaic, solar, and waste—contributed only 0.2 quads of input energy to electric utilities in 1990. Therefore, to the extent that MSW is used for future electricity generation (and all WTE facilities in the planning phases are slated to produce electricity at least in part), WTE may become a major player in the production of electricity in the coming decades.

NOTES

1. See, for example, Hershkowitz (1987), Hershkowitz and Salerni (1987), Office of Technology Assessment (1989), and Williams (1991). Hershkowitz and Salerni find that, with respect to Japan, as much as 25 percent of the cost of WTE facilities is paid by the national government in the form of grants to local governments.

2. For more on the history of WTE adoption in Europe and the United States, see, for example, Brickner (1987), Diaz, Savage, and Golueke (1982, Chapter 1), Office of Technology Assessment (1989, Chapter 6), and Williams (1991, Chapter 8).

3. Information in this subsection is summarized from Government Advisory Associates (1991). Additional details about the current WTE industry and potential factors that may have contributed to recent cancellations of WTE projects are found in Chapters 4 and 5 of this work. The reader should note that the number of facilities and initiatives referred to in Chapters 4 and 5 differ in some cases from those given in this chapter. For the analysis purposes in subsequent chapters, some facilities have been deleted from the data set; and in some cases initiatives have been summed over several years rather than taking a "snapshot" of the situation at one particular time, as is done in this chapter.

4. Recall that PURPA only applies to facilities of 80 MW or less.

5. The following chapter of this work provides additional information on curbside recycling within communities that successfully implement WTE projects and those communities that abandon those projects during the planning phases.

6. In the early 1990s the industry became more concentrated as ABB acquired Combustion Engineering and then was acquired by Ogden Martin.

7. The four-firm concentration ratio is a widely used measure of the market power held by the industry's leading firms. Concentration has been linked to various market conditions, including profit levels, barriers to entry for new firms, the development and acceptance of new technologies, and the ability to attract capital. The largest firms in a very concentrated industry are viewed as oligopolists and have some degree of control over market prices, unlike the smaller fringe firms in the industry or any firms in a competitive market structure. A movement towards a more concentrated industry may, therefore, result in higher profit levels than a competitive market would tolerate. With respect to technology change, the relationship with market structure is less clear. Some economists have speculated that excessive competition may induce premature entry of new technologies, while a monopolist may delay the introduction of new technologies. Large firms in concentrated industries may have more access to capital markets than those firms along the fringe.

8. While European companies are entering the U.S. market, U.S. WTE firms may also have opportunities in the European market. The Integrated Waste Services Association (1992b) reports that the European market for WTE services will be about $14.5 billion between 1992 and 2005, with total capacity additions of over 100,000 tons per day.

9. For more information on the domestic WTE industry see, for example, Kilgore (1988), Kiser (1991a, 1991b), Office of Technology Assessment (1989, Chapter 6), Sweetnam (1989), and Williams (1991, Chapter 8).

10. Note that Glenn (1992b) in *BioCycle* estimates that the total quantity of MSW in the United States was about 280 million tons in 1991. The current lack of data collection activities and methodology differences make estimating the total quantity of MSW an inexact science.

11. Note that it is assumed that the energy potential of MSW is not particularly sensitive to the type of WTE technology used. Curlee (1991) presents information from Diaz, Savage, and Golueke (1982) on the net system energy output per unit input of MSW for different types of combustion technologies. Their analysis shows that the outputs for waterwall, mass-burn, modular, RDF typical, and RDF advanced technologies are all about the same. If transportation energy is considered, RDF may be at a slight disadvantage. For an input of 4,500 Btus, a waterwall unit will have outputs of about 2,500 Btus. Excluding energy that may be required to transport RDF from the RDF facility to where it is burned, RDF is estimated to have an output of 2,111 Btus for an input of 4,500 Btus.

Chapter 4

Waste-to-Energy in the United States and Key Socioeconomic Factors

4.1 INTRODUCTION

A primary purpose of this work is to assess the relationship between the community's decision about WTE technologies and various socioeconomic parameters. Subsequent chapters focus specifically on financial trends that have played a key role in the decision process and present the results of four in-depth case studies that address the relationship between decisions about WTE and key socioeconomic parameters but focus more importantly on the decision-making process itself.

This chapter examines at an aggregate level a variety of potential relationships between decisions about WTE and socioeconomic parameters. In other words, whereas the case studies examine conditions at four specific sites, this part of the work takes a more general perspective in that data were collected and analyzed for all existing and most scratched/abandoned facilities, as well as the states and communities in which those projects were considered. Numerous questions are addressed. For example, does the decision to adopt or abandon a WTE project correlate with socioeconomic characteristics such as per capita income, population density, population age, educational level, and type of commercial/industrial base? Is there a relationship between population growth and WTE? Are communities with relatively high-cost waste-disposal systems more likely to consider and adopt WTE? Is there a relationship between the existence of an active recycling program and the decision about WTE? Do state legislative mandates to recycle and reduce the quantity of MSW correlate with the adoption or rejection of WTE? Is the consideration and adoption of WTE more likely to occur in states with limited landfill capacity? Is a community's ambient air quality related to its decision about WTE? These are but some of the issues addressed in this chapter.

Before examining how socioeconomic parameters may contribute to decisions to consider and possibly abandon a WTE project, a word of warning is appropriate about this analysis. Specifically, the emphasis of this work is on identifying relationships, not establishing causality. Due to data limitations and other reasons, this work cannot establish that specific decisions about WTE are "caused" by particular socioeconomic conditions. While relationships can be established, the stronger conclusion of "causality" must await future work.

4.2 ANALYSIS OF COMMUNITIES WITH WASTE-TO-ENERGY INITIATIVES

4.2.1 Background to the Analysis

Government Advisory Associates (GAA) has maintained a detailed data base on all planned, operational, and shutdown WTE facilities in the United States since the early 1980s. In more recent issues of their publication *Resource Recovery Yearbook*, GAA has also reported on scratched/abandoned WTE projects (Government Advisory Associates, 1988, 1991). For those years prior to the time that GAA kept records on scratched projects, a close examination of planned and existing facilities from one issue of the data base to the next allows the identification of scratched projects.

However, the GAA data do not easily allow one to develop a comprehensive longitudinal data base containing information about the annual status of each facility since 1980, and such a data base was not constructed for this work. A cumulative listing of counties involved with WTE initiatives was instead prepared, indicating the status of the initiatives in the county as of 1990. Information on each of the WTE initiatives contained in the GAA data bases from the years 1982, 1984, 1986-1987, 1988-1989, and 1991 were reviewed to determine the county in which the facility is or was to be located. Relatively few of the initiatives have been sponsored by multicounty organizations, although many WTE initiatives appeared to be dependent on obtaining waste from a multicounty area. In those cases where the site was not clearly defined or determined, the most populous county in the service area was chosen as it would most closely reflect the characteristics of the population primarily responsible for deciding on the facility.

This chapter's analysis makes comparisons between counties with varying WTE situations. First, counties with no WTE initiatives are compared to counties with WTE initiative(s). A county that has had some involvement with WTE during this period (e.g., planning, operating, etc.) is considered as a WTE initiative county in this analysis. Second, counties with operating WTE facilities are compared to counties that have scratched/abandoned WTE initiatives.[1] Operating facilities include all currently built and operating facilities. Scratched/abandoned facilities are either projects that never

Table 4.1 Distribution of Counties by WTE Status (number of counties)		
WTE Status of County	Metro Counties	Non-metro Counties
All Counties	722	2347
Counties with No WTE Initiative	470	2458
Counties with WTE Initiative	252	102
Counties with Scratched Initiatives	136	48

matured beyond the planning stage or facilities that were under construction but never became operational.

To assess the relationships between WTE decisions and local socioeconomic characteristics, information on the location of WTE facilities was matched with local socioeconomic data. Organizing the data by counties provides the simplest and most consistent regional unit of analysis for this study. In many regions, local waste management services are a function of county governments; in those cases the county is the appropriate spatial unit of analysis. In those cases where a large city or township provides the bulk of the service in the county, it is expected that the demographic and economic characteristics of the city will also dominate the county statistics. The independent cities of Virginia are an exception, in that their statistics are often reported separately. The approach used for the independent cities in this study was to incorporate the city data with an associated county.[2]

Summary results of this county identification process with respect to distribution of initiatives are summarized in Table 4.1. Note that because of methodological concerns some counties with initiatives were deleted from this analysis. Specifically, initiatives in Hawaii and Alaska were omitted because the county basis of analysis was inappropriate for these states. Several facilities serving military installations also were dropped. Many counties, such as Los Angeles County, California, have more than one WTE initiative. For reasons presented later in this discussion, initiatives are desegregated by metropolitan and non-metropolitan counties. Graphic depictions of the counties that are and have been involved in WTE initiatives are presented in Figures 4.1, 4.2, and 4.3. The U.S. maps are shaded to indicate the counties that have had a WTE initiative of various types during the time period covered in the GAA data bases.

Also indicated on the map in Figure 4.1 are counties with populations over 500,000 (i.e., high population). The predominance of WTE sites in populous counties, as depicted in Table 4.1 and displayed visually in the map of Figure 4.1, indicates that WTE initiatives are primarily a large-county phenomena. Indeed, early in the analysis it was found useful to conduct separate analyses based on the urban orientation of the counties. The U.S. Census Bureau classifies 722 contiguous U.S. counties as primarily metropolitan in character. These will be referred to as metro counties. The remaining 2,346 counties are referred to as non-metro. Table 4.1 presents a breakdown of counties according to their WTE status. Over twice as many metro counties (252) had WTE initiatives as in non-metro areas (102). However, only a little over a third of the metro areas have had WTE initiatives (i.e., 252 out of the 722 metro counties). Initiatives took place in a very small share—less than 5 percent—of the non-metro counties (i.e., there were only 102 non-metro counties with initiatives out of the total 2,347 non-metro counties).

Additional information on the distribution of counties with operating WTE facilities and scratched initiatives is presented in Figures 4.2 and 4.3. Again, it can be seen that the majority of WTE activity has been in the metro counties.

The structure of the county data presented in Figure 4.1 sets the stage for the two empirical questions that are addressed in the analysis of this section. The first question is: Are there any differences in the socioeconomic characteristics of the 354 counties that have been actively involved with WTE initiatives and the remaining 3,069 counties? The second question is: Do the factors identified above also differentiate between counties that followed the process through to completion (i.e., currently have one or more operating facility) and those counties that scratched the initiative along the way?

A wide variety of data was available for each county from which interesting relationships could be investigated. A primary goal of this exploratory analysis was to identify community characteristics that appeared to be supportive of WTE initiatives, as well as to identify any that were correlated with the abandonment of initiatives. For discussion purposes, it is useful to consider the information collected and analyzed in four distinct sets: (1) the spatial settlement patterns of each community, (2) the socioeconomic characteristics of the local population, (3) the local availability of waste management alternatives, and (4) the local climate for environmental concern. Analysis of each set of information is conducted in two parts. First, each

Figure 4.1
WTE Initiatives by County Size

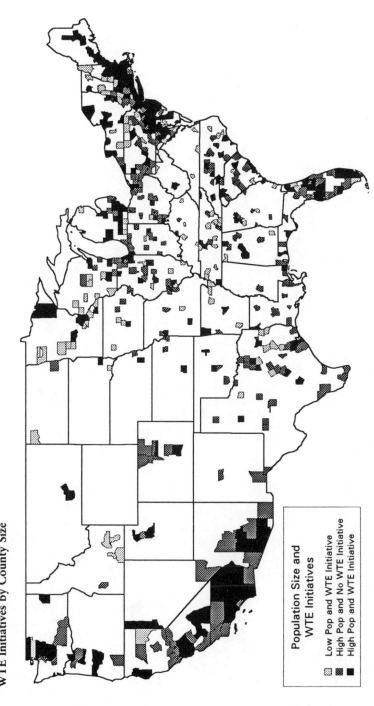

Population Size and
WTE Initiatives

Low Pop and WTE Initiative
High Pop and No WTE Initiative
High Pop and WTE Initiative

Figure 4.2
Counties with Existing and/or Planned WTE Facilities

Counties with Existing and/or
Planned WTE Facilities

Planned Facilities

Existing Facilities

Both Existing and Planned

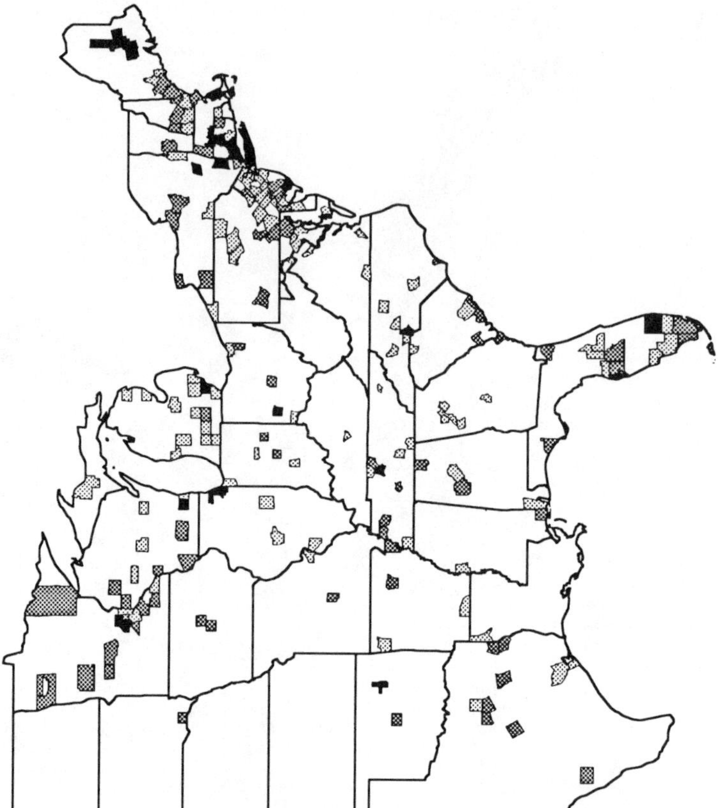

Figure 4.3
Counties with Scratched WTE Facilities

Counties with Scratched
WTE Facilities

■ Scratched Facility

of the socioeconomic characteristics is introduced and examined as to its potential relationship with the WTE status of the sample counties. The analysis is conducted as a comparison of mean scores for counties categorized by the nature of their WTE involvement. This allows the addressing of such issues as, for example, the relationship between a decision about WTE and county population growth. Second, a multiple indicator analysis is conducted that allows for the simultaneous examination of the complete set of questions that involve more than one characteristic at a time. For example, one may ask, is there a significant relationship between a decision about WTE and county population growth given that the county is also a higher income county.

The following subsections introduce each issue area and the selected characteristic variables for that area and then present a comparison of WTE initiative and non-WTE county scores for those variables. Comparisons between counties that initiate and complete a WTE project and counties that initiate and then scratch a WTE project are then presented. The final subsection completes the analysis with a discussion of the multiple regression analysis for the complete set of variables.

4.2.2 Demographic Settlement Patterns

The design size of waste-to-energy facilities has been increasing. This increase suggests that economies of scale are important in the technology or perhaps that some minimum plant size is required for profitable operations. Common sense suggests that size will be important. The catchment area should, for example, provide enough potential waste to support continuous WTE operations. Indeed, the data indicate that WTE initiatives are predominately in the larger metro counties. Additionally, if the sources of municipal waste in a region are highly concentrated due to a dense settlement pattern, the cost of collecting the waste stream may be considerably less than in sparsely settled counties.

A basic characteristic for discriminating among counties that could feasibly support a facility is suggested by settlement patterns. Large densely populated counties may, in general, be more favorable toward WTE. Thus, it is of interest to examine whether the size or compactness of the local waste stream is an important determinant in the selection of WTE options. County population settlement patterns can serve as proxies for these characteristics of the waste stream. For this analysis, the relative size of a region's waste stream is measured as simply the county population, and the density is measured by the population relative to land area (i.e., persons per square mile in the county). A second measure of spatial settlement density—the percent of the population living in rural areas—is also considered in this analysis. Finally, a growing region may place greater pressure on solid waste management capacity and may, therefore, be more likely to be involved

Table 4.2 County Population Density
(persons per square mile)
[numbers in parenthesis are standard errors of group means]

WTE Status of County	Metro Counties		Non-metro Counties	
	Mean	Std. Error	Mean	Std. Error
All Counties	727	(122)	38	(0.9)
No WTE Initiative	249	(20)	36	(0.9)
WTE Initiative	1618*	(341)	74*	(5.4)
Operating Facility	1085	(246)	56	(7.2)
Scratched Initiative	1367	(283)	78#	(7.5)

* Indicates a significant difference (>95%) in means of the WTE and non-WTE counties.

\# Indicates a significant difference (>95%) in means of counties with canceled initiatives and counties with operating WTE facilities.

with a WTE initiative. To test for this in the analysis, the percentage growth in population from 1980 to 1990 was calculated for all counties. The average population growth of all counties for that 10-year period was around 4 percent. The rate for metro counties (13.6 percent) was significantly greater than the non-metro counties (a low 1.1 percent growth rate).

In the analysis, counties that have had WTE initiatives are compared to counties that have not been involved with WTE. Counties with operating facilities are also compared to counties with scratched initiatives. Means for each of the study indicators are calculated for the different groupings of the counties required to conduct these two analyses. Tables 4.2 through 4.5 present the various WTE status group means for each of the population settlement indicators discussed above. The associated means of each indicator for all metro and all non-metro counties are also presented in the tables for reference.

Table 4.3 County Population Size (1000 persons) [numbers in parenthesis are standard errors of group means]				
WTE Status of County	Metro Counties		Non-metro Counties	
	Mean	Std. Error	Mean	Std. Error
All Counties	266	(18.9)	24	(0.5)
No WTE Initiative	129	(8.4)	22	(0.5)
WTE Initiative	522*	(47.8)	50*	(3.2)
Operating Facility	624	(128.9)	47.1	(11.1)
Scratched Initiative	591	(81.5)	50.4	(4.5)

*   Indicates a significant difference (>95%) in means of the WTE and non-WTE counties.

\#   Indicates a significant difference (>95%) in means of counties with canceled initiatives and counties with operating WTE facilities.

As an example, the first line of Table 4.2 depicts the difference between metro and non-metro counties. The next two lines present the means for all counties without and with WTE initiatives. The final two lines present the means for counties with operating facilities and scratched initiatives. The standard error of the mean for the group is presented in parentheses. Using the standard errors, one can test to determine if the difference between two means is greater than what might likely be attributed to chance. *A simplified test can be used to identify statistically significant differences (at a conservative 95% level) between two means. If the difference between the two means is greater than twice the larger of the standard errors involved, the difference can be considered significant.* Table 4.2 indicates that, as one would expect, metro counties are significantly more dense than non-metro. The average population density for metro counties is 727 persons per square mile. This is much greater than the 38 persons per square miles of non-metro counties. Since the difference between the two means is 689 (727 − 38)

Table 4.4 County Rural Population (percent rural) [numbers in parenthesis are standard errors of group means]				
WTE Status of County	Metro Counties		Non-metro Counties	
	Mean	Std. Error	Mean	Std. Error
All Counties	36.1	(0.98)	72.8	(0.49)
No WTE Initiative	44.5	(1.21)	73.4	(0.50)
WTE Initiative	20.4*	(1.12)	60.8*	(1.80)
Operating Facility	20.0	(1.98)	57.2	(2.81)
Scratched Initiative	20.8	(1.60)	62.3#	(2.92)

* Indicates a significant difference (>95%) in means of the WTE and non-WTE counties.

\# Indicates a significant difference (>95%) in means of counties with canceled initiatives and counties with operating WTE facilities.

and this is more than 244 (i.e., twice the 122 value of the metro counties standard error, the larger of the two involved), it also can be considered statistically significant. Two tests, separately conducted for metro and non-metro counties, are indicated in the tables. An asterisk (*) is used to indicate if the means of WTE counties are significantly different than non-WTE counties. A # sign is used to indicate if the means of counties with scratched initiatives are different from those with operating facilities.

A striking pattern is evident in the data presented in Tables 4.2 to 4.5. In general, for all of the demographic settlement patterns except population growth, a significant difference appears between the WTE and non-WTE counties. In other words, counties that have had a WTE initiative (i.e., a planned, operational, shut-down, or scratched facility) are significantly different from counties that have not had a WTE initiative. However, and somewhat surprisingly, no significant differences are discernible between metro counties with operating facilities and those that have scratched WTE

Table 4.5 County Population Growth (percent change 1980-1990) [numbers in parenthesis are standard errors of group means]				
WTE Status of County	Metro Counties		Non-metro Counties	
	Mean	Std. Error	Mean	Std. Error
All Counties	13.6	(1.28)	1.1	(0.29)
No WTE Initiative	13.9	(0.91)	0.9	(0.30)
WTE Initiative	13.0	(1.03)	4.9*	(1.05)
Operating Facility	11.5	(1.35)	4.2	(2.81)
Scratched Initiative	14.2	(1.54)	3.9	(1.42)

* Indicates a significant difference (>95%) in means of the WTE and non-WTE counties.

\# Indicates a significant difference (>95%) in means of counties with canceled initiatives and counties with operating WTE facilities.

initiatives. Those communities that initiate planning for a WTE facility and subsequently cancel their project are not significantly different from communities that initiate a WTE project and see their facility through to completion. As this pattern is so striking and consistent, each factor will not be discussed in great detail. Rather, the basic findings as illustrated in the tables will be highlighted by focusing on population density. To further simplify the following discussion, only metro counties are discussed in detail.

The mean population density of metro counties with no WTE initiative is 249 persons per square mile. This value is significantly less than 1,618, which is the mean of all counties with WTE initiatives.

Also of keen interest for this study is the relative ranking of counties that have operating and scratched facilities; the metro counties have densities of 1,085 and 1,367 persons per square mile, respectively. The mean population densities of these counties are also significantly greater than that of counties that have not had a WTE initiative. However, these means are not signifi-cantly different from each other.

The same pattern is displayed by county size. Metro counties with no WTE initiatives are considerably smaller than those with initiatives. This suggests that there may indeed be a minimum threshold population size for the initiation of a WTE project. Counties that have scratched WTE plans are slightly, but not significantly, smaller than counties with operating WTE facilities. Interestingly, the same pattern again shows up in non-metro counties. The non-WTE counties are significantly smaller than ones with WTE. But the large difference in population size between the average metro and non-metro county suggests that two different scales of plant (market size) may exist for WTE technologies. This observation is consistent with our knowledge that modular units are more often used in counties with smaller populations, and large mass-burn units are typically adopted in the larger metro areas.

In the average metro county, some 36 percent of the population lives in a rural environment. In non-metro counties, the average is around 73 percent rural. In a sparsely populated area distant from major cities, one would expect a mostly rural population. A county with large population and area that is located adjacent to a major city could be classified as metro but still have a significant rural population in the area far from the city. The dis-tribution of the population between the city and rural areas would be mea-sured by the rural percentage. For any given area and population size (i.e., population density) many different rural patterns could, therefore, be pres-ent. The rural composition of the population, consequently, can provide an additional dimension on the spatial distribution of the population.

For both metro and non-metro areas, the pattern for rural population is found to be the same as for population density. In metro counties without WTE initiatives, the rural population is around 45 percent, indicating more sparsely settled areas. Metro counties with WTE initiatives are significantly less rural (21 percent), and those with scratched initiatives are not signifi-cantly different from counties with operating facilities. The non-metro coun-ties show a similar pattern. Non-WTE, non-metro counties have a rural population of 73 percent, which is significantly greater than all of the means of the non-metro counties with WTE initiatives. This result, which is con-sistent with the other indicators, also indicates a dual market for WTE—one with a scale appropriate to large metro areas and the other with a scale appropriate to the larger of the non-metro counties.

Unlike other population measures, population growth during the period does not appear to have been a significant factor in inducing metro counties to consider WTE initiatives. Metro counties with WTE initiatives do not show higher-than-average growth rates. This suggests that initiatives have been pursued to meet current population needs and not future needs based on projected county population growth. Another possible explanation would be that WTE initiatives are pursued in areas where the current population can support a facility or in areas where a facility is considered as a substitute for other waste options. The lack of a significant relationship indicates that population growth has not been required as a prerequisite for the pursuit of a WTE facility. This may not be true for non-metro counties as there is a significant relationship between population growth and considering WTE.

4.2.3 County Socioeconomic Characteristics

This subsection explores possible relationships between several socioeconomic characteristics and a community's adoption of WTE. A large number of sociodemographic variables are available to classify communities. The approach of creating regional topologies is becoming more popular since it has been adopted as a strategy in market segmentation analysis. In this analysis, only a few key variables were selected that have been proven significant as county classification variables in other analyses. The factors identify differences in the population in terms of the general level of education, personal income, age structure, and population in industrial jobs.

Data and findings presented in Table 4.6 (education), Table 4.7 (per capita income), Table 4.8 (population age), and Table 4.9 (industrial employment) suggest that metro counties with a lower industrial base, a wealthier and better educated population, and with a strong representation of persons at the family-formation age are more likely to consider a WTE initiative. The differences between counties with WTE initiatives and non-WTE counties are significant with respect to all four of the characteristics. Again, however, there are no significant differences between counties that have canceled initiatives and counties that have operating WTE facilities.

In the case of non-metro counties, the test results are split. With respect to education, per capita income and population age structure, the metro and non-metro results are the same, albeit with somewhat lower values in the case of non-metro counties. However, there appear to be no significant differences in industrial employment between non-metro WTE and non-WTE counties.

In summary, population characteristics examined in this section provide results similar to those examined in the previous subsection. The selected factors do appear to discriminate between WTE-initiative and non-WTE-initiative counties. However, the factors do not differentiate those counties that have decided to scratch their WTE program from those communities that have an operating WTE facility.

4.2.4 Availability of Waste Management Alternatives

As discussed in previous chapters, WTE facilities are only one of several alternative MSW management strategies. Past perceptions of the scarcity of

Table 4.6 County Population with High School Degrees (percent with a high school degree) [numbers in parenthesis are standard errors of group means]				
WTE Status of County	Metro Counties		Non-metro Counties	
	Mean	Std. Error	Mean	Std. Error
All Counties	65.7	(0.38)	57.2	(0.25)
No WTE Initiative	63.8	(0.5)	57.1	(0.25)
WTE Initiative	69.2*	(0.5)	60.2*	(1.11)
Operating Facility	70.0	(0.8)	59.8	(2.24)
Scratched Initiative	69.3	(0.7)	61.8	(1.51)

* Indicates a significant difference (>95%) in means of the WTE and non-WTE counties.

\# Indicates a significant difference (>95%) in means of counties with canceled initiatives and counties with operating WTE facilities.

landfill space at the national, regional, or local levels may have promoted interest in WTE. Urban areas with high-cost landfills and severe difficulties in siting new landfills may have looked more favorably toward WTE. In addition, some communities may have looked to recycling as a substitute for the development of WTE. To examine these issues, several regional indicators were constructed. One set related to recycling options, and a second set examined the impact of landfill alternatives. Two recycling options were investigated: the presence of a local recycling program and the region's potential access to a materials recovery facility (MRF).

The Council for Solid Waste Solutions (CSWS) (renamed the Partnership for Plastics Progress) maintains a data base on plastics recycling programs in some 3,965 communities. The communities are further identified in terms of providing one or more recycling options, such as curbside, drop-off, or buy-back programs. The CSWS data are designed primarily to cover programs that include plastics recycling, but according to CSWS the data cover

Table 4.7 County Per Capita Income (constant 1982 dollars per person) [numbers in parenthesis are standard errors of group means]				
WTE Status of County	Metro Counties		Non-metro Counties	
	Mean	Std. Error	Mean	Std. Error
All Counties	13,408	(111)	10,848	(46)
No WTE Initiative	12,622	(112)	10,830	(47)
WTE Initiative	14,876*	(213)	11,237*	(196)
Operating Facility	14,967	(370)	11,056	(358)
Scratched Initiative	14,910	(271)	11,473	(328)

*   Indicates a significant difference (>95%) in means of the WTE and non-WTE counties.

\#   Indicates a significant difference (>95%) in means of counties with canceled initiatives and counties with operating WTE facilities.

virtually all recycling programs. For the needs of this study, all communities in the CSWS data base were located by county, and a county data base was constructed. A county was considered to have a recycling option if any community in the county had a program. Note that the intent of developing this indicator is not to measure the amount of recycling that might have taken place, but rather to provide an indicator of local perceptions about recycling as a serious waste management option. Consequently, it was assumed that the existence of a recycling program anywhere in the county suggested a community awareness of the recycling option. In developing the data base and examining the data on many of the counties with multiple community reports, it became clear that the recycling program was often a county program, perhaps in about one-fourth of the cases.

Table 4.10 presents the results of the analysis of recycling programs and WTE initiatives. The recycle indicator was 1 if there was a recycling program in the county and 0 otherwise. In this case, the means can also be interpreted

Table 4.8 County Population at Family Formation Age (percent of persons aged 22 to 39) [numbers in parenthesis are standard errors of group means]				
WTE Status of County	Metro Counties		Non-metro Counties	
	Mean	Std. Error	Mean	Std. Error
All Counties	21.1	(0.14)	17.7	(0.08)
No WTE Initiative	20.8	(0.17)	17.6	(0.08)
WTE Initiative	21.7*	(0.22)	19.1*	(0.33)
Operating Facility	21.7	(0.42)	19.5	(0.68)
Scratched Initiative	20.8	(1.60)	19.3	(0.45)

* Indicates a significant difference (>95%) in means of the WTE and non-WTE counties.

\# Indicates a significant difference (>95%) in means of counties with canceled initiatives and counties with operating WTE facilities.

as the share of counties with a recycling program. Somewhat surprisingly, counties without a WTE initiative have a smaller share of recycling programs than counties with WTE initiatives. Recycling programs are found to be positively correlated with the presence of WTE initiatives, for both metro and non-metro counties.

The number of materials recovery facilities (MRFs) in each state as of 1990 was obtained from Glenn (1991) in *BioCycle*. The number of MRFs in a state is used as the potential accessibility of any county in that state to a facility. If there are numerous facilities, then it is assumed that the average county in the state has a high accessibility. The typical metro county is in a state that has an average of about six MRFs (the mean of all metro counties is 6.5). In general, metro counties with WTE initiatives have significantly greater accessibility to MRFs than metro counties without WTE initiatives. The data show little difference between counties that have scratched and

Table 4.9 County Industrial Base (percent of employment in manufacturing, mining and construction) [numbers in parenthesis are standard errors of group means]				
WTE Status of County	Metro Counties		Non-metro Counties	
	Mean	Std. Error	Mean	Std. Error
All Counties	27.7	(0.40)	31.0	(0.30)
No WTE Initiative	29.5	(0.52)	31.0	(0.30)
WTE Initiative	24.2*	(0.54)	32.1	(1.30)
Operating Facility	24.4	(0.84)	31.0	(2.17)
Scratched Initiative	24.6	(0.75)	30.0	(1.74)

*   Indicates a significant difference (>95%) in means of the WTE and non-WTE counties.

\#   Indicates a significant difference (>95%) in means of counties with canceled initiatives and counties with operating WTE facilities.

those that have adopted WTE (see Table 4.11). The non-metro situation is somewhat cloudy with no clear and dominating pattern.

The availability of landfills was examined similarly. Initially it was thought that measures of local tipping fees and landfill capacity would be ideal indicators for the potential competitiveness of landfills. However, the development of a comprehensive data base on local landfills was beyond the scope of this project, and available alternatives appear to be fraught with problems. Current measures of capacity are not consistent across all regions, and recent environmental regulations have caused a major reassessment of potential capacity at many landfill operations. In addition, an examination of tipping fees leads one to question if tipping fees are seriously related to the current cost of landfill operations. Many landfills are subsidized. We concluded that, for the purposes of this study, landfill tipping fees are not a suitable measure of the cost of the landfill option. Conse-

Table 4.10 Recycling Programs
(indicator variable: no program = 0, recycling program = 1)
[numbers in parenthesis are standard errors of group means]

WTE Status of County	Metro Counties		Non-metro Counties	
	Mean	Std. Error	Mean	Std. Error
All Counties	0.63	(0.01)	0.17	(0.01)
No WTE Initiative	0.51	(0.02)	0.16	(0.01)
WTE Initiative	0.85*	(0.02)	0.46*	(0.05)
Operating Facility	0.86	(0.04)	0.42	(0.09)
Scratched Initiative	0.87	(0.03)	0.50	(0.07)

*   Indicates a significant difference (>95%) in means of the WTE
    and non-WTE counties.

\#   Indicates a significant difference (>95%) in means of counties
    with canceled initiatives and counties with operating WTE
    facilities.

quently, simpler alternative measures of landfill capacity and cost were
developed for this analysis.

The number of open municipal landfills in each state during 1989 is
available from *BioCycle* magazine (Glenn and Riggle, 1991a). The number
of landfills in the state is used as a measure of accessibility, similar to the
MRF analysis above. Table 4.12 presents the results of this tabulation. The
data show no significant differences between counties that have had a WTE
initiative and those that have not in either the metro or non-metro cases.
Table 4.13 develops a scaled measure of landfill access. The total number
of landfills in the state was divided by the state population to provide a
measure of the per capita availability. Even when so scaled, there are no
significant differences between the different classes of counties.

Given that reliable landfill costs are not available at the county level, a
measure of the cost of waste management practices in the typical county
was developed from data presented in U.S. Bureau of the Census, *County*

Table 4.11 Access to MRFs (number of MRFs in state) [numbers in parenthesis are standard errors of group means]				
WTE Status of County	Metro Counties		Non-metro Counties	
	Mean	Std. Error	Mean	Std. Error
All Counties	6.52	(0.35)	2.51	(0.11)
No WTE Initiative	4.97	(0.38)	4.96	(1.43)
WTE Initiative	9.42*	(0.65)	6.10*	(0.93)
Operating Facility	9.22	(1.17)	7.44	(1.47)
Scratched Initiative	9.65	(0.88)	8.54#	(1.67)

* Indicates a significant difference (>95%) in means of the WTE and non-WTE counties.

\# Indicates a significant difference (>95%) in means of counties with canceled initiatives and counties with active WTE initiatives.

Government Finances: 1989-90, where expenditures in solid waste management for counties with populations greater than 500,000 are available. These annual costs reflect operating expenditures for all waste practices in the county. These data were put on a per capita basis for analysis, and Table 4.14 presents the results of the analysis. As noted in the table, this analysis is for a small subset of the total number of counties and relates primarily to metro counties. Metro counties involved in WTE initiatives have significantly higher per capita solid waste costs as compared to metro counties with no WTE initiatives. Thus, a higher solid waste management budget is correlated with a greater likelihood of involvement in WTE projects. This result is tantalizing and suggests that high alternative waste management costs may indeed be a key inducement or facilitator to WTE initiatives. Table 4.14 also provides the only case where some discrimination among different WTE categories is observed. Metro counties with operational facilities reflect higher per capita waste costs than counties that have scratched initiatives.

Table 4.12 Access to Landfills (number of landfills in state) [numbers in parenthesis are standard errors of group means]				
WTE Status of County	Metro Counties		Non-metro Counties	
	Mean	Std. Error	Mean	Std. Error
All Counties	203	(8.8)	198	(5.3)
No WTE Initiative	207	(11.5)	199	(5.4)
WTE Initiative	196	(13.5)	171	(20.4)
Operating Facility	201	(24.1)	258	(53.8)
Scratched Initiative	205	(19.4)	159	(22.4)

* Indicates a significant difference (>95%) in means of the WTE and non-WTE counties.

# Indicates a significant difference (>95%) in means of counties with canceled initiatives and counties with operating WTE facilities.

The general conclusions that can be drawn from this section are somewhat limited. The positive correlation between recycling options and WTE initiatives may simply reflect the fact that large dense counties have considered a variety of waste management strategies, or that recycling, like WTE, is facilitated by a dense urban environment. The nebulous results on the landfill indicators may be due to the aggregate and diffuse nature of the indicators available. More detailed and rigorous analyses of landfill costs and capacities may be fruitful avenues for future research.

4.2.5 The Local Climate for Environmental Concern

The initiation and acceptance of a WTE facility may be impacted by the real and perceived status of environmental quality in the community. For example, state-mandated recycle and source-reduction goals may discourage the consideration of WTE. In addition, if local atmospheric environmental

Table 4.13 Availability of Landfills (number of landfills per 1000 persons in state) [numbers in parenthesis are standard errors of group means]				
WTE Status of County	Metro Counties		Non-metro Counties	
	Mean	Std. Error	Mean	Std. Error
All Counties	0.029	(0.001)	0.043	(0.001)
No WTE Initiative	0.030	(0.001)	0.038	(0.004)
WTE Initiative	0.027	(0.002)	0.040	(0.008)
Operating Facility	0.031	(0.004)	0.047	(0.007)
Scratched Initiative	0.027	(0.003)	0.041	(0.007)

*	Indicates a significant difference (>95%) in means of the WTE and non-WTE counties.

\#	Indicates a significant difference (>95%) in means of counties with canceled initiatives and counties with operating WTE facilities.

quality has been compromised in the past, concerns may arise about any combustion technology. These and other similar issues were examined with a final set of indicators that reflect the condition of the county's environment and local and state regulations that deal with the environment.

In the recently published book *1991-1992 Green Index*, Hall and Kerr (1991) present a wide variety of indexes constructed to represent each state's level of concern for the environment. One measure they include is membership in the Sierra Club, Greenpeace, and National Wildlife Federation in each state. Each state's total membership is scaled by dividing by the state's population (in thousands). For this study, the state value is used for each county in the state, and the counties are grouped as in the earlier tests. Table 4.15 presents the summary results. Interestingly, metro counties with WTE initiatives are in states with significantly greater representation in environmental groups than is the case for non-WTE counties. As is the case

Table 4.14 County Municipal Solid Waste Disposal Expenditures
($ per capita)
[numbers in parenthesis are standard errors of group means]

WTE Status of County	Metro Counties		Non-metro Counties	
	Mean	Std. Error	Mean	Std. Error
All Counties	13.8	(1.28)	9.3	(2.23)
No WTE Initiative	8.4	(1.19)	9.2	(3.10)
WTE Initiative	18.1*	(2.03)	9.5	(2.58)
Operating Facility	24.7	(4.21)	N/A	N/A
Scratched Initiative	14.9#	(2.41)	9.4	(2.86)

* Indicates a significant difference (>95%) in means of the WTE and non-WTE counties.

\# Indicates a significant difference (>95%) in means of counties with canceled initiatives and counties with operating WTE facilities.

for many other factors considered in this chapter, there are no significant differences between counties that have adopted WTE and those that have scratched facilities. There also are no significant differences among non-metro counties.

The influence of local environmental quality was tested by identifying those counties that were in non-attainment for carbon monoxide, particulate, ozone and/or lead. A county data base was constructed with an indicator set to 1 if any part of the county was listed as in non-attainment in the *Federal Register*'s final rule on air quality designations (November 6, 1991). Table 4.16 presents the result of this environmental quality analysis. Since a 0-1 indicator was used, the means represent the proportion of counties that are in non-attainment. Surprisingly, 51 percent of the metro counties violate the limit on one or more of the pollutants. Rural counties indeed appear in general to be considerably more pristine, with only 5 percent of them in non-attainment. Non-attainment is in general a dense population

Table 4.15 Membership in Conservation Groups (state membership per 1000 persons) [numbers in parenthesis are standard errors of group means]				
WTE Status of County	Metro Counties		Non-metro Counties	
	Mean	Std. Error	Mean	Std. Error
All Counties	7.78	(0.11)	6.93	(0.06)
No WTE Initiative	7.09	(0.13)	8.37	(0.37)
WTE Initiative	9.08*	(0.19)	8.42	(0.62)
Operating Facility	9.24	(0.33)	8.87	(2.81)
Scratched Initiative	9.32	(0.27)	8.51	(0.52)

*   Indicates a significant difference (>95%) in means of the WTE and non-WTE counties.

\#   Indicates a significant difference (>95%) in means of counties with canceled initiatives and counties with active WTE initiatives.

phenomenon. The data show that metro counties with WTE initiatives are almost twice as likely to be in non-attainment as non-WTE counties. Non-metro counties with WTE programs are similarly more likely to be in non-attainment. There is a significant positive correlation with non-attainment and WTE initiatives. It should be noted that this correlation does not imply causality. It is possible that characteristics that contribute to communities being out of attainment—dense population and industrial areas—also contribute to their need for waste management capacity and their considering alternative solid waste management (SWM) options.

The last two indicators to be examined address the level of environmental regulation present in a state. A plausible hypothesis is that more stringent regulations—with respect to environmental controls and mandated incentives for recycling and source reduction—may hinder the adoption of WTE technologies. The first policy index relates specifically to stated preferences for recycling and source reduction. The second index reflects a more general measure of environmental policy.

Table 4.16 Local Environmental Quality (Percent of counties located in non-attainment areas) [numbers in parenthesis are standard errors of group means]				
WTE Status of County	Metro Counties		Non-metro Counties	
	Mean	Std. Error	Mean	Std. Error
All Counties	51	(2)	5	(1)
No WTE Initiative	40	(2)	4	(1)
WTE Initiative	70*	(3)	18*	(4)
Operating Facility	70	(5)	12	(6)
Scratched Initiative	71	(4)	50#	(7)

* Indicates a significant difference (>95%) in means of the WTE and non-WTE counties.

\# Indicates a significant difference (>95%) in means of counties with canceled initiatives and counties with active WTE initiatives.

To construct the SWM index, state recycling regulations and policies as of 1990 were reviewed (Glenn and Riggle, 1991b). Each state was scored on six MSW policies: (1) the existence of a mandated goal of managing at least 25 percent of its waste stream by recycling, source reduction, and/or composting, (2) the existence of mandatory municipal ordinances to meet these goals, (3) state requirements for local governments to develop recycling programs, (4) state requirements that local governments meet waste reduction goals, (5) mandatory bottle-deposit laws, and (6) state financial incentives to produce recycled goods. The level of intensity on each policy was subjectively weighted and then summarized. The final score was set to 0 for states that had not enacted any of the six criteria measures, to a value of 1 for states that had enacted no more than two of the six measures, and a value of 2 for states that had enacted three or more of the measures.

The SWM policy index for a state was assigned to all the counties in the state, and then mean scores were calculated for the various county groups. Table 4.17 presents the table of means. Metropolitan counties without WTE

Table 4.17 State Waste Management Policies (high (2), medium (1), or low (0) score in state MSW policies) [numbers in parenthesis are standard errors of group means]				
WTE Status of County	Metro Counties		Non-metro Counties	
	Mean	Std. Error	Mean	Std. Error
All Counties	1.36	(0.02)	0.94	(0.02)
No WTE Initiative	1.26	(0.04)	0.93	(0.02)
WTE Initiative	1.55*	(0.05)	1.14	(0.09)
Operating Facility	1.61	(0.08)	1.18	(0.17)
Scratched Initiative	1.53	(0.06)	1.23	(0.13)
* Indicates a significant difference (>95%) in means of the WTE and non-WTE counties.				
# Indicates a significant difference (>95%) in means of counties with canceled initiatives and counties with active WTE initiatives.				

initiatives have a significantly lower score on the intensity of SWM policies than do counties with WTE programs. In other words, counties in states with few or no incentives for recycling, composting, and/or source reduction are less likely to have had a WTE initiative. Counties with scratched facilities have slightly lower scores than do counties with existing facilities, but our test does not show significance. Non-metro counties exhibit a just barely significant difference between counties with and without WTE initiatives and no significant difference between those that are using and those that have scratched WTE.

A very similar pattern is shown by the broader environmental policy index. Hall and Kerr (1991) reviewed and scored 50 environmental policies for each state and then calculated a summary score. Table 4.18 presents county means of the environmental policy index.

The positive correlation of pollution, stringent policy initiatives, and environmental activism within counties involved with WTE initiatives most

Table 4.18 State Environmental Policies (state score in 50 environmental policies) [numbers in parenthesis are standard errors of group means]				
WTE Status of County	Metro Counties		Non-metro Counties	
	Mean	Std. Error	Mean	Std. Error
All Counties	48.4	(0.51)	42.2	(0.26)
No WTE Initiative	45.3	(0.59)	42.0	(0.26)
WTE Initiative	54.1*	(0.87)	47.7*	(1.48)
Operating Facility	55.3	(1.42)	49.2	(2.67)
Scratched Initiative	54.5	(1.20)	48.8	(2.19)

*   Indicates a significant difference (>95%) in means of the WTE and non-WTE counties.

\#   Indicates a significant difference (>95%) in means of counties with canceled initiatives and counties with active WTE initiatives.

likely reflects a correlation of the problems of urban density with the need to consider a range of MSW alternatives. In large urban areas, the waste problem is more serious and, consequently, may induce interest in WTE facilities. It is also in these areas that interest in environmental issues may peak.

The analysis in this section is summarized in Table 4.19, which reports the results for WTE initiative counties compared to non-WTE counties, and Table 4.20, which compares counties with operating WTE facilities to counties with scratched initiatives. The key findings are that: (1) many of these indicators are characteristics that differentiate counties that have (or have had) WTE initiatives from those that have had no WTE initiative, and (2) these same factors do not distinguish counties who have scratched their initiatives from these that have seen initiatives through to completion and have operating WTE facilities.

	Metro	Non Metro
Table 4.19 Summary of Significant Differences of Means: Comparison of Counties with WTE Initiative to Counties with No WTE Initiative		
Population Density	+	+
Population Size	+	+
Rural	-	-
Growth	NS	+
Education	+	+
Per Capita Income	+	+
Family Formation	+	+
Industrial Base	-	NS
Recycle	+	+
Access to MRFs	+	+
Access to Landfills	NS	NS
Availability of Landfills	NS	NS
MSW Cost	+	NS
Conservation Members	+	NS
Local Env Quality	+	+
State MSW Policy	+	NS
State Env Policy	+	+

+   The mean of WTE counties is significantly larger than non-WTE counties.

-     The mean of WTE counties is significantly less than non-WTE counties.

NS   No significant difference.

	Metro	Non Metro
Table 4.20 Summary of Significant Differences of Means: Comparison of Counties with Operating WTE Facilities to Counties with Scratched Initiatives		
Population Density	NS	-
Population Size	NS	NS
Rural	NS	-
Growth	NS	NS
Education	NS	NS
Per Capita Income	NS	NS
Family Formation	NS	NS
Industrial Base	NS	NS
Recycle	NS	NS
Access to MRFs	NS	NS
Access to Landfills	NS	NS
Availability of Landfills	NS	NS
MSW Cost	+	NA
Conservation Members	NS	NS
Local Env Quality	NS	-
State MSW Policy	NS	NS
State Env Policy	NS	NS

+   The mean of WTE counties is significantly larger than non-WTE counties.

-    The mean of WTE counties is significantly less than non-WTE counties.

NS   No significant difference.

4.2.6 Multiple Indicator Analysis

In the comparison of means analysis presented above, each of the indicators were examined independently of one another. However, several of the factors are likely to be correlated with each other. A method in which the separate effects can be identified, while taking into account the other factors, is multiple regression analysis. Counties with WTE initiatives were given a value of 1 and counties with no initiatives were given a value of 0. A regression analysis could then be conducted that tested the set of factors as to their importance in contributing to a WTE initiative in the typical county. A second analysis was also conducted in which the factors were studied as to their ability to discriminate between counties with operating facilities (given a value of 0) from counties with scratched initiatives (given a value of 1).[3]

The results of the two regression analyses, along with the standard statistics, are presented in Tables 4.21 and 4.22. The most interesting result of the regression analysis is that the basic findings presented in previous subsections are confirmed. The indicators examined are able (individually or jointly) to discriminate between those counties that have had a WTE initiative and those counties that have not had a WTE initiative. Most of the coefficients in the WTE/non-WTE regression presented in Table 4.21 are statistically significant. The low R-squared coefficient for the second analysis, combined with the non-significance of the individual coefficients indicates that the factors useful for distinguishing between counties with and without WTE initiatives are not useful as predictors of the WTE project's ultimate success or failure.

The coefficients for education, family-formation age, MSW cost, and state MSW policy variables are also significantly negative in the WTE regression analysis. These variables were positively related in the means analysis. The change in sign between the two types of analysis indicates that these three variables are correlated with others in the analysis, most likely per capita income and population density. When the analysis is adjusted for associated levels of income, density, etc., the regression analysis results suggest that these factors are associated with a lower likelihood of WTE activity. For example, among densely populated, high per capita income counties, those counties with older populations, higher current cost in solid waste management, and stricter MSW policies are less likely to have WTE initiatives.

4.3 SUMMARY AND CONCLUSIONS

An exploratory means analysis and a more comprehensive multiple indicator analysis were conducted to identify socioeconomic factors associated with WTE involvement and success. Both types of analyses produced similar

Table 4.21 Multiple Indicator Analysis of All Counties

Dependent Variable:

WTE: = 0 if there was not a WTE initiative in the county
= 1 if there was a WTE initiative in the county

Mean:	0.1153	
Std. Deviation:	0.3195	

Regression Statistics:

Number of Observations:	3069
Multiple correlation:	0.564
Std Error:	0.264
R-Squared:	0.318
Adjusted R-Squared:	0.315

Analysis of Variance:

Source	DF	Sum of Squares	Mean Square	F	Prob >F
e	16	99.66507	6.22907	Value	0.0000
Model	3052	213.50208	0.06995	89.04	
Error	3068	313.16716			
Total					

Parameter Estimates:

Variable	Coefficient	Std. Error	T	Prob
Constant	0.731492	0.0940701	-7.78	0.000
Metro	0.047936	0.016461	2.91	0.004
Density	0.000012	0.000003	3.76	0.000
Log Population	0.194270	0.017220	11.25	0.000
Per Cent Rural	-0.000382	0.000272	-1.4	0.160
Pop Growth	-0.000975	0.000334	-2.91	0.004
HS Education	-0.002546	0.000625	-4.07	0.000
Per Capita Income	0.000014	0.000003	5.53	0.000
Family Formation	-0.001778	0.001396	-1.27	0.203
Industrial Base	-0.001369	0.000394	-3.48	0.001
Recycle	0.052450	0.013879	3.78	0.000
Access to MRF	0.001543	0.000906	1.70	0.089
Availability of Landfills	-0.017092	0.144203	-1.19	0.236
MSW Cost (1)	-0.004263	0.001606	2.65	0.008
Conservation Members	0.014733	0.003165	4.65	0.000
Local Env Quality	0.052586	0.017340	3.03	0.002
State MSW Policy	-0.029533	0.007631	-3.87	0.000
State Env Policy	-0.000607	0.000664	-0.91	0.361

(1) MSW cost estimates from another regression using only 262 of counties with population over 500,000.

Table 4.22 Multiple Indicator Analysis of WTE Counties

Dependent Variable:

SCRATCH:	= 1 if WTE initiative was scratched or abandoned	
	= 0 if operating WTE facility	
	Mean:	0.667
	Std. Deviation:	0.472

Regression Statistics:

Number of Observations:	276
Multiple correlation:	0.210
Std Error:	0.476
R-Squared:	0.044
Adjusted R-Squared:	0.000

Analysis of Variance:

Source	DF	Sum of	Mean Square	F Value	Prob >F
Model	16	Squares	0.1691	0.7472	0.74395
Error	259	2.7062	0.2264		
Total	275	58.6272			
		61.3333			

Parameter Estimates:

Variable	Coefficient	Std. Error	T	Prob
Constant	0.074796	0.66041	0.11	0.910
Metro	0.069782	0.0101377	0.69	0.492
Density	0.000008	0.000013	0.58	0.561
Log Population	0.075029	0.113295	0.66	0.508
Per Cent Rural	0.003799	0.002390	1.59	0.113
Pop Growth	0.002351	0.002066	1.14	0.256
HS Education	-0.000452	0.004606	0.10	0.922
Per Capita Income	0.000003	0.000013	0.22	0.823
Family Formation	0.000690	0.009358	0.07	0.941
Industrial Base	-0.000561	0.003638	-0.15	0.878
Recycle	0.073593	0.085974	0.86	0.393
Access to MRF	0.005085	0.003802	1.34	0.182
Availability of Landfills	-0.559736	0.964881	-0.58	0.562
MSW Cost (1)	-0.004324	0.002204	-1.96	0.050
Conservation Members	0.000671	0.016464	0.04	0.968
Local Env Quality	0.047930	0.084109	0.57	0.569
State MSW Policy	-0.050098	0.053461	-0.94	0.350
State Env Policy	-0.002194	0.003556	-0.62	0.538

(1) MSW cost estimates from another regression using only 108 of WTE counties with population over 500,000.

results. Three general conclusions may be drawn from this segment of the analyses. First, several factors may be used to define the set of counties likely to consider WTE programs. In particular, scores on population size, density, income, and other factors appear to act as thresholds to define the regions that consider WTE initiatives.

Second, counties that have had WTE initiatives may be grouped into two market sizes, metropolitan and non-metropolitan. The similarity of results in the mean comparisons for metro and non-metro counties is intriguing. It appears that two distinct markets exist: one market for large waste conversion facilities in large dense metropolitan areas and another market in the larger non-metropolitan counties. Variables used in the regression analysis appear to identify those counties in which waste-to-energy may be considered a feasible option.

However, the factors that ultimately lead to the success or failure of a WTE initiative are not among the socioeconomic factors considered in this part of the overall study. Perhaps it is likely that there are more subtle financial, political, and/or institutional factors that are important in determining the likely success of a WTE facility even when the basic set of feasibility criteria is met. The next two chapters investigate several possible candidates.

NOTES

1. We also looked at means of counties with planned facilities and those with permanently shutdown facilities. In general, there were no significant differences among categories.

2. This approach follows the model adopted in the National Planning Association's regional demographic and economic data used in the analysis (Terleckyj and Coleman, 1990).

3. The results presented here are based on Ordinary Least Squares (OLS) regression. A more sophisticated probit analysis, conducted to take into account some limitations of the OLS approach, gave the same basic results.

_____ Chapter 5

A Focus on Financial Issues

5.1 INTRODUCTION

In the previous chapter, the decision to abandon numerous WTE projects in the latter 1980s and early 1990s was viewed in relation to various socioeconomic parameters. This chapter focuses specifically on financial trends that occurred during this time period and on the financial barriers that may have contributed to WTE project cancellation. In addition, this chapter examines current and anticipated financial trends and their potential impacts on the long-term viability of incineration with heat recovery.

Three major financial trends played a role in decisions about WTE projects in the late 1980s and early 1990s and are the primary focuses of this chapter. First, the costs of WTE facilities escalated rapidly during this period, primarily in response to requirements for more sophisticated environmental controls and the movement toward large mass-burn and RDF technologies. Second, federal tax policy took a major turn in 1986 with the enactment of the Tax Reform Act (TRA86), which made it more difficult for local governments to finance capital-intensive WTE facilities with bonds that were exempt from federal taxes. Some projects had to turn to higher-cost financing options. Third, changes in intergovernmental aid and local fiscal policy occurred that made it more difficult for communities to finance WTE facilities, aside from their increasing costs and difficulties in obtaining tax-exempt financing. For example, communities were faced with increasing across-the-board demands from federal and state governments to respond to numerous environmental concerns, while at the same time federal and state governments were taking various actions to make the financing of those projects more difficult and costly. "Lumpy" capital expenditures, tax and expenditure limitations, and the inability of some communities to access national capital markets placed financing restrictions on some jurisdictions.

5.2 SOME BACKGROUND ON THE COST OF ENVIRONMENTAL MANAGEMENT

Before exploring the specifics of recent financial trends and the impacts of those trends on the viability of WTE, it is beneficial to review how WTE expenditures fit within the overall financial burden faced by governments in meeting environmental protection goals. In 1981, the total cost of environmental protection at the federal, state, and local levels was about $35 billion.[1] Of that amount, $26.7 billion, or 76 percent of the total public-sector costs of environmental protection, was borne by local government. By the year 2000, it is projected that expenditures of $55.6 billion will be necessary just to maintain the current level of environmental protection; local governments are expected to pay more than 87 percent of those expenditures. Expenditures on solid-waste-management (SWM) systems currently account for between $5 billion and $6 billion per year, representing 14 percent of total environmental expenditures.

By the year 2000, it is projected that municipalities will need to issue about $18.8 billion in municipal bonds for wastewater, drinking water, and solid waste projects (U.S. EPA, 1990a). This is approximately double the level of bonds issued for these facilities in the 1980s. Debt issued for environmental purposes is presently a small percentage of total debt issued by state and local governments; given the long-term fundamentals of the municipal bond market, this level of debt will not be unmanageable with respect to the ability of capital markets to absorb these additional environmental financing requirements of local governments. However, large capital-intensive environmental projects can crowd out other public-sector investments due to the "lumpy" expenditure streams of these facilities.

5.3 POTENTIAL FINANCING MECHANISMS

A variety of alternative financing mechanisms are available to communities to finance WTE facilities and other large public projects. This section reviews those mechanisms and summarizes their main pros and cons, particularly from the perspective of financing WTE facilities.

The financial approaches used to finance WTE facilities can be analyzed within the context of three major categories. The first category—traditional debt approaches—includes general obligation bonds, tax-exempt revenue bonds, taxable revenue bonds, and state and local revenue bonds. The second category is federal and state grants and revenue options. This approach consists of federal and state grant programs; federal, state, county, and municipal revenues; state loan guarantees; and various state bonding banks and authorities. The third category can be termed "innovative market approaches" to state and local financing, and these approaches can also take several forms. Many of the innovative approaches that will be discussed here are traced to operations in the taxable, corporate financial markets that have been little used in the municipal market. In addition, an innovative approach may consist of implementing a new set of relationships that combine unique features of municipal debt with economic features associated with private ownership of assets. For example, the use of alternative leasing arrangements allow municipalities to shift tax benefits that they cannot use (e.g., depreciation, investment tax credits, etc.) to private-sector entities that can use them, thus allowing a lower overall cost of facility financing.

Under traditional methods of finance, municipalities sell a fixed interest and fixed payment security, and the creditworthiness of the credit issuer is depended upon for repayment. The lender in this transaction is compensated through interest payments for the time value of money, interest rate risk, and credit risk. Innovative financing mechanisms alter the traditional risk/ return relationships by (1) shifting a portion of the interest rate risk from the lender to the municipality, (2) improving the creditworthiness of the borrower through the use of third-party credit enhancements, (3) making alternative types of returns available to investors other than regular receipt of interest payments, and/or (4) designing debt instruments that have appeal to specialized groups of investors.

5.3.1 Traditional Debt Instruments

There are two basic categories of traditional debt instruments. The first type is a general-obligation bond, and the second type is a revenue bond. General-obligation bonds are secured by the issuers "full faith and credit" or unlimited taxing authority. For most municipalities, the taxing power is limited to the property tax. However, many larger municipalities issue general-obligation bonds secured by corporate and personal income taxes, sales taxes, as well as property taxes. Should bonds be backed by the issuer's taxing authority and outside revenue sources, such as fees and other charges, the bonds are referred to as double-barrelled general obligations. Should a general-obligation bond be secured by only a portion of the tax stream, then the bond issue is referred to as a limited-tax general-obligation issue. In either case, general-obligation bonds are more risky for the community than other financing methods because the community pledges to back the bonds with its taxing authority. Due to the greater financial risks to the community, voter approval is usually required for general-obligation bonds, and state and/or local statutory limits are usually placed on the extent to which communities can issue general obligations. On the plus side from the community's perspective, general-obligation bonds are usually the municipality's least costly means of financing due to the low risk borne by the investor. In addition, in almost all cases, general-obligation bonds are exempt from federal, state, and local taxes. When the yields from bonds are tax-exempt, investors are obviously willing to accept a lower overall yield than they would require on taxable bonds.

Revenue bonds pledge revenues derived from the projects being financed, but do not obligate the issuer to use its power of taxation should the revenue stream be insufficient to meet the obligation. Revenue bonds are therefore less risky to the community than are general-obligation bonds; revenue bonds are, however, more risky to the investor and thus provide a higher yield than general obligations. Much of the financing of waste-to-energy facilities and other infrastructure is accomplished through the use of revenue bonds. Revenue bonds come under a host of different names, including industrial-revenue bonds (IRBs), private-activity bonds (PABs), and taxable revenue bonds (TRBs).

In some cases, revenue bonds are exempt from federal taxes. Under the most recent federal rules (discussed in detail below), selected revenue bonds are exempt from federal taxes if they meet certain guidelines and if the state in which the bonds are issued has not exceeded its federally controlled "cap" on the overall volume of such federally tax-exempt bonds. Voter approval for the issuance of tax-exempt revenue bonds may or may not be required, depending on rules in the particular state.

A recent development in environmental financing in the 1980s has been the increasing use of taxable revenue bonds and state and local enhancements to revenue bond issues. Thirty-three states and the District of Columbia have an income tax and exempt from taxation the interest earned on municipal bonds issued within their jurisdictions, while taxing interest earned on other municipal securities.[2] Taxable revenue bonds are thus exempt from state income taxes, although they do not always carry the federal exemption. In addition, state and local government pledges (e.g., property, sales, and other tax exemptions) enhance the creditworthiness of such an issue.

5.3.2 Grants, Revenue Financing, and Guarantee Options

To a limited extent, federal and state governments have used grants to assist the construction and operation of WTE facilities. These grants are direct outlays to local governments that are used to lower the overall cost of facility financing. Unfortunately for local governments, federal and state monies for grants are extremely limited at the present time.

State guarantees enhance the credit rating and lower the subsequent financing costs for many smaller jurisdictions. Small jurisdictions usually have no credit rating or a poor credit rating, and the higher credit rating of most states reduces financing costs for these small communities.

The establishment of state bonding banks and authorities is a similar method of enhancing facility financing, except that the state does not have a direct guarantee. State bond banks are established by the state as a quasi-state agency with the ability to issue debt on its behalf to support infrastructure financing. At least 13 states and Puerto Rico have established bond banks to help local governments access capital markets. Vermont created the first bond bank in 1969. Other states with established bond banks are Alaska, Georgia, Illinois, Indiana, Maine, Michigan, Mississippi, New Hampshire, Nevada, North Dakota, Oregon, and Tennessee. Bond banks act as a conduit between local governments and national credit markets by either (1) buying bonds from local governments and pooling them into one larger issue to be sold in the capital markets, or (2) selling bonds in the capital markets and using the proceeds to purchase bonds from local governments. The primary advantages of this method are that (1) it involves no direct government outlays other than initial capitalization in some states and (2) the direct borrowing capacity of the state is unaffected. Nevertheless, the state may inherit some contingent liability in the form of a "moral obligation." In addition, the use of bond banks for WTE and other capital-intensive financing is not presently a viable method because these banks are presently funded at inadequate levels in most states.[3]

Finally, federal, state, county, and municipal revenues are in some cases used to lower the overall cost of finance, as well as being a component to facility financing. With decreasing federal and state intergovernmental adjustments, local jurisdictions are finding it increasingly necessary to use direct local-sector resources to secure overall facility financing.

5.3.3 Innovative Market Approaches

The 1980s brought a surge of tax and expenditure limitations that made it more difficult to increase revenues for local public-sector capital projects. Sluggish economic growth and high interest rates, coupled with the movement toward tax and expenditure limitations, forced local jurisdictions to reallocate current dollars to on-going government operations and away from public-sector capital requirements. Volatile and unstable credit markets and declining federal and own-source revenues led to a surge of innovative financing for capital projects at the local level.

5.3.3.1 Third-Party Credit Enhancements. There are a number of factors responsible for the growth in third-party credit enhancements for municipal debt. Tax reform over the past decade has significantly reduced the attractiveness of debt financing, advance refunding, and escrow investment. A significant factor has been the emergence of the individual investor as the primary investor in municipal securities. Since the mid–1970s, there has been a marked shift in the ownership structure of municipal bonds.[4] Major reasons for the dramatic shift are (1) that tax policy has made it less attractive for commercial banks to hold municipal securities, and (2) the growth in municipal bond mutual funds, which have reduced risks for individual investors. Table 5.1 illustrates the changes in municipal bond holdings over the

Table 5.1 Percentage Ownership of Municipal Bonds: 1975-1990				
YEAR	HOUSEHOLDS DIRECT	FUND	COMMERICIAL BANKS	P&C FIRMS*	IMPLICIT TAX RATE** 20 YEAR
1975	30.3	0.0	47.2	14.9	21.7
1976	30.9	0.1	43.8	15.3	27.6
1977	29.6	0.6	42.6	17.2	32.2
1978	29.8	0.9	40.5	19.5	34.6
1979	30.4	1.1	39.7	20.8	35.5
1980	28.8	1.6	40.1	21.9	30.8
1981	30.0	2.2	39.2	21.6	22.9
1982	33.6	3.8	35.8	20.0	15.4
1983	37.5	5.8	32.3	17.9	20.6
1984	40.3	7.3	30.7	15.8	22.2
1985	41.7	9.8	29.5	13.5	19.7
1986	40.0	14.5	27.7	12.6	14.8
1987	42.7	16.6	21.9	13.9	19.0
1988	47.8	15.6	17.6	14.5	15.5
1989	51.1	16.2	14.6	14.0	17.9
1990	50.9	18.3	12.4	13.7	19.0

Source: Feenberg and Poterba (1991).

   *   Property and casualty insurance firms.
   ** The implicit tax rate is the tax rate of the "marginal investor" as implied by tax-exempt yields during period. The implicit tax rate is defined as:

$$\Phi = \frac{R_T - R_E}{R_T}$$

where R_T: Taxable Nominal Interest Rate
      R_E: Tax-Exempt Nominal Interest Rate

period 1975-1990. In 1975, households accounted for 30.3 percent of municipal holdings, while banks accounted for 47.2 percent of holdings. By 1990, households (direct and mutual funds) accounted for 69.2 percent of holdings, while the commercial banking share had dropped to 12.4 percent.[5]

Financial risk aversion, the inability to diversify investment portfolios, and the costs of tracking and evaluating individual municipal issues have led to the increasing use of credit enhancements. Credit-enhanced bonds reassure investors that, should an issuer default on a bond, the third-party guarantor will step in and pay off the defaulted bond debt. As much as one-third of the long-term debt coming to the market has some kind of credit enhancement.[6]

The most widely used credit enhancement has been private bond insurance. Private insurance for municipal bonds, which is irrevocable and issued for the life of the issue, is purchased at the time a bond series is sold. The premiums range from 0.1 to 2.0 percent of the total principal and interest due over the life of the issue, dependent upon the assessment of risks by the insurance company.[7] The use of private insurance has shown phenomenal growth in the 1980s. Primary reasons include shifts in the marginal investor, changes in federal tax policy that have compressed premiums for government-insured bonds, and declining insurance premiums as a result of the narrowing yield spread between Aaa/AAA and Baa/BBB securities.[8]

Although bond insurance is an effective way for a locality to lower financing costs, it is not without its risks. An insurance company may require high-reserve and high debt-coverage ratios for certain revenue-supported debt. In addition, insurance companies must spread the risk potential for capacity constraints in certain geographic regions.[9]

5.3.3.2 Letters of Credit. A letter of credit (LOC) is a commitment by a financial institution (primarily a AA- or AAA-rated commercial bank) to make principal and interest payments of a specified amount and term in the event of default by a municipal issuer. If the LOC is irrevocable, then it would behave in much the same manner as private insurance. The commercial bank would be a direct guarantor of the issuer's obligation.

A LOC is usually issued for a period of five years, which may be renewed at the discretion of the bank. If the LOC is not renewed, the investor would have the option of redeeming the bonds. The LOC requires the payment of an annual fee, ranging from 0.25 to 1.00 percent of the amount of the debt. A primary advantage to the bank is that the LOC provides a source of income for balance sheet improvement without incurring a liability that would reduce the amount of loanable funds.[10]

5.3.3.3 Leasing. The use of leasing as a method to finance WTE facilities and other public-sector projects has increased dramatically over the past decade. Lease-based financing accounted for 9 percent of the tax-exempt market in 1988, while accounting for only 4 percent in 1984.[11] In the data base used for this analysis of operational WTE facilities, leasing was a component of 7.5 percent of facility financing in 1990, while only 0.5 percent in 1984. Although leasing comes in a variety of forms (sale-leasebacks, safe-harbor leases, and leveraged leases), it requires private-sector financing of most of the investment.

A leveraged lease is a financing transaction whereby economic value in the form of tax benefits (e.g., tax credits, depreciation, and other tax benefits) are created where none existed prior to the transaction. A leveraged lease allows a public sector entity to raise equity capital to lower the overall facility costs to the local government. In a leveraged-lease transaction, a municipality is providing leverage to a private entity. The private entity uses this borrowed capital to purchase the proposed waste-to-energy facility that can then be leased to another private entity or municipality. Although tax-exempt revenue debt has been the primary vehicle used in conjunction with leveraged leasing, other types of debt instruments will emerge as financial markets and choices continue to adjust.

A leveraged lease may be structured in the following manner. Initially, a leveraged lease requires a private equity investor who will provide 20 to 30 percent of the facility cost. This equity investment is then leveraged with the tax-exempt debt financing (70 to 80 percent) for the remainder of the facility costs. It is crucial to understand at this point that the economic value of the tax benefits accruing to the private entity is the significant contribution to the proposed transaction. In a leverage lease, the greater the net present value of the tax benefits, the greater is the amount of equity provided for a required rate of return and the lower is the required lease payment.

Although the actual purchaser is a trust established to own the facility, the equity investor retains a certificate of participation. The private entity, which now owns the facility, will lease the facility for a certain period of time. The rental payments on the lease must be sufficient (1) to service the debt on the outstanding bonds and (2) to provide sufficient after-tax returns to the equity investor.

Tax laws impose several restrictions on the types of lease transactions allowed. For example, the terms of the lease cannot exceed 80 percent of the economic life of the facility. In addition, the facility must be operated by a private concern, and the purchase option must be at fair market value.

The capital costs associated with a leveraged lease are lower given the net present value of cash flows over the life of the facility. Value is created in this transaction because the equity investor can take tax credits, depreciation, and other tax benefits that a municipality cannot take. For a 20 to 30 percent equity investment, a private company can take these tax benefits for the entire value of the facility. In addition, the debt associated with a leveraged lease does not have to be counted for balance-sheet debt treatment.

The equity investor's return on investment is derived from three sources. They are (1) the net cash flows of lease rentals over debt service, (2) the tax benefits accruing from ownership, and (3) the residual value of the facility. The residual value is the ownership and use value of the facility from the end of the lease period to the end of the facility's economic life.

Tax benefits are the significant feature of leveraged leasing; however, the benefits cannot be taken until the facility is operational. Because the investor's rate of return is partially in the form of tax benefits, the effect on the cost of capital is lower than the effective net cost of debt. Before tax benefits begin accruing to the investor, the rate of return on equity requires a cash return. Therefore, leverage leasing is more advantageous for permanent, rather than construction, financing.[12] A major limitation of a leveraged-lease transaction for a WTE facility is that it is a large, illiquid investment that limits the scope of potential investors. A potential solution is a certificate of participation (COP) for lease financing. This can be structured similarly to participation certificates in the corporate markets (e.g., mortgage and asset-backed certificate pools). Under a COP, a wide range of potential investors have the right to receive payments under a lease, which are divided into certificates of participation. In addition to the advantages of a standard lease (e.g., no voter approval and no impact on debt restrictions), COPs allow the pooling of local agency projects.[13] In the case of pooling, agencies aggregate local sector requests for financing, issue COPs, and distribute the funds to pool participants. In California alone, certificate-of-participation financing increased from $265 million in 1982 to $4 billion in 1986.

5.3.3.4 Variable-Rate Municipal Debt. In recent years, homeowners have taken advantage of variable-rate mortgages to obtain interest rates lower than available long-term rates. Variable-rate municipal debt offers the same kinds of opportunities for communities considering a large purchase, such as a WTE facility. Innovative financing instruments are structured so that the cost of local-sector funds can be priced at short or intermediate yield levels. While lower interest rates can be obtained, a downside for munici-palities in this type of innovative financing is that a portion of the interest rate risk is borne by the municipality, i.e., a general increase in interest rates will translate into higher interest rates on the municipality's debt. New debt management tools have been developed to minimize this risk (e.g., hedges and interest rate swaps discussed below).

A variable-rate security is one in which the interest rate is adjusted at specific intervals. The coupon rate is pegged to indices such as the LIBOR Rate, 90-day Treasury Bill Rate, the Prime Rate, and the J.J. Kenny Index. Because of the high liquidity of variable-rate obligations, a bank letter of credit is usually required. Although the bundling of securities involving adjustable-rate securities may add additional costs to a financing package, there can be substantial savings if there is a large spread between short-term debt and long-term debt. A flattening of the yield curve, i.e., little variation between short-term and long-term interest rates, will result in diminished use of variable-rate municipal debt.[14]

5.3.3.5 Interest-Rate Swaps. Interest-rate swaps are used extensively in the corporate and financial markets as an asset-liability, debt-management tool that has begun to gain acceptance in the municipal market. An interest-rate swap is a contractual agreement between two parties calling for the exchange of interest payments on assets on a notional basis, usually for a period of 1 to 10 years. An interest-rate swap is not an exchange of the underlying assets or liabilities, but rather an exchange of interest payments only (usually a floating-rate coupon for a fixed-rate coupon). Payments in an interest-rate swap are made on a net basis.

An interest-rate swap (fixed-rate payer/floating-rate receiver) can be used as a tool to convert floating-rate liabilities (e.g., variable-rate municipal debt) synthetically into a fixed-rate liability. This results because the floating cost of liabilities is "offset" by floating-rate receipts associated with the swap. An increase or decrease in the liability cost is matched by a similar change in floating-rate inflows as long as the notional amount of swaps is equal to the principal amount of the liability. The net effect of the interest-rate swap is to lock-in the liability cost at a fixed rate.

An interest-rate swap is not without risks. Legal risks, market/basis risk, counterparty risk (e.g., counterparty unable to meet payment obligations), and the potential for reversing the swap should unforeseen economic consequences dictate must be addressed by the parties involved in the transaction.[15]

5.4 THE INCREASING COSTS OF WTE FACILITIES

The mean-adjusted, constant capital costs of all existing and advanced-planned WTE facilities in the United States increased 19.6 percent, from $43.8 million in 1982 to $52.4 million in 1990. The total dollar amount of facility costs increased from $4.9 billion in 1982 to $10.5 billion in 1990, reflecting an increase in total existing and advanced-planned facilities from 111 in 1982 to 201 in 1990. More revealing is the fact that from 1982 to 1990, the mean cost of advanced-planned facilities increased by 40.6 percent, from $62.1 million in 1982 to $87.3 million in 1990 (see Table 5.2). The total cost of advanced-planned facilities increased from $3.8 billion in 1982 to $5.3 billion in 1990, while the number of advanced-planned facilities remained constant.

There are a number of reasons for the rapid escalation of facility costs in WTE facilities over the decade. One of the most important reasons is that many of the advances in air pollution technology did not exist or were not required when earlier facilities were constructed. Further cost escalations can be expected due to more stringent environmental controls. (See Chapter 2 for more information on existing and forthcoming air emission controls.) For example, the U.S. EPA has estimated that the national annualized cost of the New Source Performance Standards (NSPS) for MSW combustion technologies (as part of the Clean Air Act) will be $190 million for new sources and $320 million for existing sources.[16]

In addition, the distribution of WTE technologies explains a substantial portion of the rapid increase in facility costs, as there is a significant difference in the planned and existing-facility design capacities (see Table 5.3).

YEAR		ALL FACILITIES	PLANNED	EXISTING

Table 5.2 Waste-to-Energy Facility Adjusted Capital Costs:
1982-1990
(in millions of constant 1982 dollars)

YEAR		ALL FACILITIES	PLANNED	EXISTING
1990	MEAN	$ 52.4	$ 87.3	$37.2
	SUM	10532.9	5323.8	5209.2
	N	201	61	140
1988	MEAN	47.2	71.6	27.4
	SUM	9476.8	6438.5	3038.3
	N	201	90	111
1986	MEAN	50.7	82.7	31.7
	SUM	9674.8	5869.2	3805.6
	N	191	71	120
1984	MEAN	39.7	65.7	27.4
	SUM	5049.9	2693.8	2356.1
	N	127	41	86
1982	MEAN	43.8	62.1	21.4
	SUM	4857.0	3787.0	1070.0
	N	111	61	50

Sources: Adapted from information in Government
             Advisory Associates, Inc., Resource Recovery
             Yearbook, 1982, 1984, 1986, 1987, 1988, 1989,
             1991.

For 1990, the mean design capacity of all planned facilities was 1,101 tons per day (tpd) as compared with 656 tpd for existing facilities.

There are several reasons for this large discrepancy. First, 27 percent of existing WTE facilities are comprised of small, modular facilities, while only 6.5 percent of advanced-planned facilities are of this design. With respect to advanced-planned facilities, 79.3 and 12.9 percent will employ large-scale, mass-burn technology and RDF processes, respectively. Only 52.8 percent of existing facilities employ such designs. Second, the design capacity of all resource-recovery facilities is increasing, regardless of the technology chosen. As of 1990, advanced-planned, mass-burn facilities were slated to process an average of 1,151 tpd, while the mean for existing mass-burn facilities was 913 tpd. In addition, regional variations with respect to design capacity explain some of the cost differences. WTE facilities, both existing and those in the advanced stages of planning, in the Northeast have generally larger design capacities than those of other regions (GAA, 1991; Kelsay, 1992).

Table 5.3 WTE Facility Design Capacities: 1990 (in tons per day)		
SAMPLE	PROCESS	AVERAGE CAPACITY
ALL FACILITIES		793
	Mass Burn	1024
	Modular	143
	RDF	1065
	Other	50
PLANNED FACILITIES		1101
	Mass Burn	1151
	Modular	242
	RDF	1333
EXISTING FACILITIES		656
	Mass Burn	913
	Modular	133
	RDF	1003
	Other	50

Sources: Adapted from information in Government
             Advisory Associates, Inc., Resource
             Recovery Yearbook, 1982, 1984, 1986,
             1987, 1988, 1989, 1991.

5.5 FEDERAL TAX POLICY

Although the tax-exempt market is widely used to finance solid and hazardous waste facilities and a host of other "quasi-public" activities, federal
tax policy has increasingly placed restrictions and limitations on federally
tax-exempt state and local financing.[17] Between 1968 and 1989, there were
17 major tax laws that significantly affected the municipal bond market
and impacted the ability of state and local governments to raise public
capital. Changes in the municipal bond market include changes in public
purpose definition, arbitrage profits, tax shelters, private capital costs, tar-
geting of beneficiaries, user restrictions, volume allocations, and other restrictions.

Table 5.4 Private Activity Bond Volume as a Percentage of Total Bond Volume (1975-1986) (in billions of dollars)		
YEAR	PRIVATE ACTIVITY AMOUNT	SHARE OF VOLUME
1975	$6.2	20.6%
1976	8.4	24.0
1977	13.1	27.9
1978	15.8	32.2
1979	24.6	51.1
1980	29.4	53.6
1981	27.4	48.5
1982	44.0	51.7
1983	49.9	71.0
1984	65.8	72.7
1985	99.4	67.9
1986	17.2	20.0

Source: Zimmerman (1990).

Beginning with the Revenue and Expenditure Control Act of 1968 (RECA), which stated that certain bonds that had an unacceptably large portion of proceeds being used for private purposes were taxable as an Industrial Development Bond (IDB), the federal government sought to limit the use of tax-exempts by state and local officials. However, this initial attempt to curb tax-exempt financing did not halt the movement toward tax-exempts. In fact, the share of private-activity bonds as a percentage of total bond volume increased from 20.6 percent in 1975 to 72.7 percent by 1984 (see Table 5.4). In order to slow this explosive growth and thus prevent further erosion of the federal tax base, Congress adopted a series of volume caps on the amount of private-activity bonds that could be issued by a state in any calendar year. Although RECA had attempted to place restrictions on certain types of tax-exempt activity prior to 1984, the Deficit Reduction Act of 1984 (DRA84) was the first piece of legislation to extend the volume caps to a large number of IDBs. DRA84 set state yearly volume caps for private-activity bonds at $150 per capita or $200 million per state, which-ever was greater. The objective was to reduce the growth in private purpose bonds, while giving the state and local jurisdictions the flexibility to decide what activities should be recipients of the volume cap.

The TRA86 has been the most far-reaching attempt to curb the volume and applications of tax-exempt, private-activity bonds. TRA86, which became effective in 1987, went a step further toward reducing the volume of private-activity bonds by establishing state volume caps of $50 per capita or $150 million, whichever was largest. (For 1987, the tax-exempt, public-activity bond cap was set at $75 per capita or $250 million.) TRA86 also further restricted the number of activities qualifying for exemption. The net effects of these various restrictions were to (1) limit the available tax-exempt financing that might be used for WTE facilities, (2) make it more difficult for WTE projects to qualify for tax-exempt financing, and, as a result, (3) increase the overall cost of WTE financing. As an aside, a measure of the attractiveness of local-sector, tax-exempt financing is the interest-rate differential between a taxable corporate bond and a tax-exempt bond, ceteris paribus. This interest-rate differential can be summarized by the yield ratio, which is the ratio of the tax-exempt yield to the corporate yield. The lower the tax-exempt/corporate ratio, the more advantageous tax-exempt state and local borrowing becomes. As this ratio approaches 1, the tax-exempt rate approaches the taxable corporate rate, with no resulting differential for state and local borrowing. Table 5.5 indicates that the differential has increased steadily from 0.62 in 1979 to 0.75 by 1990.

5.5.1 Specific Provisions of TRA86

Although tax-exempts are still used to finance solid and hazardous waste facilities under TRA86, numerous restrictions and limitations apply to the issuance of tax-exempts by or on behalf of state and local governments. In order to qualify as tax-exempt bonds under TRA86, the bonds must be classified as (1) governmental bonds, or (2) private-activity bonds that are also "qualified bonds" for solid and hazardous waste facilities. If an issuer determines that a governmental bond is superior to a "qualified" bond, it must retain an almost proprietary interest in the facility, forego its share of the tax benefits, and observe the restrictions on private use of facilities imposed by TRA86.

5.5.1.1 *Governmental Bonds.* Prior to 1986, a state or local bond was classified as an industrial development bond. With passage of TRA86, state and local bonds are now classified as either governmental bonds or private-activity bonds. Governmental bonds are tax-exempt, but private-activity bonds (PABs) are tax-exempt only if they are qualified bonds. Even if PABs are tax-exempt, they are at a disadvantage to governmental bonds because, among other things, they are subject to prior public notice and interest on PABs is treated as a preference item on alternative minimum tax (AMT)

Table 5.5 Yields on Corporate and Tax-Exempt Bonds and the Yield Ratio: 1965-1990 (Aaa bond rating)			
YEAR	TAX-EXEMPT YIELD	CORPORATE YIELD	TAX EXEMPT/CORPORATE
1965	3.34	4.49	0.74
1966	3.90	5.13	0.76
1967	3.99	5.51	0.72
1968	4.20	6.18	0.68
1969	5.45	7.03	0.78
1970	6.12	8.04	0.76
1971	5.22	7.39	0.71
1972	5.04	7.21	0.70
1973	4.99	7.44	0.67
1974	5.89	8.57	0.69
1975	6.42	8.83	0.73
1976	5.66	8.43	0.67
1977	5.20	8.02	0.65
1978	5.52	8.73	0.63
1979	5.92	9.63	0.62
1980	7.85	11.94	0.66
1981	10.43	14.17	0.74
1982	10.88	13.79	0.79
1983	8.80	12.04	0.73
1984	9.61	12.71	0.76
1985	8.60	11.37	0.76
1986	6.95	9.02	0.77
1987	7.14	9.38	0.76
1988	7.36	9.71	0.76
1989	7.00	9.26	0.76
1990	6.96	9.32	0.75

Source: Federal Reserve Bulletin (1965-1990).

calculations. Whether bonds are governmental bonds or PABs depends on a more restrictive use and security test.

5.5.1.2 Private-Activity Bonds (PABs). The 10 percent use-in-trade test states that no more than 10 percent of the bond proceeds may be used in any business other than the public entity. The 10 percent security test states than no more than 10 percent of the proceeds may be secured by an interest in the property of a private business. If an issue fails to meet both of these tests, it is classified as a private-activity bond. In addition, there is a $15 million output-facilities test that states that no more than $15 million can be used for a non-qualifying portion as defined by Section 141 of the Code.

In addition to this two-part test, TRA86 stipulated two additional conditions: (1) the unrelated-or-disproportionate-use rule and (2) the private-loan-financing rule. The unrelated-or-disproportionate-use rule states that if 5 percent or more of the bond proceeds are used to finance a non-government trade or business that is unrelated or disproportionate to the use of the government facility being financed by the bonds, then the issues must be a PAB. The private-loan-financing rule states that bonds are PABs if an amount of the bond proceeds exceeding the lesser of 5 percent or $5 million is to be used directly or indirectly to make or finance loans to non-governmental persons.

5.5.1.3 Qualified Bonds. If bonds are classified as PABs, they may still be tax-exempt if they are qualified bonds. Qualified bonds are bonds issued where 95 percent or more of the net proceeds are to be used to provide solid-waste-disposal facilities or qualified hazardous-waste facilities.

Under U.S. Treasury regulations, a solid-waste-disposal facility consists of any project involving the collection, storage, treatment, processing, and final disposal of solid waste. In recycling facilities, at least 65 percent of the waste by weight or volume of material introduced into the conversion process must be solid waste. The regulations permit the following items qualified for financing: processing equipment and structures, combustion and pollution control equipment and structures, transfer stations, site excavation and improvement, landfill improvements, and collection equipment. Project components ineligible for financing include material or energy handling or processing equipment and structures from the point where such materials or energy recovered from the disposal process have value (e.g., steam lines from a steam boiler). Qualified bonds have the following restrictions:[18]

1. 2 percent costs of issuance limitations
2. unified volume caps
3. limits on management contracts
4. extended depreciation schedules
5. arbitrage restrictions
6. public hearings

7. bond maturity limitations
8. land and existing property restrictions
9. substantial user restrictions and change-in-use rules
10. information reporting requirements
11. advance refunding prohibitions, and
12. restrictions on federal guarantees

Although it is not possible to completely disentangle the different effects of TRA86 on financing WTE facilities, it is clear that the most significant impact was the unified volume cap. As stated above, the amount of private-activity bonds that may be issued by any one state within a calendar year is limited to an amount that is the greater of $150 million or $50 per capita. The allocation formula for the volume cap is established by each state based upon its own priorities. Further, TRA86 provides that the volume cap may be carried forward for three years upon the proper election of a specified activity (housing, student loans, environmental facilities) if a state is unable to use its current allocation during the current year. The election is irrevocable, and the allocation is lost if not used.

In early 1992, a data collection exercise (Kelsay, 1992) was undertaken as part of this study to assess the impact of the unified volume cap on the states' ability to finance public investment, particularly environmental infrastructure. This was augmented by earlier survey work by Kenyon (1991), Kenyon and Zimmerman (1991), and Zimmerman (1990). Results of the data collection (Table 5.6) show that 23 states received caps in excess of $50 per capita in 1991, with Wyoming ($330), Alaska ($273), and Vermont ($266) receiving the largest per capita allowances. The largest dollar allocations were received by California ($1.5 billion), New York ($899 million), and Texas ($849 million).

An analysis of the amount of the volume caps used by the various states, not counting carryforward authority, shows that few states are exhausting their authority, which may suggest that the volume cap is not a binding constraint. Table 5.7 gives the percentages of the volume caps used by the various states, not counting any carryforward authority. (Note that the results for 1991 were not available for many states due to the timing of the data collection exercise and are not reported in the tables. However, the results from those states providing 1991 data also show that few states are exhausting their authority.)

There are several reasons why states may not be using all of their volume authority. First, most states establish strict priorities for their caps by allocating certain percentages to selected activities. Second, in many states unused authority is released in the ninth to eleventh month of the year, making a short planning horizon difficult for many activities. Third, the inflexible carryforward provisions make it difficult to allocate unused caps

Table 5.6 State Private-Activity Bond Volume Caps: Totals and Per Capita: 1989-1991 (totals given in thousands of dollars)						
	1991 CAP		1990 CAP		1989 CAP	
State	Total	Per Capita	Total	Per Capita	Total	Per Capita
Alabama	$202,050	$50	$205,900	$50	$206,350	$50
Alaska	150,000	273	150,000	285	150,000	292
Arizona	183,250	50	177,800	50	173,300	50
Arkansas	150,000	64	150,000	62	150,000	62
California	1,488,000	50	1,453,150	50	1,408,400	50
Colorado	164,700	50	165,850	50	164,500	50
Connecticut	164,350	50	161,950	50	162,050	50
Delaware	150,000	225	150,000	223	150,000	227
D.C.	150,000	247	150,000	248	150,000	242
Florida	646,900	50	633,500	50	618,850	50
Georgia	323,900	50	321,800	50	320,050	50
Hawaii	150,000	135	150,000	135	150,000	137
Idaho	150,000	149	150,000	148	150,000	150
Illinois	571,550	50	582,900	50	577,200	50
Indiana	277,200	50	279,650	50	278,750	50
Iowa	150,000	54	150,000	53	150,000	53
Kansas	150,000	61	150,000	60	150,000	60
Kentucky	184,250	50	186,350	50	186,050	50
Louisiana	211,000	50	219,100	50	221,000	50
Maine	150,000	122	150,000	123	150,000	124
Maryland	239,050	50	234,700	50	232,200	50
Massachusetts	300,800	50	295,650	50	293,550	50
Michigan	464,750	50	463,650	50	465,000	50
Minnesota	218,750	50	217,650	50	215,300	50
Mississippi	150,000	58	150,000	57	150,000	57
Missouri	255,850	50	257,950	50	256,950	50
Montana	150,000	188	150,000	186	150,000	187

	1991 CAP		1990 CAP		1989 CAP	
State	Total	Per Capita	Total	Per Capita	Total	Per Capita
Nebraska	150,000	95	150,000	83	150,000	94
Nevada	150,000	125	150,000	135	150,000	142
New Hampshire	150,000	135	150,000	136	150,000	137
New Jersey	386,500	50	386,800	50	386,000	50
New Mexico	150,000	99	150,000	98	150,000	99
New York	899,500	50	897,500	50	894,900	50
North Carolina	331,450	50	528,550	50	326,300	50
North Dakota	150,000	235	150,000	227	150,000	226
Ohio	542,300	50	545,350	50	543,600	50
Oklahoma	157,300	50	162,200	50	163,150	50
Oregon	150,000	53	150,000	53	150,000	55
Pennsylvania	594,100	50	602,000	50	601,350	50
Rhode Island	150,000	150	150,000	150	150,000	151
South Carolina	174,350	50	175,600	50	174,650	50
South Dakota	150,000	216	150,000	210	150,000	210
Tennessee	243,800	50	247,000	50	245,950	50
Texas	849,350	50	849,550	50	839,000	50
Utah	150,000	87	150,000	88	150,000	89
Vermont	150,000	266	150,000	265	150,000	270
Virginia	309,350	50	304,900	50	298,800	50
Washington	243,350	50	238,050	50	230,950	50
West Virginia	150,000	84	150,000	81	150,000	80
Wisconsin	244,600	50	243,350	50	242,900	50
Wyoming	150,000	330	150,000	316	150,000	318
Total	$14,325,400		$14,387,450		$14,178,050	

Table 5.6 State Private-Activity Bond Volume Caps:
Totals and Per Capita: 1989-1991
(totals given in thousands of dollars)
(continued)

Sources: Kenyon and Zimmerman (1991) and Kelsay (1992).

Table 5.7 State Tax-Exempt Private-Activity Bonds: Percentage of Cap Used, 1989-1990 (exclusive of carryforwards)		
State	1990 (%)	1989 (%)
Alabama	82	NA
Alaska	47	22
Arizona	65	79
Arkansas	99	85
California	86	100
Colorado	94	56
Connecticut	87	84
Delaware	0	33
D.C.	NA	NA
Florida	88	96
Georgia	96	100
Hawaii	17	29
Idaho	6	21
Illinois	NA	92
Indiana	89	87
Iowa	97	71
Kansas	98	86
Kentucky	63	64
Louisiana	83	70
Maine	100	25
Maryland	62	56
Massachusetts	87	56
Michigan	99	79
Minnesota	89	100
Mississippi	47	57
Missouri	100	100

Table 5.7 State Tax-Exempt Private-Activity Bonds: Percentage of Cap Used, 1989-1990 (exclusive of carryforwards) (continued)		
State	1990 (%)	1989 (%)
Montana	0	43
Nebraska	31	12
Nevada	64	30
New Hampshire	55	100
New Jersey	30	57
New Mexico	3	12
New York	49	67
North Carolina	54	54
North Dakota	11	74
Ohio	94	100
Oklahoma	92	100
Oregon	73	79
Pennsylvania	70	35
Rhode Island	62	6
South Carolina	95	84
South Dakota	7	38
Tennessee	19	72
Texas	100	98
Utah	96	88
Vermont	34	35
Virginia	90	62
Washington	97	62
West Virginia	78	100
Wisconsin	89	83
Wyoming	14	23

Sources: Kenyon and Zimmerman (1991) and Kelsay (1992).

from previous years. Despite the finding that volume caps often go unused, the data show significant numbers of denied and delayed requests to finance environmental infrastructure. Denials and delays for environmental infrastructure projects were found to be in excess of $4 billion over the three-year period 1989 to 1991.

Previous studies have also examined the impacts of the volume caps. For example, Pryde (1990 and 1991) conducted a survey that showed that 25 states were constrained by the volume cap and 25 states reported they were not. Of those 25 states reporting they were constrained by the cap, 10 were larger states that were subject to the $50 per capita allowance. Zimmerman (1990 and 1991) conducted an extensive survey for the Urban Institute and the U.S. Advisory Commission on Intergovernmental Relations to examine whether the volume caps do reduce private activity bonds. Zimmerman provides partial evidence that the volume caps may be constraining. In comparing private-activity bonds from 1984 to 1986 with 1989 levels, private-activity bond volume fell substantially. In addition, Zimmerman reported that 27 states had to delay or deny bond-financed projects because of inadequate volumes. Kenyon (1991) reports regression results that show the volume cap to be a partially binding constraint on the issuance of private-activity debt in 1989 and 1990. For an incremental dollar per capita of volume cap that a state has, per capita issuance of private activity bonds were found to increase by $0.62. However, there is little evidence in the data and early empirical work that shows the volume caps to affect the overall level of public capital investment.

5.5.2 The Use of Local Debt Instruments

There has been a marked shift in the type of state and local debt instruments used to finance public investment. The use of general-obligation debt has declined dramatically with respect to revenue bonds over the last 20 years (Table 5.8). In 1970, revenue bonds accounted for 33.9 percent of new issue volume. This has increased steadily over the last 25 years, with revenue issues accounting for 75.4 percent of new issue volume in 1985, before declining slightly to 67.2 percent by 1990.

General-obligation debt can be viewed as "public activity," while revenue bond issues are financing "private activity" to a large extent. The use of general-obligation debt has decreased due to several factors: (1) constitutional and statutory restrictions on state and local governments to issue general-obligation debt, (2) referendum requirements for many general-obligation issues, and (3) the belief that debt repayment of revenue bond issues will not ultimately fall on the local taxpayer. Another contributing factor to the growth of tax-exempt, revenue-bond activity is that much of the activity is done on "behalf of issuers," e.g., dependent agencies. These de-

Table 5.8 U.S. Volume of Long-Term Tax-Exempt Debt (in millions of dollars)			
Year	General Obligations	Revenue Bonds	Revenue Bond Share (%)
1965	7177	3517	32.9
1966	6804	3955	36.8
1967	8985	5013	35.8
1968	9269	6517	41.3
1969	7725	3556	31.5
1970	11850	6082	33.9
1971	15220	8681	36.3
1972	13305	9332	41.2
1973	12257	10632	46.5
1974	13563	10212	43.0
1975	16020	14511	47.5
1976	18040	17140	48.7
1977	18042	28655	61.4
1978	17854	30658	63.2
1979	12109	31256	72.1
1980	14100	34267	70.8
1981	12394	35338	74.0
1982	21094	58044	73.3
1983	21566	64855	75.0
1984	26485	80156	75.2
1985	52622	161567	75.4
1986	46346	100664	68.5
1987	30589	71818	70.1
1988	30312	84210	73.5
1989	35774	77873	68.5
1990	39610	81295	67.2

Source: Federal Reserve Bulletin (1965-1990).

pendent agencies (special districts, special funds, and authorities) issue bonds on behalf of governments because they lack an independent taxing authority. It is this type of non-guaranteed debt, which is not subject to volume and public-activity restrictions at the state and local level, that the federal government has sought to constrain.

5.6 OTHER FINANCIAL CONSTRAINTS ON LOCAL JURISDICTIONS

The 1980s presented a dual problem for local governments with respect to financing capital-intensive, waste-to-energy facilities and other public infrastructure—i.e., increasing federal and state mandates for improving environmental protection in combination with constraints on funds to accomplish these mandates. Gold (1991) reports that revenues from taxes and fees and federal aid fared much better for state governments than for local governments. Federal aid to county and municipal governments during the period 1980 to 1988 decreased by 46.6 percent and 37.9 percent, respectively. At the same time, property taxes and non-property taxes increased substantially, more than doubling over the period at the county level. Because many local governments face real or perceived tax and expenditure limitations, the increasing demand for environmental capital may crowd out other local public investments. Most WTE facilities are financed through some type of revenue-bond mechanism; and if the debt service is greater than the user fees generated from a bond issue, the overall credit rating of the community may be impaired. It is generally agreed that a community's ability to raise user fees to support facility debt will be constrained once user fees reach an aggregate of 1 to 2 percent of median household income.[19]

In addition to tax and expenditure limitations as a constraint on local finance, small jurisdictions face additional problems. First, because of potential economies of scale involved with some WTE technologies and other waste management technologies, the regionalization of waste sheds may be necessary so that the cost of capital will be manageable for local jurisdictions. Second, revenue-bond financing, which is the primary source of capital for these facilities, may be approaching constraints at the local level. The Environmental Financial Advisory Board (1991a) reports that households spend 0.32 percent of their annual incomes on solid waste management and about 1.30 percent for all environmental media. Third, Woodward (1992) points out that WTE projects often do not fit within the business priorities of major potential suppliers of funds. Therefore, communities must be creative in their financing and may have to increasingly utilize a variety of funding mechanisms and tap various sources of funds to successfully finance their proposed WTE projects.

5.7 ADJUSTMENTS IN THE FINANCING OF WTE PROJECTS

State and local governments are adjusting to altered financial conditions and increasing demands for environmental infrastructure by taking a four-prong approach to successfully finance WTE facilities. First, in order to successfully finance large capital expenditures, local jurisdictions are using a combination of several financing mechanisms. Second, jurisdictions are increasingly using local-sector resources for financing (e.g., city and county revenues and taxable revenue bonds). Third, as traditional debt options become less viable because of restrictions imposed by, for example, TRA86, innovative and new methods of finance are being used to adjust to altered market conditions. Fourth, private-sector participation is being used more extensively. Private-sector participation allows local-sector resources to be reallocated elsewhere for other public good consumption and acknowledges the constraints imposed by federal legislation, such as TRA86. Tables 5.9 and 5.10 reflect these adjustments at the local level during the 1982 to 1990 period.

5.7.1 Advanced-Planned and Operational Facilities

The use of private equity to finance WTE projects continues to grow. In 1990, 44.8 percent of all existing and advanced-planned WTE facilities reported the use of equity capital as a component of their finance packages. The use of revenue bonds (both tax-exempt and taxable) have also increased over the decade, with 10.8 percent of 1982 facilities and 47.2 percent of 1990 facilities reporting these methods of finance.

Federal grants have declined over the period from 1982 to 1990, from a high of 13.4 percent in 1982 to 8.5 percent in 1990. State grants have increased from 10.2 percent in 1982 to 17.4 percent in 1990. The use of city, municipal, and county revenues has also increased over the period from 4.7 percent in 1982 to 11.0 percent of all existing and advanced-planned facilities in 1990. State loan guarantees and state bonding authorities were a financial component in 6 percent of facilities in 1990, up slightly from the 1982 level.

Leasing and other innovative types of finance (e.g., bond insurance, letters of credit, and variable-rate debt) are emerging as a primary source of finance. Leveraged leasing or bank leasing was a component in the financing of 7.5 percent of facilities in 1990, while 16.9 percent of existing and advanced-planned facilities report some type of credit enhancement in their financing package.

With respect to the advanced-planned facilities, IDB use has increased as a financing component, from 25.0 percent in 1984 to 36.1 percent in 1990 (Table 5.10). Municipal revenue bonds have increased from 12.5 percent

Table 5.9 Waste-to-Energy Capital Finance: Historical Trends of Finance (% of facilities using method)*					
METHOD OF FINANCE	1990	1988	1986	1984	1982
Private Equity	44.8	24.4	27.4	25.0	26.3
Tax-Exempt Revenue Bonds**	36.3	11.4	7.7	10.6	10.8
Taxable Revenue Bonds	10.9	-	-	-	-
IDBs**	34.3	26.0	26.5	16.7	12.4
State Grants	17.4	9.8	9.1	9.7	10.2
General-Obligation Bonds	16.4	9.3	11.1	13.0	15.6
Federal Grants	8.5	4.5	7.4	9.3	13.4
City or Municipal Revenue	7.5	3.7	3.7	4.2	4.3
Leverage Lease or Bank Lease	7.5	3.2	-	0.5	-
Federal Revenues	4.0	2.4	2.6	4.2	-
County Revenues	3.5	1.9	1.1	0.5	-
State Loans or Loan Guarantees	3.5	1.6	0.8	-	1.6
State Bonding	2.5	1.6	1.4	2.3	2.3
Other	2.0	0.3	1.1	2.3	3.2

Sources: Government Advisory Associates, Inc., Resource Recovery Yearbook, 1982, 1984, 1986-87, 1988-89, 1991.

* Multiple responses: firms reported multiple forms of finance.

** "Tax-Exempt Revenue Bond" and "IDB" are used interchangeably and many local officials do not distinguish between the two. A tax-exempt revenue bond generally refers to municipal financing (tax-exempt) for a municipal project. An IDB generally refers to tax-exempt financing of a private-sector project which a municipality views as beneficial for a municipality.

in 1982 to 55.7 percent in 1990. With respect to existing facilities, the use of IDBs and municipal-revenues bonds has increased from 12.5 percent and 9.7 percent in 1984, to 33.6 percent and 27.9 percent in 1990, respectively. Private-equity investment has more than doubled during the period, increasing from 18.8 percent in 1984 to 39.3 percent in 1990. State and federal grants have declined substantially during the period, reflecting decreased intergovernmental revenues.

For successful WTE facilities, private-equity capital, tax-exempt bonds, and taxable municipal bonds are the major sources of finance. More im-

Table 5.10 Alternative Methods of Finance: Advanced-Planned and Existing WTE Facilities: 1984-1990 (% of facilities using method)*				
STAGE OF DEVELOPMENT	1990	1988	1986	1984
Advanced Stage				
Private Investment	57.4	33.7	42.9	37.5
IDBs**	36.1	36.1	40.6	25.0
Municipal Revenue Bonds**	55.7	13.6	6.0	12.5
General Obligation Bonds	4.9	4.7	3.8	9.7
Existing Plants				
Private Investment	39.3	16.8	17.9	18.8
IDBs	33.6	17.8	17.9	12.5
Municipal Revenue Bonds	27.9	14.2	8.7	9.7
General Obligation Bonds	21.4	13.0	15.6	18.7
State and Federal Grants	8.2	14.7	23.4	21.5

Sources: Government Advisory Associates, Inc., Resource Recovery Yearbook, 1984, 1986-87, 1988-89, 1990.

*   Multiple responses: some firms reported multiple forms of finance.

**   "Tax-Exempt Revenue Bond" and "IDB" are used interchangeably and many local officials do not distinguish between the two. A tax-exempt revenue bond generally refers to municipal financing (tax-exempt) for a municipal project. An IDB generally refers to tax-exempt financing of a private-sector project which a municipality views as beneficial for a municipality.

portantly, an emerging trend among successful facilities is the use of multiple financing mechanisms. As WTE participants adjust to a changing financial environment, innovative methods and a combination of several financial instruments are increasingly found in the financial packages of successful projects. In order to assess which financing mechanisms have accounted for the largest dollar volumes of total WTE financing (in contrast to their frequency of use), a data collection exercise (Kelsay, 1992) was undertaken to augment the GAA data base. Table 5.11 summarizes these results for 1990.

When viewed from the perspective of total dollar financing, a somewhat different pattern emerges. IDBs and tax-exempt revenue bonds accounted for 46.3 percent and 21.4 percent, respectively, of total dollar volume. This reflects the predominant use of tax-exempt mechanisms prior to the 1986 tax reforms and the large lag time in facility planning. Private equity ac-

Table 5.11 Waste-to-Energy Capital Finance Mechanisms: 1990			
Method of Finance	Number of Facilities Using Method*	Amount (in billions of dollars)	% of Total Finance
IDBs	73	$ 7.893	46.3
Tax-Exempt Revenue Bonds	38	3.642	21.4
Private Equity	61	2.142	12.6
General-Obligation Bonds	29	1.143	6.7
Taxable-Revenue Bonds	15	0.524	3.1
State & Federal Grants	21	0.203	1.2
City & County Revenues	11	0.107	0.6
Adjustable-Rate Muni Bonds	2	0.081	0.5
Lease-Revenue Bonds	15	1.300	7.6
Total	265	$17.035	100.0%
Credit Enhancements** (Letters of Credit, Bond Insurance, and Guarantees)	27	$ 2.824	16.9%

Sources: Government Advisory Associates, Resource Recovery Yearbook, 1991 and Kelsay (1992).

  * Some facilities use more than one method of finance.

 ** Credit enhancements are not a financing method but rather are a means of improving the viability of the finance methods listed above.

counted for 12.6 percent of the total dollar amount. State and federal grants and city/county/municipal revenues were found to represent a small, but important, component of finance packages. In addition, there is a trend toward the increasing use of innovative financing. For example, lease-revenue bonds and other types of lease structures account for 7.6 percent of total financing; and the use of third-party credit enhancements (e.g., letters of credit, bond insurance, and guarantees) were involved in 16.9 percent of all transactions. A growing emphasis on minimizing the financial risks to the local community (due to political and other objections) and general difficulties with the use of traditional financial instruments suggest that the use of these innovative risk-spreading mechanisms will increase over time.

5.7.2 Scratched and Abandoned Facilities

This chapter began with a supposition that financial changes in the latter 1980s played a role, possibly a key role, in the recent cancellations of WTE facilities. While there is clear evidence that the direction of change in financial markets in the latter 1980s was toward making financing more difficult and costly, the importance of financial constraints in the actual decisions to abandon a WTE project is less clear. This subsection reviews the information that is available with respect to this question.

First, consider once again where WTE cancellations have occurred. Table 5.12 presents summary data on the location and potential design capacity. of canceled WTE facilities in the United States. Seven states account for 45.7 percent of canceled facilities—California, Florida, Michigan, New Jersey, New York, North Carolina, and Pennsylvania. California and Pennsylvania alone account for over 22 percent of cancellations. With respect to design capacity, five states account for 50.1 percent of cancellations. They are California, Florida, New Jersey, Pennsylvania, and Texas. Together California and Pennsylvania account for 26.5 percent of canceled design capacity.

It is difficult to assess the magnitude of the impact of selecting a particular financing mechanism on the decision to cancel a WTE project because (1) it is not possible to disentangle the effects of financial barriers as compared to barriers presented by other factors considered in this work, and (2) many facilities that were canceled had not yet gotten to the financing stage or had no specific financing mechanism yet selected. Finance mechanism data are almost non-existent for cancellations that occurred at early decision points (e.g., cancellation after preliminary investigation and cancellation at the conceptual stage). Nonetheless, data on the financing mechanism chosen by many advanced-planned facilities are available and were collected for this work. Tables 5.13 and 5.14 summarize these results.

In terms of the financing method used, private equity was a component in 31.9 percent of canceled facilities for which data are available. IDBs and tax-exempt revenues were identified as potential finance components in 28.6 percent and 13.2 percent of projects, respectively. General-obligation bonds were identified in 8.8 percent of canceled projects. Upon examination of methods of finance with respect to total dollars, the data show 75.8 percent of facilities planned to use IDB and tax-exempt revenue bonds. Local sector revenues, adjustable rate bonds, and lease financing were insignificant or zero.

Possibly the most important finding here is that innovative methods of finance (e.g., lease arrangements, adjustable-rate debt, and third-party credit enhancements) were not present in any of the financial packages put together or considered for facilities that were eventually canceled. It is unclear if the absence of multiple and innovative financing mechanisms was a contributor

Table 5.12 Location of Scratched/Abandoned Facilities by State: 1986-1990				
STATE	NUMBER OF FACILITIES	%	POTENTIAL CAPACITY (tpd)	%
AL	2	1.00	850	0.7
AK	1	0.5	750	0.6
AR	3	1.4	370	0.3
AZ	2	1.0	3050	0.5
CA	30	14.5	19365	15.8
CO	2	1.0	615	0.5
CT	4	1.9	1600	1.3
FL	10	4.8	9397	7.5
GA	3	1.4	449	0.4
HI	1	0.5	274	0.2
IA	2	1.0	1000	0.8
ID	2	1.0	220	0.2
IL	8	3.9	4640	5.7
IN	2	1.0	280	0.2
KS	2	1.0	1400	1.1
KY	4	1.9	1040	0.8
LA	2	1.0	350	0.3
MA	8	3.9	3780	3.0
MD	7	3.4	6200	5.0
ME	2	1.0	1100	0.9
MI	9	4.3	2230	1.8
MN	1	0.5	180	0.1
MO	5	2.4	2250	2.0
MS	1	0.5	150	0.1
NC	9	4.3	3114	2.5

Table 5.12 Location of Scratched/Abandoned Facilities by State: 1986-1990 (continued)				
STATE	NUMBER OF FACILITIES	%	POTENTIAL CAPACITY (tpd)	%
ND	2	1.0	160	0.1
NH	7	3.4	3550	2.9
NJ	10	4.8	10324	8.3
NM	1	0.5	NA	-
NY	11	5.3	3930	3.2
OH	3	1.4	2500	2.0
OK	1	0.5	249	0.2
OR	1	0.5	1200	1.0
PA	16	7.7	13321	10.7
PR	1	0.5	1000	0.8
RI	1	0.5	400	0.3
SC	2	1.0	525	0.4
TN	3	1.4	1700	1.4
TX	8	3.9	9674	7.8
UT	1	0.5	650	0.5
VA	6	2.9	3225	2.6
VT	2	1.0	200	0.2
WA	5	2.4	4650	3.7
WI	4	1.9	1950	1.6
TOTAL	207	100.0	124482	100.0

Sources: Government Advisory Associates, Resource Recovery Yearbook, 1982, 1984, 1986-87, 1988-89, 1991, and Kelsay (1992).

Table 5.13 Waste-to-Energy Capital Finance Mechanisms at Scratched/Abandoned Facilities: 1986-1990		
METHOD OF FINANCE	NUMBER OF FACILITIES USING METHOD	% OF FACILITIES USING METHOD
Private Equity	29	31.9
IDBs	26	28.6
Tax-Exempt Revenue Bonds	12	13.2
General Obligation Bonds	8	8.8
Taxable Revenue Bonds	4	4.4
State Grants	7	7.7
Federal Grants	2	2.2
City & Municipal Revenues	2	2.2
Lease or Bank Leases	1	1.0
Total	91	100.00

Sources: Government Advisory Associates, <u>Resource Recovery Yearbook</u>, 1982, 1984, 1986-87, 1988-89, 1991, and Kelsay (1992).

* Information on financial methods used was available only for those facilities that were in the advanced stages of planning. Facilities in the conceptual stages or before had not decided on a finance mechanism.

Table 5.14 Waste-to-Energy Capital Finance Mechanisms at
Scratched/Abandoned Facilities by Finance Amount: 1986-1990

METHOD OF FINANCE	NUMBER*	AMOUNT (in billions of dollars)	% of TOTAL FINANCE
IDBs	21	2.511	51.2
Tax-Exempt Revenue Bonds	12	1.20	24.6
Private Equity	19	0.781	15.9
General-Obligation Bonds	7	0.249	5.1
Taxable Revenues	2	0.087	1.8
State & Federal Grants	6	0.021	0.4
City & County Revenues	1	0.010	0.2
Adjustable Rate Municipal Bonds	-	-	-
Lease or Bank Leases	1	0.038	0.8
Totals	75	$4.904	100.0%

Sources: Government Advisory Associates, Resource Recovery Yearbook, 1982, 1984, 1986-87, 1988-89, 1991 and Kelsay (1992).

* Finance amounts were available only for those facilities that were in the advanced stages of planning. Those facilities in the conceptual stages or before had not decided on a finance mechanism. The number of facilities in Tables 5.13 and 5.14 differs because some facilities had decided on the financing mechanisms but not the dollar allocation toward each method.

to the failure of the project, or if these projects simply did not get far enough down the development path to consider these innovative and possibly less obvious financing strategies. To the extent that public opposition arose to the WTE project on the basis of increased financial risk to the community, the absence of these innovative approaches, which are designed primarily to lower the community's level of financial risk, may have played a role in project cancellation. Unfortunately, data do not currently exist on the degree to which financial risk to the community played a role in the various project abandonments. This issue is addressed further in the next chapter as part of our case studies.

Although financing data are limited for scratched facilities, an analysis of large capital facilities (i.e., those greater than $80 million) reveals that a large share of the proposed financing was to be public financing. If two canceled facilities that had proposed 100 percent equity financing are deleted, the total amount of public-sector financing (e.g., IRBs, IDBs, and general-obligation debt) is more than 87 percent, compared to about 75 percent overall. Nine large abandoned projects reported that 100 percent of their financing was to be public. To the extent that the public viewed their community's financial risk to be increased by a WTE project that depended almost entirely on public debt, the reliance on public financing may have played a role in the decision to abandon the project.

With respect to restrictions placed on tax-exempt financing by TRA86, the situation is again less than clear. Recall that TRA86 (1) imposed caps on the amount of tax-exempt financing a state can issue to support projects such as WTE facilities and (2) imposed more severe restrictions on the types of projects that qualify for tax-exempt financing particularly with respect to the degree to which private firms are allowed to be involved in the project. There is little doubt that the restrictions imposed by TRA86 played a significant role in escalating the rate at which WTE projects were introduced in the latter 1980s. Some projects that might have developed at a more leisurely pace were no doubt "moved along" to avoid the impending financing restrictions of TRA86. If TRA86, in fact, resulted in an upward surge in the number of WTE projects being considered in the latter 1980s, a follow-on argument is that the number of cancellations also increased even if the probability of a project making it through to operation remained unchanged. Further, to the extent that projects were hurried in their development, a case can be made that some projects met cancellation because they were simply "pushed too fast." In this case, changes in financial markets may have contributed indirectly to some WTE project cancellations.

With respect to the caps imposed by TRA86, six of the nine states that contributed more than 49 percent of all project cancellations came close to fully using their allotted caps on tax exempts (see Table 5.7).[20] Further, this work has found that more than $750 million in solid-waste financing requests were denied in 1991 in those states as a result of the unified volume caps. However, three of those states—New Jersey, New York, and Pennsylvania—did not use more than 70 percent of their allocations in either 1989 or 1990, and Pennsylvania used only 35 percent of its allotment in 1989.[21] Therefore, analysis of the data in this area does not lead to any hard conclusions about the effects of the TRA86 caps on WTE cancellations.

5.8 SUMMARY AND FUTURE OUTLOOK

This chapter has examined how financial constraints changed during the 1980s and the impacts of those changes on decisions to abandon WTE projects and on the overall viability of WTE. Three trends were particularly important. First, increasing facility costs led to very large financing packages, which for many communities were the largest financing packages ever considered. For advanced-planned WTE facilities, constant adjusted capital costs increased by more than 40 percent during the period 1982 to 1990. Second, state and local tax and expenditure limitations and changes in the tax-exempt market forced adjustments in the risk/return relationships necessary for successful finance. These adjustments led to more innovative methods of finance including leasing arrangements, adjustable-rate debt, letters of credit, municipal-bond insurance, and other third-party credit enhancements. Third, states and local communities have been faced with increasing demands for more expenditures on environmental infrastructure at the same time they have faced more difficult financing conditions. Federally imposed unified volume caps and severe restrictions on tax-exempt financing have led communities to adopt non-traditional and, in some case, more expensive methods of finance. In addition, the extremely large capital outlays required for some WTE facilities have forced some communities to make hard decisions about where they allocate their limited credit lines. Communities are sometimes forced to make trade-offs between funding environmental infrastructure and more traditional activities, such as housing and education. And although the costs of all MSW management options are expected to rise, the decisions of communities about WTE have not been, and will not be, made easier by WTE cost escalations resulting from mandates for stricter environmental controls.

The fundamentals of the long-term bond market are generally positive over the next decade, and, therefore, capital markets should show little strain in funding future expenditures for local environmental projects, such as WTE. The problem is whether local jurisdictions will have the financial ability and, in some cases, the political will to take on higher levels of debt burden. Large, capital-intensive WTE facilities can crowd out other local investments, and some small communities may face obstacles in accessing capital markets.

On the positive side, however, innovative financial instruments are increasingly available that overcome to some extent the financial obstacles imposed during the 1980s. Adjustments on the parts of capital markets and communities to new financial realities are likely to improve the financial viability of capital-intensive projects, such as WTE facilities. Although financing constraints will continue to be problematic, especially for those communities with questionable credit ratings, financial constraints are not expected to be a "show-stopper" as the overall viability of WTE is determined in the 1990s.

NOTES

1. See U.S. EPA (1990a) for an overview of the projected costs of environmental regulations and expenditure trends for 1981 through 2000.

2. Lovely and Wasylenko (1992) provide a review of studies of state taxation and municipal borrowing costs. Using a large sample of individual bonds, their

results suggest a 1 percentage point reduction in the tax rate on in-state municipal interest reduced yield required to finance public borrowing by 3.9 basis points. The ratio of losses to savings indicate that about one-half of a state's debt must be held by non-residents for losses to be matched by interest savings.

3. The TRA86 took away many of the advantages of bond banks. It barred earning investment income on bond proceeds, which many bond banks used to pay issuance and administrative costs. However, the states of Tennessee and Maine are exceptions. The Tennessee Local Development Authority (TLDA) is a quasi-government agency established under this concept. In fact, the Davidson County, Tennessee, WTE facility was financed with a $60.475 million loan from TLDA.

4. For a thorough discussion of the participants in the municipal bond market and the changes in ownership over time, see Feenberg and Poterba (1991).

5. These percentage holdings are consistent with the implied tax rate theory of the "marginal investor." From 1975 until 1986, the implied tax rate as computed by Feenberg and Poterba (1991) closely tracked the statutory corporate tax rate. With the passage of TRA86 and the shift in the marginal investor to the household sector, the implied tax rate tracked the top individual marginal tax rate.

6. Third-party credit enhancements include letters of credit (LOC), state and federal guarantees in bond banks, and private bond insurance.

7. The municipal bond insurance industry is dominated by four companies. Reported market shares in 1989 were (1) Municipal Bond Investors Assurance Corporation (MBIA 36.6%), (2) American Municipal Bond Assurance Corporation (AMBAC 31.6%), (3) Financial Guaranty Insurance Company (FGIC 16.7%), and (4) Bond Investors Guaranty Insurance Corporation (BIG 13.7%) (McLoughlin and Holstein, 1989).

8. McLoughlin and Holstein (1989) report that in 1982 the yield spread was 160 basis points (i.e., 1.6 percent). By 1989 this spread had compressed to 49 basis points.

9. It was recently reported that bond insurance is reaching capacity constraints in certain geographic regions for bonding municipal debt. For example, Washington, D.C., which has an A-rating from Standard and Poors, has insured debt of $1.6 billion of the total $3.8 billion of direct debt outstanding. FGIC reports that capacity problems for bond insurance are present in the Northeast and may be approaching in the Southwest and California (Mitchell, 1992).

10. For a general discussion of bank credit enhancements, see Hough and Petersen (1983) and Petersen (1991).

11. Tax and expenditure limitations have forced municipal issuers to adopt more innovative methods to finance public investment. Lease-based financing is a direct response to these limitations as they do not require voter approval and are not classified as long-term debt in the calculation of debt.

12. For example, the city and county of Honolulu sold its WTE facility in a leveraged-lease transaction. The transaction raised $80 million in equity financing for the city of Honolulu (Turbeville, 1990).

13. Barzel (1988) gives examples of certificate-of-participation programs as a mechanism for public-sector investment. In this type of agreement, a number of local agencies participate in one financing issue, which results in a substantial decrease in financing costs.

14. Petersen (1991) reported that adjustable-rate municipal debt accounted for

20 percent of municipal bond volume in 1985, but had declined to 7 percent by 1990 as a result of the flattening of the tax-exempt yield curve.

15. The city of Columbia, Missouri, addressed these issues in structuring an interest-rate swap in 1987 involving $22.1 million of obligations and leases (Boldt, 1988).

16. Edwards (1990) reports that these NSPS would result in national average cost increases of $13/ton and $12/ton, respectively for waste burned at new and existing sources. These figures represent about a 20 percent increase in the cost of WTE technology.

17. For an excellent review of tax-exempt bond legislation over the 1968 to 1989 period, see Zimmerman (1991).

18. For a discussion of the restrictions on qualified bonds under TRA86, see, for example, Zimmerman (1991).

19. For a thorough discussion of the financial options available to finance environmental facilities, see Environmental Financial Advisory Board (1991d).

20. The data show that five states, California, Florida, Illinois, Texas, and Washington, which exhausted or came close to exhausting their volume caps, account for 38.5 percent of facility cancellations with respect to total design capacity. The same five states account for 29.5 percent of facility cancellations.

21. Due to the inherent problems of the unified-volume-cap limitations (e.g., short-planning horizon, carryforward provisions, dedicated activity allocations, etc.) some states have, in effect, exhausted their volume caps if they utilize more than about 75 percent of their allocations.

Chapter 6

Case Studies: Community Decision Making

6.1 INTRODUCTION

Previous chapters have established that the management of municipal solid waste clearly is an issue of increasing public concern. Proponents of WTE see it as a solution to this country's solid waste management (SWM) problem. However, many proposed WTE facilities have not been built in municipalities across the country.

This chapter attempts to describe the range of factors that influence decisions regarding WTE made by municipalities but does not seek to judge the correctness of the decisions. Influential factors include the technical and financial issues previously discussed as well as social and political issues. Separately investigating these kinds of issues may not provide a composite or synthetic picture of the factors leading to decisions about WTE facilities in any one community. Detailed case studies, in contrast, allow a broad perspective about the decision-making process within communities. Describing this broad perspective is the primary objective of the case studies discussed in this chapter.

Decision making involves at least two components: the decisions that are made, which we label *outcomes*, and the *process* of making decisions. In the case of WTE, the outcomes of interest are decisions whether or not to proceed with the incinerators and the degree to which those decisions are supported within the relevant municipalities. A municipality may decide to build a WTE facility without having the strong backing of citizens or politicians, as an example. The process of decision making involves the activities undertaken in the course of reaching an outcome. Process decisions include procedures for choosing host sites, whether and when to hold public meetings, whether to hold public referenda, and the like. Process clearly is linked to outcome, but like processes need not lead to like outcomes.

The study reported here sought to discern the factors that are critical to decisions about WTE by examining and comparing two cases in which formalized decisions were made to proceed with the facilities with two cases in which formalized decisions were made not to proceed with WTE facilities. The framework for the study, which emphasizes the context within which decisions were made and the process of decision making, was developed from relevant literature primarily on WTE incinerator planning and implementation, public involvement, and the siting of controversial facilities in general.

The U.S. EPA and several other agencies and authors discuss WTE in addition to other waste management alternatives. The U.S. EPA's *Decision-Maker's Guide to Solid Waste Management* (1989) provides information for public officials to use in evaluating various waste management alternatives. The Office of Technology Assessment (OTA, 1989) and Velzy (1990) also outline WTE's role in integrated SWM programs. The OTA report provides background information and suggestions for federal funding and incentives for implementating integrated waste management programs. Blumberg and Gottlieb (1989) also consider WTE's role in integrated waste management systems but hold a much less favorable attitude about WTE than OTA, arguing that a true hierarchical strategy that emphasizes and subsequently funds waste reduction, reuse, and recycling is a better option than WTE.

Technical and economic profiles and status reports about numerous WTE projects were reviewed. Articles about individual projects discuss a Tulsa resource-recovery facility (Richmond, 1987; Van Fleet, 1989), a San Diego project (Clay, 1987), an Indianapolis facility (Stevens, Henderson, and Tulli, 1990), a multijurisdictional Massachusetts facility (Yaffe and Wooten, 1984), a Connecticut RDF facility (Kiser, 1989) and two Florida projects, Palm Beach County (Burr, 1990) and Broward County (Allen, Foye, and Henderson, 1990). A compilation of brief profiles of numerous WTE facilities also was consulted (Richards et al., 1990).

Environmental issues associated with WTE facilities are examined by several authors.[1] Coverage of several issues including air emissions and ash and problems with the regulation thereof is provided by Blumberg and Gottlieb (1989) and *Newsday* (1989). Human exposure to toxic air emissions from WTE facilities is discussed by Jones (1987) and Travis and Hattemer-Frey (1989). Florini, Denison, and Ruston (1990) and Denison and Silbergeld (1988) argue that potential adverse health effects of WTE can be reduced by implementing other components of integrated waste management, i.e., source reduction (for toxic metals), separation, and recycling. Kiser (1992a) provides an overview of recent ash management actions, and Cook (1989) discusses ash management from a state's perspective and makes recommendations for reducing toxicity by controlling input in addition to existing emissions control technology.

Several authors have provided guidance for planning, implementing, and siting WTE projects. Some focus on a single aspect of WTE projects such as financing mechanisms (Chen, France, and Howard. 1990; Hilgendorf, 1989), assessing a project's economic feasibility (Russell, 1982), host community compensation mechanisms (Binder and Minott, 1989), public approval (Steisel, 1987), legal issues associated with negotiations, contracts, and ownership (Mishkin, 1987), identifying markets (Gershman, 1987), and permitting (Alexeeff, Marty, and Lipsett, 1989). Broiles (1988) also discusses permitting and demonstrates how a bifurcated permitting process, i.e., having separate risk and environmental impact assessments, can stimulate confusion and controversy. Others provide cursory advice about numerous aspects of project planning and implementation based on first-hand experience with one project (Lewis, 1987; Buhler, 1987). Project planning and implementation activities discussed in such articles include meeting regulations, selecting from ownership options, technical siting considerations, and public involvement.

Public involvement in WTE planning and implementation is the focus of several articles and documents. For example, as a companion to its *Decision-Maker's Guide to Solid Waste Management* (1989), U.S. EPA has published a guidebook for public involvement in decision making about SWM activities, including WTE (U.S. EPA, 1990c). The guide is directed at public officials and provides public information and participation techniques in addition to advice on building credibility and effectively communicating technical information. Konheim (1989) and Luderer (1990), dealing specifically with WTE, also address the difficult task of conveying highly technical information and provide suggestions about the relationship between trust in the process of decision making and overall support of the decision. Luderer (1990) specifically recommends that public involvement programs ensure that the concerns of officials and the public are clearly understood by all parties and that sufficient information is exchanged to allow informed decisions. Bealer and Crider (1984) add that an appreciation of the total context should be gained, including history, defined as past events and previous relations among participants.

Other researchers have identified information needs of various segments of the public neighboring a European WTE facility according to their knowledge and demand for information (Wiedemann, Schutz, and Peters, 1991). This research correlates "personal relevance," a likely proxy for proximity to a proposed facility, with individuals' desire to participate in the decision-making process. This correlation could, in part, explain greater activism among persons residing in close proximity to proposed facilities.

As pointed out previously, very little of the literature examines all activities related to WTE facility planning and implementation. One notable exception is U.S. EPA's (1990c) guide for public involvement, which divides the siting process (from identifying a waste problem to building, operating, and eventually closing the facility) into three phases. The first phase is planning and includes identifying the problem, choosing a technology, and choosing site selection criteria. The second phase is site selection and facility design. In this stage the site is selected, the facility permitted, mitigation plans prepared, and the facility constructed. The final stage, termed implementation, encompasses facility operation, management, and eventual closure. Each stage includes important decisions and considers critical issues. We adopted a similar strategy for information collection so that the occurrence of particular issues and the conduct of particular decision-making activities might be correlated.

It also is the case that few documents about WTE or other SWM alternatives focus their attention on decision making. There are, however, three exceptions. One is Popp, Hecht, and Melberth (1985). These authors explicitly discuss resource-recovery decision making, aiming to identify the most significant variables in that process. They distinguish the following three idealized categories of decision maker: rational, intuitive-emotional, and quasi-rational. Rational decision making is essential in the resource-recovery arena, although time, the cost of information, incompatible goals, structural obstacles (e.g., fragmented authority in multijurisdictional settings), and political feasibility impede a rational decision-making process, according to Popp, Hecht, and Melberth. The authors recognize that participants in the decision-making process go well beyond elected, formal decision makers to include non-elected governmental administrators, business and industry representatives, community or neighborhood organizations, and the like. However, in discussing the variables that are critical to resource-recovery decision making, Popp, Hecht, and Melberth delineate primarily technical and economic variables. They tend to specify the decisions that must be made in the course of planning and implementing resource-recovery options instead of discussing the decision-making process or the links between interim decisions and outcomes. For instance, one variable they consider to be critical to decision making is facility siting. The authors cite the proximity of the market for steam and potential transmission losses as highly important and also state that "there will be the inevitable emotional issue of public acceptance to contend with" (p. 131). They recommend that public awareness programs and citizen advisory group participation should begin in project planning and persist throughout the course of the project.

Much of Popp, Hecht, and Melberth's book is prescriptive, suggesting factors that ought to be considered in the course of developing and implementing resource-recovery projects. Similarly, U.S. EPA's *Decision-Maker's Guide to Solid Waste Management* (1989) offers practical guidance to communities involved in solid waste management, including WTE. Much of U.S. EPA's guide grapples with decisions that are necessary for project planning and implementation such as developing an integrated solid waste program, technical aspects of SWM (e.g., waste-stream assessment, collection and transfer of solid waste), and a variety of waste management strategies. The chapter on municipal waste combustion focuses on technical (e.g., facility type, facility sizing), administrative (e.g., facility ownership and operation), and economic (e.g., the market for steam, financing options) aspects of that waste management option. In addition, a sidebar in that chapter addresses facility siting and a different chapter prescribes public education and involvement measures. Nonetheless, U.S. EPA's guide tends to discuss details about which decisions must be made, rather than stages in the decision-making process. It also does not describe links between components of decision making (either stages or factors) and outcomes.

In contrast, Chertoff and Buxbaum (1986) explicitly explore the factors that lead to public acceptance or rejection of WTE facilities with the goal of recommending measures to surmount public animosity toward the technology. These authors undertook case studies of 30 medium- and large-scale projects that were started from the late 1960s through the early 1980s, conducting interviews with project managers or their surrogates. Among the interview questions were why the WTE option was selected, how it was announced publicly, what public responses were, and why the public responded in that fashion. These questions did not aim to investigate the role of the decision-making process in outcomes. Chertoff and Buxbaum concluded that the two factors that had the greatest effect on public support were the perceived need for a facility (i.e., the absence of additional landfill capacity) and the existence of groundwater problems caused by existing landfills.

Relevant literature generally failed to regard WTE planning, implementation, or decision making chronologically. Because WTE decision making is a process that occurs over time, we adopted a chronological organizational framework for studying factors involved in WTE decision making. We hypothesized a sequential framework to allow us to distinguish when during the course of events particular issues came to the fore, for example. The hypothesized stages in the chronology are listed below.

- Identifying the need for the facility
- Project planning
- Selecting finalist site(s)
- Attempting to site the facility
- Project implementation
- Formalized decision

Each stage was envisioned to build upon the previous stage(s). Researchers recognized the likelihood that two elements would cut across all the stages—the sociopolitical environment in which decisions are made and history (e.g., community and regional history of attitudes toward, and interactions with, waste management alternatives and with industries already in place or that wish to locate).

The chronological framework assumed that the WTE decision-making process would start with identifying the need for a facility. Existing waste management policies, the status of current and projected waste management practices (including the need for facilities and the operational effectiveness of existing facilities), and regional population size and growth trends are among the elements that may contribute to the identification of WTE as a serious waste management option. Once WTE is proposed, researchers hypothesized that project planning would begin. Components of project planning include decisions about the size of the facility, the technology that would be used, and preferable financing options. The next hypothesized stage in some ways is a subset of project planning, namely identifying likely sites for the WTE facility. This stage was separated from the others because of its hypothesized importance in both the decision-making process and in the outcomes of that process. Local population density, population composition, income, and the geographic extent of any potential adverse health impacts are among the considerations that may influence the identification of likely sites. Finalist sites may be selected by examining their environmental context (e.g., other sources of industrial pollution) through a technical screening process.

The next hypothesized stage in the sequence is project implementation, which includes vendor negotiations, steps to obtain financing, and activities to effectuate siting. These latter siting activities, such as obtaining zoning changes and permitting, may encourage the most public aspects of the decision-making process and may include both formal and informal decision making. It is during this stage that meetings, news media coverage, and public participation in decision making may approach their peak. The last hypothesized chronological state stage, the formalized decision, is defined by a clearly recognized decision point, perhaps in the form of a public referendum or the execution of a vendor contract.

The remainder of this chapter discusses the methods used to conduct and analyze case studies, describes each of the case studies, and analyzes all of the case studies. The chapter concludes by portraying future trends in WTE decision making.

6.2 METHODS

Two methods were used to study the factors that contribute to WTE decisions within a community context—a literature review and case studies. The literature examined focused on WTE planning and implementation and on the siting of controversial facilities in general. Secondarily, literature on related topics such as public involvement and risk communication also was reviewed. Results of this literature review were summarized in Section 6.1.

A case-study approach was adopted to allow a detailed examination of communities' WTE decision making. To discern the factors distinguishing "proceed" outcomes from "not proceeding" outcomes, the case-study approach also was comparative. Time and budgetary constraints limited the number of case studies to four—two sites where formalized decisions were made to proceed with WTE and two sites where the opposite decisions were made. While a sample size of four does not allow statistically meaningful generalizations or comparisons to be made, four detailed case studies do allow qualitative analyses and inferences.

6.2.1 Selection of Case-Study Sites

Several criteria were used to select appropriate case-study sites. First, because of the comparative approach taken in the study, there had to be two sites in which formalized decisions were made to proceed with WTE and two sites in which decisions had been made not to proceed with WTE. Second, such decisions had to be made relatively recently because the passage of time makes reconstructing the decision-making process increasingly difficult due to faulty memory and the influence of later events. Also, recent decisions—especially decisions not to proceed with WTE—would enhance the likelihood of locating key participants to interview. Third, the sites had to be geographically diverse, even though four sites could not represent every part of the nation. Fourth, to optimize comparisons to the extent practicable with four sites, variation was sought in such characteristics as regional population size and growth trends, local population density (i.e., in close proximity to the proposed site), and general degree of industrialization. The four case-study sites—Broward County, Florida; Oakland County, Michigan; Knox County, Tennessee; and Monmouth County, New Jersey—are depicted in Figure 6.1.

6.2.2 Data Collection

Extensive background research was undertaken for each case-study site. Available Government Advisory Associates (GAA) data, journal articles, progress summaries in solid waste publications, and newspaper articles were examined. Preliminary telephone and facsimile contacts were made with people familiar with the local history of WTE. Researchers then conducted a series of face-to-face interviews with key informants (i.e., people who are knowledgeable about the topic and who may represent the views of a group of people) in each case-study location. All persons who were interviewed, as well as some key people who declined to be interviewed, were sent drafts of their case-study descriptions (see Sections 6.3-6.6) for their comment and

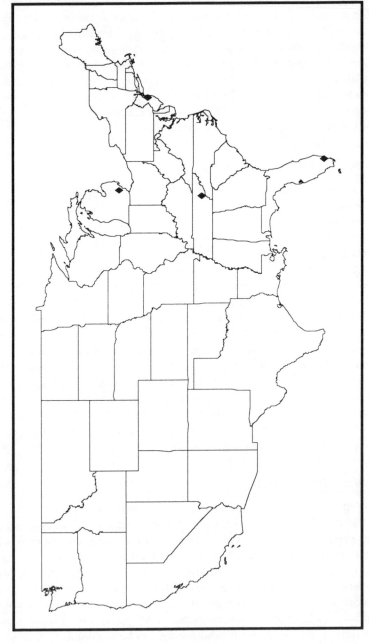

Figure 6.1
Case-Study Site Locations

review. Corrections and comments subsequently were incorporated into the text.

6.2.2.1 Selection of Respondents. The research design specified a goal of conducting 10 extensive interviews during each site visit. In a departure from Chertoff and Buxbaum's (1986) strategy of interviewing only the project manager (or a surrogate), we sought to interview a wide range of the many participants in WTE decision making (see also Popp, Hecht, and Melberth, 1985). Background research revealed enough about each case study's decision-making framework for researchers to identify categories of people involved, e.g., committees, government offices, and public groups. Criteria then were developed to select the people who should be interviewed. Researchers sought representation by WTE proponents and opponents. The people interviewed ideally included elected county and municipal government officials, appointed officials (e.g., participants in solid waste departments or authorities), relevant civic, religious, or environmental organization representatives (e.g., local environmental groups or neighborhood associations), and representatives of the news media. Respondents were contacted by telephone, facsimile, or letter to make interview appointments. Participation in the study was voluntary. Respondents were informed before participating that their names would not be used in subsequent publications. Most interviews were tape-recorded, with respondents' consent, to ensure that no information was lost in the course of note-taking.

6.2.2.2 Interview Protocol. The interview protocol was developed in conformance with the chronological organizing framework for case studies (see Section 6.1). A protocol is a tool that structures interviews by specifying the topics to be covered, but that also allows interviewer discretion in the sequence and phrasing of questions. The protocol, reproduced in Appendix B, was divided into the following five sections: (1) demographic information, (2) context factors, (3) decision-making process, (4) decision-making issues, and (5) the resolution of the decision-making process.

Demographic information comprised background details about individual respondents, some of which were noted without overt questions (e.g., gender, approximate age). This section of the interview elicited information of the respondent's role with regard to WTE. The portion of the interview on context examined previous siting controversies, siting issues, waste management policies and practices, and community characteristics. Questions about the decision-making process centered on the sequence of events in the course of WTE planning and implementation, the groups involved, their degree of agreement during the course of events, public participation, offers of mitigation and compensation, and the role of regulations. Respondents were encouraged to discuss relevant decision-making issues at different points in time without prompting. Among the issues that could be mentioned are disposal costs; financing alternatives; regulations; site selection; public attitudes; mitigation and compensation; waste management and environmental practices and regulations; relations between proponents, citizens, and municipalities; and WTE technology. Interviewers followed the respondents' lead with regard to the order in which topics were raised, but prompted respondents when they did not otherwise discuss relevant issues. The last part of the interview asked what decisions were made and how the decision-making process could be improved.

6.2.3 Analytical Methods

Data gathered from case-study interviews and documents were analyzed qualitatively. Information from each site was examined to determine the sequence of decision-making events, the key players involved in WTE decision making over time, the issues raised by different parties over time, and the resolution of, and satisfaction with, the decision-making process. These elements are detailed in the descriptions of case-study sites in Sections 6.3-6.6. The accuracy and completeness of these descriptions were improved by incorporating comments on drafts of the descriptions that had been solicited from respondents at each site. In addition, comments on draft text were obtained by some individuals who played important roles in the decision-making process, but who declined to be interviewed.

Case-study descriptions formed the basis for comparisons among case-study sites. Sites in which decisions were made to proceed with WTE were compared with each other, as were sites in which the opposite decisions were made. And, the two sites at which WTE was accepted were compared to the two sites at which WTE was rejected. These comparisons served two purposes. First, they helped determine the key factors influencing WTE decision-making outcomes, i.e., the factors that distinguish WTE acceptance from WTE rejection. Second, comparisons helped discern the factors that are critical to the WTE decision-making process.

6.3 BROWARD COUNTY, FLORIDA

Located on south Florida's Atlantic coast (see Figure 6.2), Broward County is home to 1.25 million people. Population is dense along the coastal one-third of the county, but the uninhabitable Everglades swamp occupies the western two-thirds of Broward County. Broward's burgeoning population—a 100 percent increase between 1970 and 1990—is largely the result of droves of emigrés attracted by the subtropical climate. In 1980, less than 20 percent of Broward's population were native Floridians.

Broward's economy is predominately service-oriented, a result of the vast tourism industry of south Florida. The computer industry, primarily software development, also is prominent in the county's economy. Several respondents suggested that the fragile environment of south Florida is unable to support heavy industry.

Figure 6.2
Broward County, Florida

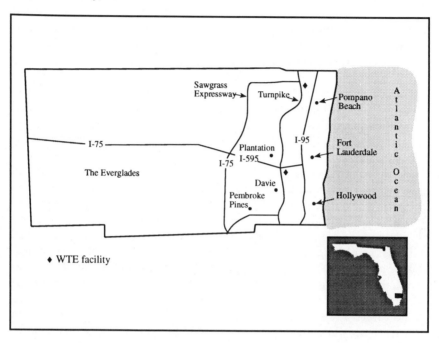

♦ WTE facility

Broward is governed by a seven-member board of commissioners; only two new members have been introduced since 1984. There are 28 incorporated municipalities in Broward. Leaders of each of these cities have membership in the Broward League of Cities, the countywide counterpart to the Florida League of Cities. The League provides avenues for cooperation among cities and for lobbying the cities' needs to county and state government.

6.3.1 Case-Study Summary

Broward County generates approximately 1.6 million tons of solid waste annually, an average of 4,400 tpd (1987 estimate). Based upon the recommendation of its consultants, in early 1983 the Broward County Commission approved the use of mass-burn incineration at two sites to handle its solid waste; service would be provided by full-service vendors. Each WTE facility would have an accompanying landfill on site, the capacity to handle 2,250 tpd, and be expandable to 3,000 tpd (size was not finalized until after negotiation with the vendors; the final project included only one on-site ash monofill). In April 1983, vendor selection began, and in July 1985 the commission selected Wheelabrator as vendor for the southern site and Waste Management, Inc. (WMI) for the northern site.

Site selection activities also began in early 1983 when county consultants identified possible locations for the proposed facilities. In the spring of 1983, the county selected two sites, one each in north and south Broward County. Pompano Beach, which neighbors the northern site, annexed and zoned the northern site to preclude the siting of the WTE facility and the landfill. Once the county selected WMI as the northern site vendor, it entered an agreement to locate a larger WTE facility at the site of WMI's landfill in northern Broward County.

Project implementation proceeded with arranging waste guarantees and project financing. Interlocal agreements guaranteeing delivery of waste to the WTE facilities were negotiated with the cities intermittently over a one-and-a-half-year period. A rough agreement was reached in early 1985, and eventually 23 of Broward's 28 municipalities signed the finalized interlocal agreement. The project was financed primarily by municipal bonds issued in December 1984 and held in escrow until project activities proceeded sufficiently to allow them to be converted to industrial development bonds. Vendor equity and interest from the bonds also contributed to project financing. Total project costs exceeded $750 million.

Despite some organized opposition to the project, including a court challenge of the bonds that financed the facilities, and additional emissions control equipment required by U.S. EPA, the county acquired all necessary permits in 1986 and 1987. Construction at both sites began in early 1989, and the WTE facilities opened in mid–1991.

6.3.2 Waste Management Policies and Practices

Solid waste management activities in Broward County have included landfilling and incineration, and now include recycling. Mixed waste composting in Broward County was begun in 1992 by Reuter, Inc., which provides service to four of the municipalities that elected not to participate in the county's program.

Recently operating landfills in Broward County include a county-owned facility in the city of Davie, a WMI facility near Pompano Beach, and a new county-owned facility near Pembroke Pines. The city of Davie initiated efforts to have the county close its landfill in 1982. But it was not until 1988 that the county closed the landfill, after the Florida Department of Environmental Regulation (DER) intervened because of seepage and resulting water contamination. Its 1983 listing as a Superfund site has heightened public awareness about possible environmental impacts of landfills. The WMI landfill near Pompano Beach opened in the late 1960s and was the only solid waste disposal site open in Broward County during much of 1988. In September 1988, a new county landfill opened on a 588-acre site northwest of Pembroke Pines. It was termed an "interim" or "emergency" landfill because it would provide waste disposal capacity until the county's WTE facilities were built. It now receives bypass waste from the southern WTE facility and the Reuter composting site.

Four solid waste incinerators operated in Broward County until the late 1970s. Two county-owned facilities, a Fort Lauderdale incinerator, and a Hollywood incinerator were closed because they failed to meet state air emission standards. Respondents described these facilities as having emitted black smoke but suggested that public awareness of the facilities was low.

Only small-scale recycling, primarily at drop-off centers, was occurring in Broward when it began WTE planning. The 1988 Florida Solid Waste Management Act mandates that 30 percent of Florida's waste stream be recycled by the end of 1994. Composting and construction fill materials are included as recycled materials. Pilot curbside pickup programs began in 1988, and currently most municipalities provide some level of curbside pickup. In late 1991, Broward had achieved a recycling rate of approximately 28 percent.

6.3.3 Previous Siting Controversies

When its incinerators became unavailable in the late 1970s, Broward County began landfill siting activities but soon discontinued them when siting became a political issue (respondents were not involved in this process and had no details). No other recent siting controversies were recalled by respondents. The numerous medical waste incinerators in Broward County recently have caused considerable controversy because regulations governing their emissions were lax and not well enforced.

6.3.4 Decision-Making Process

6.3.4.1 Events. In 1982, the Broward County government acted to provide disposal capacity for its solid waste.[2] At the time there was no state legislation to encourage or require certain solid waste disposal activities, although the DER informally encouraged the use of incineration to minimize reliance on landfills. The process of adopting WTE technology began when Broward County consultants reviewed waste disposal technologies and recommended mass-burning incineration with energy production capacity. The commission accepted the recommendation and in January 1983 approved the use of WTE technology at two sites, provided by full-service vendors. Each site was to host a WTE facility, an ash monofill, and a landfill for bypass waste. Broward's contingency landfill and use of the WMI landfill reduced the need for additional landfill capacity. Only one new landfill site—for the ash monofill associated with the southern WTE facility—was developed.

County staff initiated the vendor selection process immediately. In March 1983, county staff and consultants selected three firms from among those who replied to the request for qualifications. The commission appointed a committee on which the county and cities were equally represented to review the proposals and select a vendor. Requests for proposals were issued to qualified vendors in the summer of 1983. One vendor refused to respond, claiming that the request for proposals unfairly favored other vendors. The commission subsequently voiced concerns that the procurement process had been mishandled. As a result, in the fall of 1984, the commission reviewed the entire program and reaffirmed the use of WTE facilities, hired a new project director, and revised and reissued the request for proposals. In July 1985, the vendor selection committee suggested and the commission approved a vendor for the northern site and another for the southern site. The county purposely selected proposals from two different companies so that competition between them would keep waste disposal costs down. However, in April 1990, WMI, the northern site vendor, acquired controlling interest in Wheelabrator, the southern site vendor, giving WMI a monopoly on solid waste disposal in Broward County.

The solid waste disposal site-identification process and the technologies review that identified WTE as the preferred method occurred concurrently. Site recommendations were based on two primary considerations—location in unincorporated areas and proximity to areas of waste generation. In April 1983, the county approved two recommended sites, one in northern Broward County neighboring Pompano Beach and one in southern Broward County neighboring Davie. Pompano Beach immediately annexed the northern site and initiated rezoning activities that would preclude the siting of the WTE facility and its accompanying landfill. County efforts to rezone the northern site to allow the WTE facility failed. Consequently, one month after selecting vendors, the county entered negotiations with WMI to site the northern WTE facility on WMI property[3] and agreed to accept a WTE facility larger than originally proposed by the county.

The county commission decided in April 1984 to finance up to $590 million in project costs using tax-exempt industrial development bonds. However, by late 1984 project activities had not proceeded sufficiently to qualify for industrial development bonds. The commission therefore agreed to a project financing plan developed by county staff and consultants that authorized the issuance of up to $590 million of tax-exempt municipal bonds to be converted to industrial development bonds when vendor selection was completed. In December 1984, the county issued over $520 million in tax-exempt municipal bonds, which then were held in escrow. In a process called bond validation, every bond issuance comes before a judge with the state attorney's office acting as an adversary to ensure that the proposed bond issuance is legal. A local group, organized to oppose the project, joined the state attorney's office to challenge the bond issuance. Its claim was that the municipal bonds could be issued legally only if the county intended to operate the project itself. A court twice ruled against the bond issuance. But, in its final ruling on the matter in October 1988, the Florida Supreme Court ruled that the bonds could be issued legally. The bonds were converted to industrial development bonds, not reissued, and were therefore grandfathered in under tax laws that granted them tax-exempt status. County staff and officials asserted that a decision against the bonding would have increased project costs by $156 million but would not have stopped the project.

The county sought permits for the two facilities under a consolidated permitting process required for all power plants over a threshold size in Florida. Although the facility was permitted as a power plant only, rather than as a solid waste management (SWM) facility, the consolidated permitting process addressed all state and federal regulations applicable to WTE facilities. Discussions between the county and permitting agencies (Florida's DER and the Army Corps of Engineers) began in the fall of 1983, long before the county actually filed permit applications in April 1985 and February 1986 for the southern and northern sites, respectively. During the review process for the southern WTE facility, the DER recommended additional air pollution control equipment, i.e., acid gas scrubbers and baghouses. The county objected, arguing that performance standards and not particular types of equipment were requisite. In June 1986, the governor and cabinet certified the southern site including only county-proposed air pollution control equipment. The same certification was granted the northern site in January 1987. A permit for dredge and fill activities, required for the southern site from the Army Corps of Engineers because of wetlands protection, was obtained in November 1986.

The U.S. EPA notified the DER in October 1986 that all permits should contain limits that require the installation of acid gas controls. Two meetings with U.S. EPA representatives failed to gain an exception for Broward County facilities, and in December 1986 Broward entered negotiations with its two vendors regarding the installation and cost of acid gas controls. In May and July 1987 the U.S. EPA issued permits for the southern and northern sites, respectively.

Because the county had no control over waste flow, agreements with Broward cities guaranteeing their participation in the project, i.e., delivering their waste to the county facilities, were required. The county project team (including staff and commissioners) began negotiating interlocal agreements with the cities in late 1983, through representatives of the Broward League of Cities. The original county proposed agreement included a put-or-pay clause for each city. Strong objections from the cities resulted in a League of Cities counterproposal in which each contract city guaranteed delivery of all—but no specific tonnage—of its waste other than that expressly targeted for recycling programs. (Additional information about negotiations that led to adoption of the interlocal agreements is included in Section 6.3.4.3.) County representatives met individually with each Broward city in the spring of 1985 to work out specific details and encourage cities' participation. The commission implemented the interlocal agreements in early 1987, at which time 20 cities qualified. Three other cities joined later, bringing the number of participating cities to 23. These cities chose representatives to serve with county commissioners on the Resource Recovery Board that oversaw construction and now oversees operation of the WTE facilities.

6.3.4.2 *Participation*. During the entire WTE decision-making process, approximately 30 public hearings were held relating to the site zoning, bond issuance, DER air quality permit, and wetlands permit. These and county commission meetings were the only avenues for citizen input during the process. Some meetings and hearings attracted up to 300 people, a turnout characterized by some respondents as enormous relative to most meetings and hearings. There were no planning committees that included general citizens, although there now exists a technical advisory committee to the Resource Recovery Board that does include a position for an environmentalist.

One citizens' group formed early in the WTE decision-making process. It began as a neighborhood association located approximately one mile from the southern site, and now has a membership of almost 300 Broward County residents. The group's activities are led by a core group of 15 persons. The group opposed the facility primarily because of potential health effects resulting from air emissions and possible leachate from the ash monofill into the aquifer beneath the southern site. Representatives of the group obtained information in a piecemeal fashion. They conducted research and acquired information from persons involved at other incinerator or WTE sites nationwide. The group sent representatives to plead its position at public hearings, but characterized the permitting agencies as unreceptive to its arguments. To advocate its position, the group distributed fliers. Initially the group had difficulty obtaining media coverage that would have captured a larger audience. Its most visible and most costly (approximately $35,000) activity was supporting the suit against the county's issuance of the bonds. Its stated purpose for becoming involved in this litigation was to stop the project or slow it long enough for new emissions control technologies to be required. The group also hosted and presented to the county four proposals for alternative SWM facilities in which each vendor agreed to establish a demonstration facility at no cost to the county.

A second local group, formed in late 1990 with a goal of preventing the WTE facilities from opening, has 100 active members who oppose the WTE facilities because of potential health effects. It has worked to inform the public about the facilities by distributing literature and holding public information meetings that have drawn as many as 200 people. The group also obtained more than 10,000 signatures on a petition to require a referendum to mandate recycling 60 percent of Broward's waste stream, with the ultimate intent of making the WTE facilities unnecessary.

National groups, including Greenpeace and Clean Water Action, began active opposition to Broward's WTE facilities only recently. Prior to 1990 they had remained relatively silent about the facilities, but recently have organized protests and demonstrations including forming a human barricade at the southern facility.

Other key participants in the decision-making process were the cities within Broward County and the Broward League of Cities. Although most chose to take part in the county's system, five cities chose not to participate. When the county threatened to deny non-participating cities access to the county landfill, one city sued the county but withdrew the suit when it and the county struck an agreement allowing it use of the landfill. A second city, Pompano Beach, strongly asserted its position against the county's system when it denied the county access to the proposed northern site by annexing and rezoning the site. The Broward League of Cities played a key role as liaison between the cities and the county. Despite the League's position and political strength, some respondents asserted that many city government officials were dissatisfied with their opportunities to influence decisions about WTE facility size and monitoring.

6.3.4.3 Agreement Among the Participants. Basic decisions about adopting and implementing WTE were made by Broward County Commissioners. Commissioners sometimes had heated debates about the facilities but voted, almost without exception, in favor of them. The degree of agreement between the county and cities varied considerably. While some cities were satisfied with the county's plans for SWM capacity, others were concerned about costs and environmental effects. The county sometimes struck informal deals with cities during the process of negotiating interlocal agreements. For example, the county built a park in the town of Plantation in exchange for the municipality's support of the facilities. Several respondents suggested that county coercion and threats to deny non-participating cities access to its landfill were serious enough to make some cities sign interlocal agreements.

Disagreements between the county and permitting agencies (DER and U.S. EPA) about the air pollution control equipment were resolved in different ways. The county successfully argued its position with the state but was unsuccessful in attempts to negotiate a compromise position with U.S. EPA.

Litigation (and threats of litigation) was required to settle disagreements between the county and other parties. One non-participating city challenged county threats to deny access to the landfill with a suit that was settled in the city's favor out of court. Disagreements between the county and the WTE opponent group regarding project financing were litigated, in this case, in the county's favor.

6.3.4.4 *Mitigation.* Mitigation of WTE facility impacts involved wetlands restoration. Because the southern facility is constructed on "jurisdictional wetlands," a determination based on soil type, the U.S. Army Corps of Engineers permit required extensive on- and off-site wetlands restoration: for each acre destroyed, four were developed. Additional mitigation included tree planting. County compensation to neighboring municipalities appears to have been negotiated informally and was limited to one park provided to the municipality downwind of the southern facility.

6.3.4.5 *Regulations and Laws.* Although county planners considered state and federal regulations from the project's outset, the evolving environmental and financial regulatory climate had a significant effect on WTE facility planning. For instance, because the county and its vendors anticipated now existing requirements for double-lined ash monofills, they upgraded the originally planned single-lined monofill to one that employs a liner consisting of clay sandwiched between two geotextile membranes. Requirements for acid gas controls were imposed by U.S. EPA after facility design was underway, and state permits had been obtained. Baghouses were installed on the facilities to further keep emissions within permitted levels. These additional pollution control measures added over \$32 million to the facilities' cost.

Because of tax law changes—particularly the Deficit Reduction Act of 1984 (DRA84)—and the county's desire to obtain favorable financing, Broward hastily issued bonds in December 1984. It faced a protracted legal battle because of this action, although the financing eventually was approved. (See Section 6.3.5.2 for a complete discussion.)

6.3.5 Decision-Making Issues

The county's decision to use WTE technology was driven by a desire to provide long-term solid waste disposal capacity with proven reliability, one that would minimize the use of landfills and their resultant environmental impacts. County actions were proactive but responsive to dwindling solid waste disposal capacity in Broward.

Issues that caused concern among opponents of the WTE facilities centered primarily on the potential for adverse environmental and health effects from the facilities' air emissions. Opponents and the municipalities who did not participate in the project also were greatly concerned about the cost of the facilities, particularly as translated into tipping fees.

6.3.5.1 Environmental and Technology Issues: Site Selection and WTE Technology.

Site selection. The county's siting strategy focused on two criteria. The first criterion was that the two sites be centrally located to minimize transportation costs. The second criterion was that sites be located in unincorporated areas. This criterion was established to minimize political obstacles to siting, such as zoning and municipal regulations. Other criteria such as technical and geologic factors were considered secondarily in the county's site identification process.

Pompano Beach's reaction to selection of the northern site was immediate and intense and forced the county to select a different site (see Section 6.3.4.1). The southern site did not draw an immediate response but it has drawn the attention of WTE opponents for two main reasons. First, it neighbors a lower middle-class community. Second, its location above the aquifer that feeds the county's water well field and disagreement over the direction in which the aquifer flows has prompted concern for water quality effects. The county argues that salt water intrusion occurs in the portion of the aquifer over which the facility is located, and it is therefore not a drinking water source.

WTE technology. The county characterizes its previous experience with solid waste incineration as proof of the method's reliability and safety. Such experience—coupled with the improvements in available incineration technology and decreasing availability of land suitable for landfills—suggested to county officials and staff that WTE facilities were the best proven method for SWM.

Opponents of the WTE facilities doubted reliability and safety. They cited explosions and emissions violations at the Dade County facility, breakdowns at the Pinellas County facility, and numerous startup problems at incinerators nationwide as evidence. These doubts persisted, with claims of flawed workmanship by construction contractors at Broward's WTE facilities. However, opponents' primary concerns were and are environmental and health effects from WTE facility air emissions, particularly dioxin and mercury. Citizens' and environmental groups are expressly concerned that the cumulative impacts of mercury emitted from Broward WTE facilities, permitted at up to 13,500 pounds per year, and from other south Florida incinerators will seriously damage the Everglades ecosystem, particularly wildlife. High levels of mercury in Everglades fish have prompted restrictions against eating them, and high levels of mercury in a black panther were the suspected cause of its death. However, no direct link between the incinerators and high mercury levels has yet been established.

The size of Broward's two WTE facilities was a contentious issue for the facility vendors, the county, and the public largely due to the financial consequences of facility sizing (see Section 6.3.5.2). Vendors protested that the originally proposed size of the facilities was not economically viable because it neither maximized the facilities' power production capacity nor allowed an adequate profit margin for the vendors. In response, the county reevaluated the proposed facilities' capacity and determined that the county's waste stream mandated additional capacity. An additional upgrade in size occurred when WMI allowed the county to locate the northern facility on the existing WMI site. The county originally asserted that the facilities were sized appropriately for Broward's existing waste stream, but later argued that the facilities had been intentionally oversized so that excess capacity could first be marketed and later would accommodate the increasing waste stream of the county (vendors can market excess capacity on a short-term basis). Proposed facility size remained unchanged despite the recession of the late 1980s, which slowed population growth and thus Broward County's waste stream, and the 1988 Solid Waste Management Act that mandated recycling. The county's reevaluation of facility sizing, in light of Solid Waste Management Act requirements, determined that reduced volume would not affect the financial viability of the WTE facilities.

6.3.5.2 *Economic Issues.* Because a "put-or-pay" clause is included in the county's contract with WMI, the county incurs a financial penalty of $53.50 for each ton under the 1.1 million ton minimum quota. The Resource Recovery Board that monitors facility operation and establishes tipping fees (within contract parameters) also is empowered to levy a special fee on all improved property in the event that a shortfall occurs. Furthermore, the vendor can market excess capacity (with some contractual limitations) at a tipping fee less than that paid by Broward County. Opponents and representatives from several municipalities argue that this level of financial risk is unacceptable and that Broward would in effect subsidize other counties' waste disposal.[4]

County officials stated that Broward selected vendor ownership of the facilities to insulate the county from capital risk. Under a vendor ownership system, Broward's total financial liability is delivery of waste, or a "put-or-pay" penalty, plus costs incurred when future federal and state regulations require additional pollution control equipment. Opponents of the county's project suggested that vendor ownership was selected to allow financing with industrial development bonds. Because these bonds, unlike general-obligation bonds, do not require a referendum for approval, opponents assert that this financial option was selected to allow the county to circumvent requirements for public approval.

Economic issues were the primary reason why municipalities elected not to participate in the county's WTE facilities. The county's unwillingness to offer a firm tipping fee until late in the planning stages caused considerable uneasiness among municipal officials. Although numerous activities, such as a power sales agreement, are prerequisite to establishing a tipping fee, some officials were concerned that the county had allowed its vendor too much control over tipping fees. Tipping fees originally projected to be approximately $28 per ton had risen to $62.50 per ton when the facility opened. Annual increases in tipping fees will be determined according to the consumer price index and the cost of electricity production.

Project financing became an issue of contention when the state and a citizen's group opposing the project argued that the bond issuance and conversion had occurred illegally (see Section 6.3.4.1 for additional information). Although project financing was not the primary reason why citizens' groups opposed WTE, they used the issue to attempt to stop or delay the project. The resulting litigation delayed the project up to one and a half years. Inflation and delays caused by the lawsuit are estimated to have added $33.7 million to the facilities' price.

6.3.5.3 Public Attitudes and Participants' Relations. It is apparent that attitudes about WTE in general and Broward's WTE program specifically differ among elected public officials. Some officials wholeheartedly supported WTE, some accepted it because they believed that there is no viable alternative, and others opposed it altogether. Some municipal officials supported the concept of WTE but disapproved of the county's system or the county's handling of the WTE decision-making and planning process.

General public attitudes are more elusive to gauge than are officials' attitudes. Public apathy about solid waste disposal issues prevailed in Broward County in the mid–1980s. Public concern about solid waste increased in the late 1980s in Broward and nationally, particularly with regard to awareness of and demand for recycling. However, despite relatively high public attendance at meetings and hearings regarding the county's WTE facilities and media coverage that began in 1983, most respondents described the general public in Broward as still somewhat apathetic and uninformed. There have been no surveys of public attitudes about WTE technology or Broward's proposed system. In Broward's 1990 election for county commissioners, an incumbent and supporter of WTE was opposed by a candidate who ran a single-issue campaign against WTE. The WTE opponent was trounced.

A recent newspaper survey and respondents characterize public trust in government, locally and in general, among Broward County residents as being extremely low. In a 1991 local newspaper survey, 53 percent of the respondents said they trusted government less than they did five years ago.

Respondents characterized municipalities' trust in and relations with county government generally as fair-to-good prior to the WTE decision-making process. Broward County government has managed large public service programs on behalf of its member municipalities and worked with the Broward League of Cities to consider city interests in county government. However, Pompano Beach was enraged when Broward County government moved a regional court out of the city's jurisdiction. And, county moves several years ago to establish a Metro Broward government outraged city governments.

The county's handling of solid waste planning has created acrimonious relations between some municipal officials and county officials. The county's acquiescence to vendors regarding facility size and its failure to negotiate a "put-or-pay" clause more favorable to the county has caused considerable mistrust of county staff. In fact, some municipal officials and media representatives indicated that county staff members on occasion have deliberately misinformed them to gain acceptance for the WTE facilities. Methods used by the county to convince municipalities to participate in the project, including what have been characterized as threats of discontinued services, and the consultants' history of support for WTE are additional reasons for the mistrust that currently exists.

6.3.6 Improving the Decision-Making Process

Respondents' suggestions for improving the decision-making process differed somewhat, but almost all respondents asserted that an informed public is an essential element in good decision making. Public participation in any form, including committee service and public referenda, is contingent upon the public's ability and willingness to become informed. There were no clear suggestions about how the public should become informed.

Some respondents suggested that all decisions about SWM should consider the interrelationship among components of an integrated system, including strong mandates for recycling. They asserted that decisions about WTE facilities in the absence of an integrated waste management plan simply were premature.

Some respondents, including county staff members, suggested that county ownership of the WTE facilities would eliminate the arduous negotiation process between the county and the vendor. Respondents other than county staff asserted that the county would then be more responsive to the opinions of the public and less so to the vendor.

One-half of the respondents suggested that a decision that affects every household and requires the expenditure of hundreds of millions of dollars should be the responsibility of the general public. These same people did not, however, think that a public referendum, or any of the other suggestions to improve the decision-making process, would necessarily change the outcome of the decision-making process.

6.4 OAKLAND COUNTY, MICHIGAN

Oakland County, Michigan, with a population of approximately 1.1 million, lies just north of Detroit (see Figure 6.3) and has long been home to the American automobile industry. The thousands of jobs provided at several automotive plants in Oakland County were cut significantly with the

Figure 6.3
Oakland County, Michigan

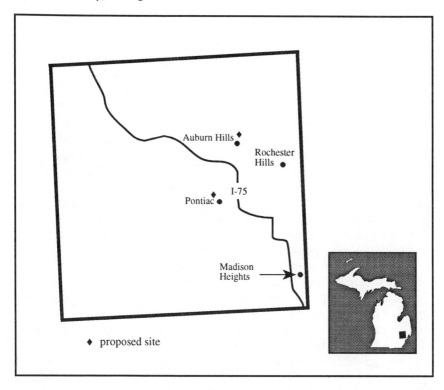

closure of two major General Motors (GM) plants in the mid- and late 1980s.

Before the auto industry faltered, diversification had already begun in the county, softening the blow and keeping unemployment below the national average. Oakland County's employment base now is comprised primarily of service and commercial companies. Research and development operations, some related to the auto industry, also have ventured into Oakland County. The Oakland Technology Park, neighboring Oakland University in Auburn Hills, features the new Chrysler Technology Center and is the focal point of economic development in Oakland County. Also in Auburn Hills is the newly constructed Palace, home of Detroit's National Basketball Association team, the Pistons.

Economic development activities are led by the 61 individual municipalities in Oakland County with some assistance provided by the county's 28-member board of commissioners and the county executive. County assistance takes the form of infrastructure development. The move away from manufacturing industries and to commercial- and service-related companies in part reflects national trends. It also reflects some municipalities' desire to steer away from "smoke-stack" industries. Some municipalities have enacted zoning ordinances that make siting heavy industrial facilities difficult.

6.4.1 Case-Study Summary

Countywide use of WTE was first formally proposed in Oakland County's 1982 state-mandated SWM plan. Oakland's second state-mandated plan included the current proposal for a 2,000-tpd WTE facility, as well as waste reduction and recycling goals and programs. The plan was approved by Oakland County Commissioners, the Michigan Department of Natural Resources (DNR), and over two-thirds of the county's municipalities.

In 1989 the county selected Westinghouse to design, build, and operate the WTE facility and filed for DNR air quality permits. Because of internal conflict and restructuring at DNR and a DNR review of existing mercury contamination, the permits are still pending. The site first selected by Oakland County was opposed by the municipality in which it was located. As a result, the county selected an alternate site in Auburn Hills (see Figure 6.3), offering substantial financial incentives.

Project implementation also included the arranging of waste guarantees. Interlocal agreements, drafted with some input from representatives of Oakland municipalities, have been revised to reflect major changes in the project. Most of Oakland's municipalities, despite having approved the SWM plan, have not agreed to participate in the county project.

Because the project was stalling and political pressure was mounting, the county commission decided that a public referendum would be held to approve project funding by general-obligation bonds. The project vendor and local groups actively campaigned prior to the November 1991 referendum. The project was approved by a margin of less than 200 votes. Despite this decision to proceed, project implementation was stymied in March 1992 when Westinghouse withdrew from its contract.[5]

6.4.2 Waste Management Policies and Practices

As in development activities, most municipalities handle solid waste disposal independently. Until recent state mandates forced some county activity, Oakland County had little involvement in managing the 3,600 tpd of waste it produces. Some municipalities contract with private companies for solid waste pickup and disposal; some are not at all involved but allow individual residents to contract for waste pickup. Two consortia have formed to handle the solid waste of their member municipalities. The Southeast Oakland County Resource Recovery Authority (SOCRRA) includes 14 municipalities in southeast Oakland County and was formed in the early

1950s; the Resource Recovery and Recycling Authority of Southwest Oakland County (RRRASOC) serves municipalities in southwest Oakland County and was formed in 1990.

Four landfills operate in Oakland County. The city of Pontiac operates a landfill that accepts waste generated only in Pontiac. The heavy cutbacks in the auto industry have considerably reduced waste production in Pontiac so that the landfill is now expected to remain open for approximately 15 years. The other three landfills are privately owned and have a combined estimated remaining lifetime of approximately 6 years (as of mid–1992). The largest of these landfills is owned by WMI with whom Oakland County has executed an agreement to reserve its capacity for county use. In addition to these operating landfills are 62 closed and abandoned landfills scattered throughout the county, only a few of which have been capped. Four of the closed landfills have been listed as Superfund sites after causing groundwater contamination; the sandy soils and high water table in the area make waste isolation difficult.

Solid waste incineration is not new to Oakland County. The SOCRRA consortium originally was formed to own and operate a 600-tpd incinerator that opened in 1957. The incinerator was retrofitted twice with emissions control equipment. However, in 1988 the DNR Air Pollution Commission closed the incinerator based on complaints from area residents who feared that the incinerator was injurious to the health of students in the school and residents of the nursing home neighboring the incinerator. Tests later showed the facility was exceeding emissions limits on some pollutants. SOCRRA plans to upgrade its incinerator and add an energy-producing plant, at a projected cost of $85 million. This upgraded incinerator is included in Oakland County's SWM system. Nevertheless, a group of local citizens and the city council of Madison Heights, where SOCRRA's incinerator is located, oppose its reopening.

A second WTE facility in Oakland County is located at a GM bus plant. It is used strictly for waste from area GM plants, primarily cardboard packaging materials. There is little, if any, public opposition to GM's incinerator.

Vegetative composting also is used in Oakland County. SOCRRA led the county's composting efforts when it began vegetative composting in 1971. SOCRRA's composting facility is located in Rochester Hills, which sued in 1990 to have the facility closed because of odor problems. The composting facility is located in an area that was zoned for residential use after the composting facility opened. Numerous municipalities very recently have instituted yard waste composting programs; disposing of yard clippings in landfills will be completely phased out by 1995 in accordance with Michigan law.

Recycling programs, available in most Oakland County municipalities, range from drop-off centers to curbside pickup of commingled recyclables.

Although less than 10 percent of Oakland County's waste stream currently is recycled, Oakland's goal is to recycle approximately 35 percent of its waste by 2005. Oakland's waste reduction goal is 10 percent by 2005.

Oakland exports 27 to 30 percent of its waste including all construction and demolition debris, much waste previously handled by SOCRRA's incinerator, and RRRASOC's waste. Although some importation occurs, Oakland County is a net exporter of waste.

In 1978 Michigan enacted the Solid Waste Management Act (also known as Act 641). Act 641 required each county to develop a SWM plan demonstrating the availability of a 5-year waste disposal capacity and planning for 20-year capacity. Although capacity could be provided by any number of means, including waste exportation, no waste could be exported unless the receiving county had accounted for it in its 5-year plan, thereby limiting the flow of waste across county borders.[6] Act 641 directed solid waste planning activities to be led by a solid waste planning committee composed of county and municipal officials, representatives of the waste industry, representatives of environmental groups, and general citizens. Members are recommended and approved by the county commission.

A decade after the enactment of Act 641, Michigan established a solid waste policy whose goal was to reduce waste going to landfills to 10 percent of the waste stream by 2005. Landfilling was to be used only for materials for which "no other environmentally sound management alternatives exist." The policy called for WTE to manage 40 percent of the waste stream, while other waste reduction methods (recycling, reuse, source reduction, and composting) were to manage 50 percent of the waste stream.

6.4.3 Previous Siting Controversies

In the mid–1970s, a hazardous waste incinerator was proposed for Oakland County. Just as necessary DNR permits were obtained, local awareness peaked. A loosely organized group emerged to oppose the proposed site, which was located immediately adjacent to Interstate 75. The city of Auburn Hills responded by establishing a pollution control review board that set stringent guidelines for hazardous waste facilities. The proposal ultimately was abandoned.

Pontiac was considered seriously as a site for a new state penal facility in the 1980s. The site was to be in close proximity to the county's campus-like group of administration buildings located in Pontiac. The city's protest of the proposed facility site was based on its demographic profile; Pontiac has a greater percentage of minority and low-income residents than other areas of Oakland County. The state, for reasons unrelated to the siting controversy, did not proceed with the facility.

Oakland County also sought to identify site(s) for a county-owned landfill that would be an integral component of the SWM planning activities (in addition to the WTE facility). A 25-member siting committee, assisted by technical consultants, initiated a blind siting process. County consultants used published data to identify candidate areas. The following features were mapped: protected farmland and open space, public recreational areas, airport restrictions, lakes and streams, wetlands, surficial geology, land use, historic and cultural areas, areas experiencing new and rapid growth, and threatened and endangered species habitats. The landfill siting committee established weighted criteria for ranking sites, but members were unaware of candidate site locations. When the locations of the 10 top-ranked candidate sites were revealed, protests immediately emerged from representatives of municipalities where sites were identified. A simple mathematical error in totalling scores of the weighted criteria caused two sites' rankings to change and, in the minds of some, cast doubt on the credibility of the whole siting process. Local opposition groups, soon formed in each township where a site was identified, focused on the credibility of the process and the accuracy of the geological data used. They claimed that the data were not technically accurate, had not been verified, and that in some cases better data were available. The county chose not to proceed with landfill siting activities.

6.4.4 Decision-Making Process

6.4.4.1 Events. Although Oakland County considered incineration in the early 1970s, the proposal for Oakland County's WTE system originated in the early 1980s as part of the Act 641, state-mandated, countywide, SWM plan. The original plan proposed one large and three small (approximately 200 tpd each) WTE plants, and included two incinerators and several landfills already operating in the county. The plan was approved by the county commissioners in 1982 and subsequently by over two-thirds of the county's municipalities and the DNR. By 1985, 30 municipalities had signed intergovernmental agreements (IGAs) committing their waste to the county system. (Because the county did not control the flow of waste in the county, these flow-control agreements were required to determine the size of the facility and to guarantee to the financier and the operator that the facility would be viable.) Implementing the plan was delayed because there was no provision in Michigan law for a county executive form of government to issue bonds for such a system. Special legislation therefore was passed in 1989. However, the recession of the early 1980s rendered some of the proposed WTE facilities no longer viable. Potential users of steam scaled back operations or simply were no longer interested.

The state requires that the SWM plan be updated every five years. When work on the second plan began in 1987, before the 1982 plan was implemented, awareness of recycling was increasing, and a change in state law required Act 641 plans to include recycling. The second plan set a goal of reducing the waste stream 30 percent by 1995 and 50 percent by 2005 through waste reduction, reuse, and recycling (exceeding Michigan solid waste policy requirements). Increased emphasis on recycling lessened the need for WTE facilities, and the new plan included the two existing incinerators in the county (SOCRRA's and GM's) and one proposed 2,000-tpd WTE facility. A new 40-year landfill originally in this plan was dropped, and instead the county planned to rely on expansions of existing landfills. Public hearings regarding the plan were held, and this second Act 641 plan, like the first, was approved by county commissioners, DNR, and over two-thirds of the county's municipalities.

The county then developed an implementation plan and began to carry it out. In 1989, the county selected Westinghouse from among the WTE proposals to design, build, and operate the WTE facility. Environmental impact and health risk assessments were completed by county consultants as part of the air quality permit application, which was filed with the DNR in December 1989. DNR delayed action on the permit application while it studied existing mercury contamination in Michigan waters and reviewed its mercury emissions policies to determine what limits should be included in future permits for WTE and other facilities. Also slowing progress at the DNR was the governor's attempt to restructure the DNR and disband several of its commissions, including the Air Pollution Control Commission where public hearings regarding the WTE facility permit would be held. The court's reversal of restructuring has been appealed to the Michigan Supreme Court.

The site first selected to host the WTE facility was near the county government complex in Pontiac. Opposition to this site arose in 1985 when Pontiac came under new administration and sued the county to prevent siting the WTE facility there. The county, wanting to avoid long delays, rethought its decision and in 1989 selected Auburn Hills as the site for the WTE facility. It is unclear whether Auburn Hills volunteered to host the facility (as is suggested by county officials and staff) or was selected by the county (as is suggested by Auburn Hills officials). The chairman of the county commission who represented the northern portion of Auburn Hills realized the project was stalling and pushed to identify a new site. The chairman and Auburn Hills' mayor maintained a cordial relationship, and together they negotiated a host community agreement allowing the facility to be built in Auburn Hills. The Act 641 process does not require the approval of the municipality in which the facility is sited, and Auburn Hills' officials believed it was in their best interest to get involved, rather than allow the county to build the facility without Auburn Hills' involvement. The original Act 641 plan was amended to include the new site. The host community agreement stipulates that Auburn Hills will do nothing to hinder project development. Additional information about siting issues is found in Section 6.4.4.4.

In late 1990, the county drafted new IGAs reflecting the changes in the county's SWM plan and excluding the "put-or-pay" clauses that originally were included in them. The county asked the municipalities to commit their waste (no specified tonnage) to the county's proposed SWM system. Although more than two-thirds of the municipalities previously had approved the county's SWM plan, only 18 of the 61 municipalities signed IGAs, together committing approximately 400 tpd of waste.

There are various reasons why so few municipalities signed IGAs. For example, SOCRRA communities chose to take no action until DNR made a decision regarding air quality permits for their incinerator. Some communities were hesitant because of DNR's mercury emissions review, emerging public opposition to the WTE component of the system, and other existing and less expensive waste disposal opportunities being offered by a WTE facility in Detroit and private landfill owners. Other communities expressed concern that specific landfill capacity was not identified in the plan. Also, some municipalities were using the IGA as a bargaining tool to gain county support for non-WTE-related agendas.

Staff and elected officials became concerned that the plan was stalling and responded with several activities. First, the county contracted with WMI for sole use of the expansion of its landfill in Orion township. Second, there was much discussion about implementing the SWM plan in two phases. The first phase would include waste reduction education and recycling; the second would be the WTE facility. No agreement to implement the plan in separate phases resulted because it was unclear whether this plan would meet Act 641 requirements, whether signing on to the first phase mandated participation in the second, and what would happen if the tonnage commitments required for the second phase were not achieved. Last, the county commission decided to hold a public referendum to approve the bond issue funding the SWM system.

Michigan law allows the public an opportunity to approve all tax increases by public referendum. However, limited tax general-obligation bonds to be paid by project-generated revenues do not require public referendum approval. Though the project initially was to be funded by limited tax general-obligation bonds, mounting political pressure and the county commission's desire to take some action to revive the program caused it to opt for general-obligation bonds and place the issue on the ballot.

During the summer and fall months before the November 5, 1991, referendum, local groups opposed to the facility actively distributed literature and held public rallies. A committee funded primarily by Westinghouse began advertising in support of the project in late August, spending several times the amount of money expended by groups opposing the WTE facility.

The election had a voter turnout of approximately 15 percent, an average turnout for a local election. The proposed system was approved by less than 200 votes. However, voters in 76 percent of the Oakland County's municipalities approved the referendum. In general, those areas where WTE facilities (including the SOCRRA incinerator) were sited experienced higher voter turnout and voted against the proposed system. Revised IGAs were issued to municipalities after the election.

In March 1992, Westinghouse exercised a pull-out clause in its contract and withdrew from the project, citing the lengthy permit application time and, according to most respondents, the absence of IGAs. Respondents also suspected that recent financial trouble at Westinghouse (the parent corporation) may have contributed to its withdrawal. The county then considered several options, including rebidding the project, selecting the runner-up from among the original bidders, dropping the WTE portion of the plan (which would require securing additional landfill capacity) and continuing with the other portions of the solid waste plan, or ceasing to be involved altogether. In the latter case, the state mandates that first municipalities, then the regional planning agency, and then the DNR must try to develop a SWM plan for the county.

6.4.4.2 Participation. The Act 641 planning process mandates the composition of the Solid Waste Planning Committee—county and municipal officials, representatives of the waste industry, representatives of environmental groups, and general citizens (usually with a technical background related in some way to SWM). An advisory committee that included members of the public also was formed; it apparently had little influence over the decision to use WTE and did not serve as a conduit for information to the public. Other opportunities for public input to the Act 641 plan included public comment and questions at each committee meeting and at hearings held once the Act 641 plan was completed.

Municipalities could participate in the Act 641 planning process through their representatives on the planning committee and by providing comments at committee and public meetings. Also, county and municipal representatives drafted the first IGA, and county staff together with county and municipal attorneys drafted the second. Some municipalities began to participate actively only when public opposition to the WTE facility became organized and vocal.

At the state level, DNR is the primary participant in Act 641 planning. DNR reviews all 641 plans, makes recommendations, and requires changes.

Beyond the Act 641 process, various existing and newly formed groups played roles in WTE decision making through their opposition to the county's proposed and existing solid waste disposal practices. Despite the existence of an umbrella coalition, these opposition groups mostly acted independently. The first organization to oppose the county's plan focused on environmental and health effects of incineration and poorly sited and operated landfills. The group's original membership was countywide, but personality conflicts caused it to splinter. When the group rebuilt, its membership and leadership were based in the residential community closest to the proposed incinerator and neighboring a privately owned landfill. The splinter group was a loosely organized, small number of residents from throughout Oakland County whose environmental activism preceded their involvement in the first group. The splinter group opposed the county's proposed incinerator on the basis of environmental, health, and financial considerations.

Another long-standing but loosely organized local environmental group, although not categorically opposed to solid waste incineration, found the county's proposed system unacceptable for environmental and waste management reasons. This organization originally formed in response to the hazardous waste incinerator proposed more than 10 years earlier.

A third group based in Auburn Hills and Rochester Hills (the town neighboring the incinerator and the host of an existing ash landfill) had a significant number of active members, received the most media attention, and received considerable support (through information and manpower) from two national environmental organizations to oppose the county's proposed incinerator. This group emerged when the site in Auburn Hills was selected. Its opposition was based primarily on health effects. This group also was closely affiliated with a similar group in Madison Heights that was instrumental in having the SOCRRA incinerator closed.

Each group provided comments at the Act 641 committee meetings and at the public hearing regarding the county's proposed system. They also distributed fliers expounding their reasons for opposing the incinerator. Other tactics differed, however, with some groups quietly collecting and disseminating information and others intentionally disrupting county and city government meetings. The members of the most active group attended and provided input at meetings when various city councils were considering IGAs and, with the assistance of two national environmental organizations, held public rallies and conducted door-to-door surveys and campaigns. Members of this local group continued their activities even after the election and Westinghouse's withdrawal.

Other primary participants in the WTE decision-making process included administrations of cities who would have affected the outcome by their decisions to join (or not) the county's system. Some municipal administrations who opposed the WTE aspect of the county's proposal took highly visible actions against it, including litigation, mailing newsletters to residents, and hosting proposals from companies promoting other waste management technologies.

Westinghouse, as the vendor of the WTE system, also was an important participant providing information to the county and its consultants. Westinghouse (through a committee) campaigned heavily for the county's system beginning in late August 1991.

6.4.4.3 Agreement Among the Participants. The degree of agreement among various participants in the county's solid waste planning activities declined as the project progressed. The majority of 27 county commissioners originally supported the project, but disagreed on various aspects of implementation, including siting and a gradual phasing in of the new facilities and management practices. Municipalities demonstrated reduced support for the system by approving the county's plan and failing to sign an IGA, or signing an early IGA and failing to act on a later version. Although the Act 641 planning process provided opportunities to negotiate disagreements, some municipalities characterized these opportunities as negligible. Municipalities also had minimal representation on the Solid Waste Planning Committee and did not act in concert to have their concerns represented during the planning process. Municipalities' decisions on signing IGAs apparently became their only way to say yes or no to the county's system.

It is unclear whether there was agreement among the groups that opposed the project about the county's system, particularly the WTE facility. For example, the various groups opposed the project for different reasons, some focusing on economic issues, others believing project economics were not an issue altogether. Also, there was no significant cooperation among the various groups.

The greatest apparent change in concordance occurred between Auburn Hills (the WTE host community) and the county. One year after negotiating a host community agreement with the county, the city council of Auburn Hills considered withdrawing from it, citing the county's unwillingness to negotiate monitoring and control (i.e., shutdown) procedures. To avoid litigation, Auburn Hills did not withdraw from the host community agreement and has since approved the IGA.

6.4.4.4 *Mitigation and Compensation.* Although no community host agreement was negotiated with Pontiac for the original site, an agreement was offered to Auburn Hills in exchange for allowing the WTE facility and a proposed materials recovery facility to be sited there (a comparable agreement was negotiated with the municipality hosting the landfill expansion). Considerable financial compensation was extended to Auburn Hills, contingent upon the facility being built there. The cash payments and forgiven debt totalled over $9 million and a community host fee of $1.50 per ton would be paid in lieu of taxes. The community host agreement provided that the county would consider comments from the city. However, the county did not allow Auburn Hills any input into facility monitoring or control, factors key to the city council's later consideration of withdrawing from the project.

6.4.4.5 *Regulations and Laws.* Michigan DNR holds permitting jurisdiction over the proposed incinerator. Michigan's Act 64, which governs hazardous waste disposal, defines ash as a non-hazardous waste that requires disposal in a double-lined monofill. No ash testing is required. No county agencies require permits. Although some municipalities, including Auburn Hills, have some form of pollution control board that establishes standards for facilities in the municipality, Michigan Act 641 states that municipal ordinances are not applicable to facilities included in the Act 641 plan.

County staff considered all federal regulations early in the planning process when it requested qualifications from vendors. Proposals were requested only from companies who demonstrated an ability to meet these standards.

6.4.5 Decision-Making Issues

The single most important issue to which Oakland County responded in its Act 641 plan was the need to reduce reliance on landfills. Contaminated groundwater resulted from several landfills in the county and heightened public awareness of the possible environmental impacts of landfills in general. As early as the 1970s, municipalities in Oakland County approached county government asking it to provide an alternative that would reduce use of landfills. Furthermore, the county was proposing an alternative to complete landfill reliance because it had experienced difficulties in landfill siting.

Providing SWM alternatives that would reduce reliance on landfills was a general concern of all participants, including groups opposing the county's WTE facility. However, opponents expressed concern that the county's WTE plant would affect the health of residents adversely and should be considered only after recycling programs and waste reduction education are fully implemented in Oakland County.

6.4.5.1 Environmental and Technology Issues: Site Selection and WTE Technology.

Site selection. Oakland County government is located in Pontiac and is housed in a number of buildings situated in a manner similar to a college campus. The county originally planned to locate the WTE facility near this "campus" so that it could take advantage of the steam to heat its buildings and to demonstrate that the facility was an integral component of county government and services.

The first site was selected from among several sites all located adjacent to or near the county complex. Land uses in the area are mixed, including commercial, industrial, and residential. Forty-five percent of Pontiac residents are minorities, and neighborhoods in the site area are inhabited by both minority and non-minority residents.

Pontiac protested the site selection arguing that it was being forced to accept an unwanted activity because its population, being poorer and heavily minority, was less powerful than other county municipalities. The city also was alarmed that property was being removed from its tax rolls without its approval. Pontiac sued the county to prevent the WTE facility from being built there.[7]

As a result, the county rethought its position and began to search for another site. A site comprised of county-owned and non-county-owned land in Auburn Hills was selected as the site as a result of negotiation between the chair of the county commission and the mayor of Auburn Hills. No alternative sites were considered seriously. The site is located in a primarily industrial area that includes a GM facility, an animal shelter, an existing landfill, and a penal facility. Approximately one mile from the site is the closest residential neighborhood, a mobile home park located on the border of Auburn Hills and Orion Township.

The response of Auburn Hills city government changed from begrudging acceptance to outright disapproval of the siting. Auburn Hills city council has since considered withdrawing from the contract, but took no action on the advice of its legal counsel. The site stirred citizen opposition in Auburn Hills and neighboring Rochester Hills. An environmental group not based in either of these cities opposes the site because it suspects air inversion conditions to exist there and because it considers a main access route to the site to be unsafe for truck traffic.

WTE technology. The primary issues associated with WTE technology are possible adverse environmental and health affects. In Oakland County there was considerable disagreement regarding the health and environmental impacts resulting from incinerator emissions. County staff and officials supporting the facility were confident in the safety of the technology and the accuracy of the health risk analysis, which concluded that health risks would be minimal.

WTE opponents believed its emissions would threaten people's health and argued that the county should have the responsibility of proving that there is no risk to residents' health. They were concerned primarily about potentially adverse health consequences of exposure to lead, mercury, and toxins created in the incineration process, i.e., dioxins and furans. Some opponents cited information about a high number of childhood leukemia cases among students near the SOCRRA incinerator and used information obtained from national environmental organizations that links municipal waste combustors (MWCs) with increased respiratory problems. They argued that mercury emissions from existing incinerators had contaminated lakes and made fish inedible, and that additional mercury emissions were unacceptable. They also thought that the technology chosen by the county would not segregate hazardous waste sufficiently and that Westinghouse's emissions controls were not the best available.

Opponents argued that reduction, reuse, and recycling strategies should be fully implemented before WTE is considered and certainly before its size is determined. Despite county officials' and staff members' belief that the WTE facility was correctly sized to account for a possible reduction of 50 percent of the waste stream, opponents armed with information from nationally known anti-incinerator activists voiced concerns that recyclable items would be burned to meet shortfalls in fuel for the facility and that the viability of other waste reduction activities would be diminished by WTE.

An issue of great concern to Auburn Hills government is facility operation procedures. With the assistance of an environmental consultant, the city has expressed 11 points of concern focusing on emergency shutdown procedures and monitoring. It is the city administration's general opinion that the county (or Auburn Hills) should have greater control over the facility than existing plans indicate.

6.4.5.2 Economic Issues. The county's proposed WTE facility accounted for approximately $300 million of the $500 million total SWM system. The amount included all construction costs, host community payments, and development and planning activities related to the system. The county estimated that in the first few years of operation tipping fees at the incinerator would exceed landfill tipping costs, but the pattern would soon reverse.

Costs were a major issue for only one opposition group who believed the county had significantly underestimated tipping fees at the proposed WTE facility. Municipalities, however, were concerned about tipping fees at the proposed facility because the fees were estimated to be much higher than current landfill disposal costs, described by the county as artificially low.

The county selected to own the WTE facility and contract its construction and operation to a private vendor. Project financing was to be repaid by system revenues and fees. Though the county originally planned to use limited general-obligation bonds because a vote is not required, public pressure forced the county to use general-obligation bonds approved by referendum. Oakland County has an excellent bond rating. Oakland County staff and government thought that the SWM system, providing 20-year capacity, would only enhance its financial situation.

6.4.5.3 Public Attitudes and Participants' Relations. Until Act 641 mandated otherwise, all SWM activities were under the purview of the municipalities. Oakland County historically has had little involvement in other controversial municipal activities or other large-scale, high-visibility projects that mandated full public disclosure and close negotiation with its member municipalities. County officials and others involved in the solid waste planning process originally relied on traditional sources of information about public attitudes: direct contact with community members and media reports that followed county solid waste planning activities from the outset. In early 1991 additional information about public awareness and attitudes regarding solid waste disposal was provided by county consultants who conducted focus groups and telephone surveys. These consultants found that awareness among residents about existing and planned solid waste disposal practices was mixed, but almost all believed that Oakland County was facing a major waste disposal problem. Further, the consultants found that opinions about the county's proposed waste management plan, including the WTE facility, mostly were favorable. A separate survey conducted by a national environmental group, however, found that 57 percent of those polled disapproved of the county's planned WTE facility.

An official in Auburn Hills commented that, during his extensive door-to-door campaign in the fall of 1990, only a very few residents raised the WTE facility as an issue. The low voter turnout in November 1991 suggests apathy among most Oakland County residents about SWM activities.

The results of the referendum in November 1991 also are suggestive of patterns of public attitudes about the county's proposed system. Voters in municipalities that would host or neighbor various facilities, particularly the landfill and the WTE facility, experienced high voter turnout and rejected the bond proposal. Municipalities in the north and west of the county supported the county's system. Various officials and the local media interpreted these votes as indicating opposition to landfills as much as support for the WTE facility. The margin of 186 votes was slim, but gave the county the mandate to proceed with WTE.

Pre-election activities caused some county residents to mistrust the county's efforts. Among these activities were the county's hiring of a public relations firm without the commission's approval;[8] a county-sponsored informational brochure distributed in local newspapers that did not acknowledge its funding source; Westinghouse's large campaign expenditures directed through a pro-WTE committee; and the pro-WTE committee's incorrect claim that the county's WTE facility was supported by a particular local environmental group.

6.4.6 Improving the Decision-Making Process

All participants in the research believed that improvements to the decision-making process were necessary. Some of these improvements would require changes to Act 641, which structures county-level SWM activities. Some major themes, related to the decision-making process itself, emerge.

One such theme is improving representation on the county's solid waste planning committee. Several of the participants thought that environmentalists should be given better (not necessarily increased) representation by allowing local environmental groups to select or guide the selection of the environmentalists on the committee. (Representatives of environmental groups who participated in the research could not identify the "environmentalists" on the Act 641 committee.) Participants also believed that municipalities, particularly those where facilities are or would be located, should be given increased representation.

A second major theme is the availability of information. Most participants agreed that early and full disclosure of information should be an essential aspect of any SWM planning. Some distinguished between public information or education and public relations. The former includes full disclosure

Figure 6.4
Knox County, Tennessee

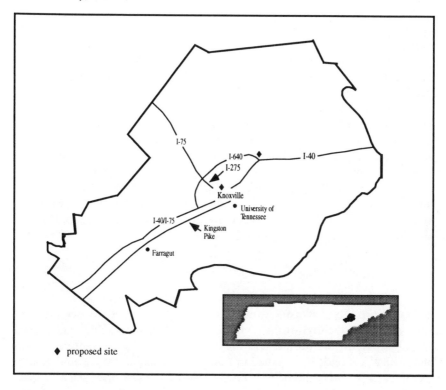

♦ proposed site

and acknowledges shortcomings, while the latter attempts to "sell" the plan by highlighting only its most positive features. Opponents of the facility suggested that readily available, accurate information will build trust.

Other suggested improvements included full implementation of recycling and waste reduction strategies before sizing and building a WTE facility and providing mitigation measures (in addition to financial compensation). Mitigation measures might include, for example, removing mercury from the waste stream and increasing land buffers between the facility and residential areas.

6.5 KNOX COUNTY, TENNESSEE

Knox County is nestled in the protected valley between the Cumberland Mountains and the Great Smoky Mountains of eastern Tennessee. Its principal city, and home to half of Knox County's 336,000 residents, is Knoxville. Farragut, with a population of approximately 13,000, is the only other incorporated municipality in Knox County (see Figure 6.4).

Knoxville's economy has been dominated historically by a pair of large industrial facilities, apparel factories, the Tennessee Valley Authority, and the state university. Jobs lost due to scaled-back industrial production and apparel manufacture have been replaced by service-oriented jobs and research and development activities, some of which are associated with the U.S. Department of Energy's facilities in neighboring counties. Much of Knox County remains devoted to low-density residential development and agricultural use.

Population has decreased more than 5 percent in Knoxville during the last decade, but increased by 5 percent in the county as a whole. The greatest population growth has been experienced in Farragut. Having incorporated in 1982, Farragut now is home to 63 percent more people than in 1986.

Knox County is governed by a county executive and a board of commissioners; Knoxville has a mayor and council. Antagonism between Knox County and Knoxville is prevalent and is demonstrated by disagreements over annexation, funding infrastructure projects, and past school consolidation.

6.5.1 Case-Study Summary

In 1986, at the suggestion of the Knox County Executive, the Metropolitan Knox Solid Waste Authority (MKSWA) formed to develop and oversee a WTE facility. At the invitation of Knox County, Knoxville agreed to participate in the project and the county and city were represented on the MKSWA. Bonds were issued in August 1986 so that they would qualify as tax-exempt and could be reinvested to fund MKSWA planning activities.

Siting activities began in 1987. In April 1988 the MKSWA approved a site located near the center of Knoxville (see Figure 6.4). The site was not zoned to accommodate a WTE facility. Opposition to the WTE proposal and site arose, and both the Metropolitan Planning Commission and Knoxville's city council failed to approve the site for the WTE facility. A second site already zoned for industrial use and located outside of Knoxville was identified and approved by the Metropolitan Planning Commission in January 1989.

In April 1989, the bonds were due to be reissued. Because no vendor had been contracted and permits had not been obtained, the bonds were reissued for one year. In the summer of 1989, Foster Wheeler was selected to design, construct, and operate a 900-tpd WTE facility for the MKSWA. All permits were obtained by April 1990, and a contract for the sale of electricity was signed with the Tennessee Valley Authority.

In April 1990, immediately before the bond remarketing, the mayor of Knoxville notified the bond insurer that the city was withdrawing its support for the project. This withdrawal caused the bonds to be uninsurable and in effect ended the MKSWA's WTE project.

6.5.2 Waste Management Policies and Practices

Knox County traditionally has relied on landfills to dispose of its solid waste. A privately owned landfill in Knox County opened in the mid–1970s and accepted most of Knox County's and Knoxville's waste until it reached capacity in the mid–1980s. Tennessee has no restrictions on intercounty transport of waste (although such a bill was being considered in the state legislature during the late 1980s). When the landfill reached capacity, waste was transported to and disposed at a privately owned landfill in a neighboring county. That landfill was within five years of reaching capacity, but permits for expansion later were acquired during the course of Knox's WTE planning.

Some operational problems have occurred at the Knox County landfill, including difficulties with noise, truck traffic, and one methane fire. Changes in operating procedures, e.g., constructing a transfer station and modifying operating hours, were instituted to address the problems. Most respondents characterized these problems as minor. With the exception of residents neighboring the landfills, public awareness of the facilities was extremely low.

Knoxville contracts with a private company to provide its residents weekly garbage pickup and disposal. Knox County provides only regional drop-off centers and allows its residents to contract independently for waste pickup.

No recycling activities were sponsored by either the county or the city prior to WTE planning. During WTE planning, the MKSWA began pilot recycling programs. These programs included curbside pickup in a limited area within Knoxville and regional drop-off centers in the city and county. A private waste hauling and disposal company also began limited recycling at commercial and industrial facilities in 1989.

6.5.3 Previous Siting Controversies

A private company's attempt to site a new landfill in the mid-to-late 1980s met considerable opposition from area residents who relied solely on wells for their water. After the site was purchased by the company, the metropolitan planning commission refused zoning. The company appealed the decision to the county commission, which also denied the siting.

Public outcry about air emissions from two local industries preceded and encouraged state regulations on air emissions and contributed to eventual closure of one facility and scaled-back operations at the second. Although not specifically a siting controversy, the public's involvement demonstrates some concern about local environmental quality.

6.5.4 Decision-Making Process

6.5.4.1 Events. In the mid–1970s and again in the early 1980s an eastern Tennessee regional development agency, on the behalf of several counties, examined SWM alternatives and identified WTE as a feasible option. No initiative ensued immediately, however.

During travels to Europe, the Knox County executive toured WTE facilities and was impressed with their operation and the municipal officials' satisfaction with the facilities. Consultation with a county financial advisor revealed that favorable tax status for such facilities would soon expire. This official first presented his idea for developing a WTE facility to other county officials and then requested the assistance of Knoxville. In early 1986, an informally organized group of county and city officials formed, visited existing WTE facilities, and decided to pursue the use of WTE.

In August 1986, the Knox County Commission and the Knoxville City Council formed by resolutions the nine-member MKSWA to plan and implement WTE use. The county retained its role as lead agency. MKSWA members, selected by the county executive and city mayor according to their experience with public works projects and willingness to support WTE, were approved by their respective governing bodies. The MKSWA was composed mostly of elected officials (city and county). It also originally included a seat for the MKSWA director, who resigned in February 1988 because of conflict of interest and was replaced by a university professor. Another citizen appointee was a veteran local government staff member.

MKSWA, based on its own facility cost estimate, issued $175 million in tax-exempt bonds in August 1986. The bonds were guaranteed by the city and county. Subsequent MKSWA planning activities were funded by arbitrage of the bonds. The bonds were reissued in April 1989 and were up for reissuance again in April 1990. In June 1989 and August 1989, respectively, the county commission and city council voted to back MKSWA spending in 1989–1990.

Project planning continued with the MKSWA hiring a consulting engineering firm to examine the technical and economic feasibility of the proposed WTE facility. In addition, the consultants estimated the waste-stream size and recommended facility siting procedures.

The WTE facility originally was conceived as a regional facility that would accept waste from neighboring counties. Accordingly, a 1,200-to-1,500- tpd facility was planned. Neighboring counties failed to respond to invitations to participate primarily because of cost considerations. The size of the facility was adjusted to 750 to 800 tpd, but readjusted to 900 tpd when county consultants reestimated the size of the waste stream. Because Knoxville provides solid waste pickup through a contractor, reasonably accurate tonnage data were available. Such information was not available for Knox County, and its waste stream was estimated according to the waste stream size of Knoxville and other cities. The size of the total waste stream originally was estimated to be 800 tpd and was projected to grow to 970 tpd by the turn of the century. Current waste production estimates were upwardly revised to over 1,050 tpd based on additional information from private haulers and landfill operators.

In January 1988, a new mayor took office in Knoxville. He immediately suggested he would ask for a three-month delay from the MKSWA to review the project. It became apparent through the news media that MKSWA would deny his request, and consequently he never made it. The mayor did, however, delay by one month the city council's vote on the flow control agreement. He also called for a new project director (hired in October 1988) and enlisted the U.S. Department of Housing and Urban Development (HUD) to conduct an independent review of the project. The mayor made his support for the waste-flow control agreement contingent upon it including HUD's findings. HUD recommended the development of a recycling program, formation of a citizens' advisory committee, reevaluation of the proposed site, and more extensive air and traffic studies. In March 1988, the Knoxville city council approved the flow control legislation that included HUD's recommendations.

Candidate sites were identified in 1987 based primarily on technical criteria: easy transportation access and proximity to the center of the waste stream. Three sites, all within Knoxville city limits, were identified. One was not given serious consideration ostensibly because of transportation problems, but perceptions that residents of the area would oppose the site contributed to its quick dismissal. Another site neighbored the University of Tennessee and was considered primarily because the university was a potential steam user. The university determined that it was not economically feasible to purchase steam from the facility for two reasons. The university would have to maintain redundant capacity in the event of a facility shutdown, and it could produce steam less expensively than it could purchase steam. The third site was in an area of light industrial and commercial use but that neighbored residential areas.

MKSWA identified the latter site as the preferred alternative and in March 1988 began activities to rezone the site for heavy industrial use. A second review of sites by MKSWA (as called for in Knoxville's waste control agreement) concluded that the site was acceptable. A third review of the site, conducted by the University of Tennessee, determined that a WTE facility constructed on the site could meet environmental requirements but suggested that a more thorough study might have identified additional sites for consideration. MKSWA approved this site—the Baxter Avenue site—in late April 1988. In June 1988, the Metropolitan Planning Commission, under public pressure to deny rezoning, disregarded the recommendation of its professional staff and voted almost unanimously to deny rezoning. MKSWA appealed the decision to the city council, which denied the rezoning in July.

MKSWA resumed site identification and selection activities almost immediately and developed site-selection criteria after consulting various business organizations. Consultants identified 22 potential sites; MKSWA narrowed the list to 4, all of which were outside Knoxville city limits in east Knox County, and identified a preferred site. The preferred site drew the most protest at two public hearings on site selection criteria primarily because it was the site of a Civil War battle and fort. MKSWA reconsidered and selected another site bordering the Holston River, which the Metropolitan Planning Commission approved in January 1989.

Site identification for a new ash and bypass waste landfill was resumed by MKSWA. A plan dividing the county into regions and preventing the siting of the WTE facility and a new landfill in the same region was considered, refused, and then restored. In November 1989, two private companies in a neighboring county bid on disposal of incinerator ash, although MKSWA took no definitive action. In the spring of 1990, MKSWA identified a landfill site.

Vendor procurement activities occurred concurrently with WTE facility site selection. Three companies responded to the authority's 1988 request for proposals, with Foster Wheeler Power Systems, Inc., submitting the lowest bid at approximately $83 million for construction and $4.4 million annually for operation. The proposals were evaluated for conformance with the authority's guidelines and willingness to accept risk in late 1988. Negotiations with Foster Wheeler ensued during the summer of 1989, and a contract was signed in July. Because a vendor had not been contracted by the April 1989 bond-refinancing date, bonds were reissued for a one-year term.

During the summer of 1989, MKSWA heard various proposals for alternatives to its WTE facility. Proposals included landfilling at a yet unpermitted site and a central waste separation and recycling facility; the authority determined that the technology for the facility was unproven. Firm cost estimates of the alternatives were not available and MKSWA decided to proceed with its WTE plan. However, an authority member later resigned his position because he favored the recycler's proposal. Also clouding the authority's decision were new extended life estimates of the landfill that was receiving the bulk of the county and city's waste. Estimates showed that capacity remained for 9.5 years of operation, and a proposed expansion would extend landfill life to 16 years.

The county commission and the city council in February 1990 endorsed state legislation allowing authorities to bill users directly—in effect, a vote of confidence for the project. However, in the month preceding the April 1990 financing deadline, much remained to be done. A contract for sale of energy was finalized with the Tennessee Valley Authority in March 1990 and state permits were acquired (after having been filed in October 1989).

Methods to repay the bonds were being considered as early as 1986. The first plan, to add a facility user fee to every utility bill, required state legislation. The legislature failed to approve this fee assessment legislation. MKSWA then sought authorization to directly assess fees to city and county residents and businesses. This plan, too, required special legislation that was turned down in the legislature on April 11, 1990.

Because MKSWA had been denied the authority to collect fees, the bonds would have to be repaid by assessments, levied directly by the city and county, possibly in the form of increased taxes. Faced with this possibility, and harboring concerns about the cost and potential environmental impacts of the project, the mayor of Knoxville called the New York bond insurer two days before the April 19 deadline for bond remarketing. He informed the insurer that "the administration of the city of Knoxville no longer supports the project." As a result, the bond insurer withdrew, leaving the bonds unmarketable, effectively ending the project.

6.5.4.2 *Participation.* Participating in the formal decision-making process by planning and approving project activities were the Knox County executive and commissioners, the Knoxville City mayor and council, and MKSWA. Engineering consultants, a lawyer to MKSWA, securities brokers, and, eventually, a financial advisor advised these decision makers. The Metropolitan Planning Commission reviewed land use.

A 15-member citizens' advisory committee was formed by MKSWA in mid–1988. Its members found the committee's role in the process unclear. Meeting attendance generally was low (some meetings were attended by only four members) and, during a nine-month period in 1989, no meetings were held. The committee received no funding and had no staff.

The role of state legislators in project development was noteworthy considering the volume and character of legislation, filed during the course of MKSWA's WTE planning, that affected the WTE project. Examples of such legislation included a bill requiring authorities to be subject to sunshine laws, to have their decisions approved by a two-thirds majority vote of the councils and commissioners of participating cities and counties, and to allow state review of bond issuance. Two proposals for fee assessments to repay bonds were defeated in the legislature. Another bill under consideration early in 1990 would have closed county borders to out-of-county waste.

A number of church groups, neighborhood associations, and groups concerned with inner-city development and quality of life, all based near the first proposed WTE site, coalesced when they were informed by their city council member that a site in their neighborhood was being considered to host the WTE facility. Members of this coalition acknowledged that individual members and groups opposed the WTE facility for different reasons. A minority of coalition members did not want the facility sited near their churches or residences. Others opposed the WTE facility because it was being considered before a recycling program was developed, because they had been unaware that the city and county were planning a WTE facility, or out of concern for adverse environmental and health effects. A minority of coalition members continued to actively oppose the WTE facility after the first siting attempt failed.

Another local group, much smaller than the first, formed to protest the second proposed WTE site. It was an association of east Knox County residents who maintained that eastern Knox County, having hosted most of county's landfills, was again being treated unfairly. The group's leaders asserted that east Knox County, as a region, was selected to host the facility because its population includes a disproportionate number of African Americans even though most of the residents near the second site are white.

A consumer advocacy group focusing on energy issues opposed the WTE facility because of potential adverse environmental and health effects, a belief that recycling and waste-reduction programs should be implemented first, and projections that the facility would raise solid waste disposal costs considerably.

Public awareness of MKSWA's activities and the proposed WTE facility was extremely low until late 1987, despite votes that had occurred in county commission and city council and occasional print media coverage. Most people neighboring the first proposed WTE facility site were unaware of planning activities until they were notified by the chance call of their city council person after their neighborhood had been selected to host the facility. Until 1988, concerned groups and individuals were not allowed to comment at MKSWA meetings. No public participation activities were undertaken by the MKSWA until mid–1988 when the citizens advisory committee was formed. A public relations firm was hired in February 1988 to conduct public information activities, but was dismissed the following month.

Public hearings were held in 1989 by MKSWA regarding site selection criteria and in 1990 by the Tennessee Department of Health and Environment regarding permits. The three opposition groups and individual member groups of the first neighborhood coalition hosted forums, held rallies, attended meetings, and lobbied the city council, the Metropolitan Planning Commission, and the state legislature. A suit filed by the first neighborhood coalition in April 1989 against MKSWA was dismissed before the bond remarketing. Another suit was threatened by the second neighborhood group immediately before the 1990 bond remarketing.

MKSWA contacted a large organization representing both city and county businesses to inform it of the WTE proposal. The business organization supported the WTE plan and, on at least two occasions before important votes, submitted letters to commissioners and council members indicating its support but requesting additional information. Two local newspapers supported the MKSWA WTE facility but advised careful planning.

6.5.4.3 *Agreement Among the Participants.* The degree of agreement among participants in the formal decision-making process varied. Respondents reported bickering among MKSWA staff as well as disagreements between staff and authority members, citing the resignations of authority staff and members. One member resigned because of the "political haggling" over the project; the other discontinued his support for the WTE proposal in favor of mechanized recycling at a central location. However, respondents reported that, through 1989, MKSWA members agreed on substantive issues and project implementation activities.

Throughout the planning process there were calls from city council members and county commissioners (not serving on the MKSWA) to reevaluate the site, the size, and the need for the project and to include additional persons on MKSWA, particularly a woman or minority. Some MKSWA members alleged that while WTE planning was underway, other MKSWA members were secretly investigating alternative SWM proposals.

Various actions taken by the new mayor, though not demonstrating disagreement with the MKSWA proposal, suggested a lack of full agreement. These actions include the HUD review and delaying important votes on the proposal. The final and foremost demonstration of his lack of agreement came when the mayor announced that he no longer supported the WTE project.

6.5.4.4 Mitigation. When a garment manufacturer neighboring the first site claimed its product potentially would be contaminated by odors emanating from the WTE facility and threatened to relocate its facility, MKSWA considered providing an air filtration system to the non-air-conditioned building. Concerns about parking and worker safety were addressed by offering reserved parking space for employees and planning a crosswalk.

When concerns about property value depreciation arose, MKSWA consultants examined property values in neighborhoods around existing facilities and found that there had been no negative impact. Therefore, no mitigation strategies were proposed.

6.5.4.5 Regulations and Laws. MKSWA's August 1986 issuance of project-financing bonds preceded other project-planning activities in order to obtain favorable financing, available before the enactment of TRA86, i.e., the ability to finance activities through arbitrage and tax-exempt status for the project. However, bond restrictions had the effect of imposing a project implementation schedule. For instance, to maintain tax-exempt status, 85 percent of construction funds had to be expended within five years of issuance. Also, final bond issuance required that a contract with a vendor be in place and that all permits be obtained. Because these activities were incomplete in 1989, the bonds were reissued temporarily. The April 1990 date for final bond reissuance established a deadline by which both the county and city were forced to make a financial commitment to the project. Knoxville's mayor withdrew his support one day before reissuance was to occur because increased property taxes were the only remaining plausible mechanism for repaying the bonds and because of uncertain project costs and impacts.

Engineering consultants to MKSWA considered the possibility of future stricter environmental regulations, particularly new U.S. EPA emissions standards, when requesting proposals from contractors. The request for proposals was drafted to require emission standards comparable to California's, recognized as among the most stringent standards in the country. Once U.S. EPA standards appeared in draft form, MKSWA staff and the vendor reviewed the proposed emissions equipment and determined that emissions would meet the new standards. Facility opponents disagreed, asserting that the facility would exceed the standards or require additional emissions control equipment that would escalate facility costs.

6.5.5 Decision-Making Issues

The major decision-making issues for county and city WTE planners were limited landfill capacity and reducing reliance on landfills to conserve land and minimize future landfill sitings. Members of the public focused on a wider array of issues than did the planners. Issues of most concern to the public were controlling solid waste disposal costs, controlling emissions and thus potential environmental and health effects, providing comprehensive waste management, and the lack of public information.

6.5.5.1 Environmental and Technology Issues: Site Selection and WTE Technology.

Site selection. The site-selection process and the first site selected (Baxter Avenue site) were the focus of much concern. The number of reviews of the Baxter Avenue site conducted after it was selected is indicative of that concern. Site-selection criteria focused on technical characteristics such as proximity to the waste stream and transportation, giving little regard to neighboring land uses and sensitive receptors. Within two blocks of the first site were residential areas occupied disproportionately by minorities, churches, and a nursing home. The lack of full consideration of one potential site located in an area occupied by relatively affluent residents spurred accusations that a major factor leading decision makers to select the Baxter Avenue site was that they anticipated no objections to it. Nonetheless, the site selection drew opposition from neighboring residents, churches, and a manufacturing company.

The second site-selection process placed more emphasis on neighboring land uses and sensitive receptors than did the first site-selection process. Further, siting criteria were considered in two public hearings. The second site was more rural than the first and outside of Knoxville's city limits. Most of the population in the area surrounding the proposed site was white. However, minorities are disproportionately represented in the eastern section of the county in which the second site was located. Opponents to this site claimed that the decision to site in the eastern section of the county was made because of the minority population located there.

WTE technology. Technical issues also influenced the decision-making process. Project supporters and opponents disagreed on whether using WTE to manage solid waste would minimize the health effects of SWM. Project opponents and representatives of the National Park Service (NPS) expressed concern about air emissions. The groups were concerned that adverse health effects would result from the heavy metals and toxins emitted. Representatives of the NPS thought that emissions could exacerbate environmental damage occurring from acid precipitation at the upper elevations of the Great Smoky Mountains National Park, located 25 miles southeast of Knoxville.

The size of the proposed WTE facility relative to the size of the waste stream, and changing estimates of the waste-stream size caused considerable concern that the facility was oversized. Originally, existing waste-stream size was estimated to be 800 tpd; the second estimate determined the size to be approximately 1,050 tpd. Several respondents challenged the procedure used to derive the estimates. Opponents thought that an oversized facility could preclude further implementation of recycling and could force MKSWA to buy solid waste from other counties or subsidize their waste disposal. (Opponents argued that, because disposal at various landfills was much cheaper than the projected disposal cost at the WTE facility, counties would not voluntarily dispose of their waste at the WTE facility without incentives.) According to many respondents, an important issue was the decision makers' failure to plan a comprehensive SWM system whose goal would be to minimize environmental impacts of waste disposal.

6.5.5.2 Economic Issues. WTE planners and decision makers acknowledged that during early operations, disposal costs at the WTE facility would exceed those at area landfills. But decision makers also thought that the reverse situation would occur as soon as landfill capacity decreased. Disposal fees first were estimated to be approximately $25 per ton and later were escalated to over $35 per ton. By comparison, tipping fees at landfills were less than $10 per ton. Opponents argued that a cost-benefit analysis of SWM alternatives was needed.

Another issue affecting WTE decision making was authorizing MKSWA, an authority whose members were appointed not elected, to access fees. This issue concerned project opponents and, apparently, some legislators who defeated two proposals that would have allowed it. Opponents of this authorization thought that the authority would have less incentive to control costs than the city council or county commission would.

6.5.5.3 Public Attitudes and Participants' Relations. Polls taken during the course of WTE planning indicated the public generally favored the concept of WTE over landfilling. A mail survey conducted by the city of Knoxville in the fall of 1987 showed 82 percent of city residents supporting incineration. A June 1988 poll of residents in a five-county area found that 68 percent of persons polled preferred incineration to landfilling and another poll in November 1988 showed 86 percent of persons polled in Knox County supported incineration.

However, perceptions of public attitudes about the WTE facility varied among the media, city council members, and county commissioners. Some judged opposition to be lessening in 1989 and 1990 as a result of a newly introduced recycling program and the selection of a second site, construed by opponents to be more acceptable than the Baxter Avenue site. Others thought that WTE opposition groups reflected public attitudes.

The relationship between the city of Knoxville and Knox County historically has been characterized by animosity and bickering. Issues such as annexation and funding for infrastructure have made county and city administrations icy toward each other. County officials often accused the mayor of attempting to undermine the WTE project. Project opponents and the media questioned the relationship between the county executive and one firm underwriting the bonds. At issue was the substantial profit made by the firm during each annual bond remarketing and the firm's role in initiating the project.

WTE-planning activities themselves, particularly the lack of information provided to the public and lack of opportunities for public involvement, became an issue of contention for WTE opponents. Because so many of the WTE-planning activities had occurred before the public became aware of them and because obtaining information about the project was difficult, some persons became opposed to the project or their opposition became firmly entrenched simply because they were excluded from the decision-making process. WTE planners on several occasions scheduled meetings in the morning or early afternoon, contributing to a public perception that they were intentionally avoiding interactions with the public.

6.5.6 Improving the Decision-Making Process

The consensus among respondents was that an improved decision-making process would include early activities to inform and involve the public. Some respondents indicated that although some segments of the public still would be likely to oppose a WTE facility, informing and involving the public could build trust and confidence in WTE decision makers and decisions. Some suggested that explaining technical issues early on would allow the public to make an informed decision about the specific proposal and to assess alternative proposals that would invariably be made during the decision-making process.

Some respondents pointed to Knoxville's solid waste task force, established after the WTE project folded, as exemplary of improved public involvement in SWM planning. They specifically recommended involving community members with substantial experience in various SWM issues in SWM planning.

Another recommendation, almost unanimously made, was to approach SWM comprehensively. This approach might include a thorough assessment of the community's needs and preferences and a complete review of alternatives, possibly including a cost-benefit analysis of alternatives.

A final recommendation was to organize project planning and implementation so that the financing is the last step. This sequencing would avoid arbitrary project deadlines and allow time for all decision makers to become fully informed and confident of their decisions.

6.6 MONMOUTH COUNTY, NEW JERSEY

Monmouth is a county with two faces. Its eastern margin is dominated by the Atlantic Ocean and the highly developed tourism and fishing industries that the ocean front spawns. The remainder of the county is far less densely populated and developed; small cities and towns are interspersed with horse farms and rural agricultural areas that account for New Jersey's nickname, "the Garden State." Within the bounds of Monmouth County are 53 individual municipalities.

The economy is service-oriented, even in portions of the county away from the tourism-oriented eastern coast. High-technology industries have settled in Monmouth County, but large, heavy-industrial facilities common in Newark, approximately 20 miles north of Monmouth County, are not present here.

Just over one-half million people reside in Monmouth County; less than 13 percent of these people are of minority races. Population growth during the 1980s was approximately 10 percent. The county is home to many emigrés from crowded New York and northern New Jersey, and also serves as a bedroom community for people commuting to jobs in New York and Philadelphia.

The county historically has been predominantly Republican but experienced democratic control during the late 1970s and again in the early 1980s. County government is headed by a five-member Board of Chosen Freeholders, who currently are all Republicans. These Freeholders choose a county administrator, a job that has remained more managerial than political in nature. The Freeholders and county administrator manage an annual budget of $270 million.

6.6.1 Case-Study Summary

In 1988, after reviewing SWM alternatives, Monmouth County Freeholders selected incineration with heat recovery combined with a front-end separation system as a means of reducing the county's reliance on landfills and providing long-term disposal capacity. Negotiations with vendors occurred in 1989, and in 1991 Westinghouse was contracted to design, build,

Figure 6.5
Monmouth County, New Jersey

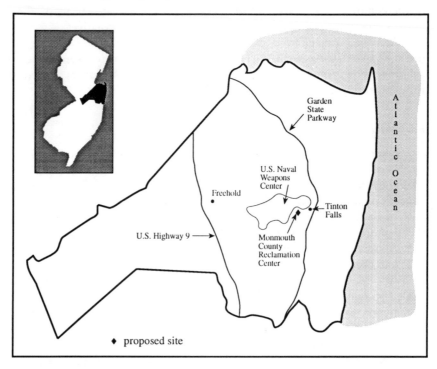

and operate a 1,700-tpd WTE facility. The facility was to be located on the site of the county's landfill in Tinton Falls (see Figure 6.5).

Opposition from citizens' groups and municipalities neighboring the proposed facility arose. The state mandated regionalization of the proposed facility. These factors left some on the Board of Freeholders reluctant to proceed with project implementation and others concerned that the project would stall. Consequently, the Freeholders decided to submit the proposal to public referendum.

The election was preceded by numerous forums hosted by municipalities and civic groups throughout Monmouth County where the county staff and project opponents presented information. In November 1991, 52 percent of the voters opposed the project. Immediately thereafter, the Freeholders withdrew from the facility contract.

6.6.2 Waste Management Policies and Practices

The proposed WTE facility in Monmouth County must be viewed in the larger context of SWM. The primary SWM methods in the county are landfilling, recycling, and vegetative composting. All participants in the research indicated that the landfill is well operated and has had minimal adverse environmental effects, and indicated a belief that the public holds the same opinion. Apparently, the general public perceives both composting and recycling as environmentally benign.

Monmouth County became involved in SWM and disposal in the early 1970s when it commissioned a study of the amount and disposition of waste generated in the county to determine future disposal needs. Acting before the New Jersey Solid Waste Management Act of 1975 required each county to plan for its solid waste disposal, Monmouth County acquired land for a landfill and in 1976 opened the Monmouth County Reclamation Center (MCRC)[9]. Other privately owned landfills that had been operating in the county were closed by 1983 primarily in response to stricter regulations and requirements of the New Jersey Department of Environmental Protection (NJDEP).

The first, 50-acre phase of MCRC reached capacity in 1983. A second phase comprising 100 acres now is operating. Because NJDEP recently granted a permit to increase the landfill height by 50 feet, capacity at the second phase is expected to last until April 1995. During the time when the county was planning the solid waste incinerator, a third phase of the landfill also was being planned. Although as many as 125 acres potentially were available, NJDEP was assessing the lands for their status under the New Jersey Wetlands Protection Act (1989). NJDEP subsequently has determined that approximately 30 acres (in several separate parcels) can be used as landfill. Based on the achievement of 60 percent recycling, the new landfill space should last five to seven years.

The first phase of the landfill was unlined but included monitoring wells. These wells identified minor contamination in the upper of two aquifers beneath the landfill possibly due to the landfill or the Naval Weapons Center adjacent to it. Phase One then was retrofitted with a leachate collection system that apparently is the cause of intermittent odor problems being experienced by residents neighboring the landfill. Phase Two of the landfill includes a leachate collection system and a methane-venting device.

When the county identified the MCRC area, Tinton Falls was deemed suitable because it was bordered on two sides by the Naval Weapons Center, centrally located in the county, and relatively sparsely populated. Population density in 1980 in Tinton Falls was 509 persons/sq. mile, half the average density of Monmouth County and had been declining (U.S. Bureau of the Census, 1983, 1992). However, in recent years Tinton Falls has experienced rapid growth, with its population increasing almost 60 percent between 1980 and 1990. Large, new housing developments are now located within one-half mile of MCRC. Further, although Tinton Falls zoned land adjacent to the landfill for manufacturing to create a buffer around the landfill, landfill expansions now occupy buffer areas.

County- and state-mandated recycling began in 1987 and targets newspaper, glass, aluminum, and tin. Non-residential establishments also must recycle white office paper and corrugated cardboard. It is likely that recycling additional materials will be mandated soon. Each municipality is responsible for providing for recycling either by drop-off centers or curbside service, or by contracting for these services. The county acts only to assist the municipalities and to identify markets for the recycled materials.

In 1990 the New Jersey Emergency Solid Waste Task Force, convened by Governor Florio to make recommendations on the future of SWM in New Jersey, established a goal of recycling 60 percent of the total waste stream by 1995. In 1990, the municipalities of Monmouth County reported recycling 25,000 tons per month, double the amount recycled the previous year. The amount of waste accepted annually at the county landfill has declined more than 40 percent since its usage peaked in the late 1980s. The overall recycling rate in Monmouth County (using New Jersey state criteria) exceeds 50 percent.

Vegetative composting of approximately 80,000 tons per year occurs at 20 municipal sites in Monmouth County. Numerous farms and one county-operated facility accept leaves for composting from residents and municipalities. Leaves were banned from the landfill in 1987, and a ban of grass is anticipated.

6.6.3 Previous Siting Controversies

MCRC siting drew little, if any, controversy for reasons related to site suitability described previously. The other major industrial facility in the county is the Naval Weapons Center, in existence since World War II. Although the lack of full disclosure about activities at the Navy depot has engendered some speculation about storage of nuclear weapons there, it is not a community issue.

Attempts to site noxious facilities include a 1986 state effort to identify a site for a hazardous waste incinerator. A potential site in Millstone Township (in west Monmouth County) received considerable opposition from local residents; one protest drew approximately 5,000 persons. Opponents argued that siting criteria were ignored so that Millstone, where little opposition was expected, could be included. The MCRC site also was considered for the hazardous waste incinerator, but New Jersey state law exempted it from consideration because the site already had been targeted for a solid waste disposal facility.

6.6.4 Decision-Making Process

6.6.4.1 Events. In the mid–1970s New Jersey responded to increasing amounts of solid waste and garbage exportation, tighter landfill regulations, and closing landfills by calling on its counties to begin solid waste planning.

The 1975 Solid Waste Management Act (PL 1975, chapter 326) required each county to handle its own solid waste problems and plan for 10 years of disposal capacity. Through 1989, under Governor Kean's administration, NJDEP encouraged the use of solid waste incineration. The NJDEP review of Monmouth County's SWM plan of the early 1980s found it deficient because it did not include the "maximum practicable use of resource-recovery procedures." The plan did not identify a specific resource-recovery method, e.g., mass-burn incineration or a refuse-derived-fuel (RDF) facility, although it suggested pursuing resource recovery in the future.

Responding to this criticism, consultants to Monmouth County conducted a study that analyzed resource-recovery technologies (i.e., incineration and composting) for their suitability in Monmouth County and developed a strategy the county could use to implement a resource-recovery facility (including management, procurement, and financing). As a result of this study, Monmouth County's July 1985 amendments to its SWM plan identified WTE as the favored technology. The next amendments, of August 1986, called for a project team composed of Freeholder representatives and county department heads to review the need for such a facility and determine the best approach with which to proceed. The identification of a favored technology was dropped entirely from the SWM plan. In early 1986, however, the Freeholders designated available land at MCRC as the site for any centralized resource-recovery facility the county would choose. (Additional information is found in Section 6.6.5.1.)

In late 1986, the county began a full-scale study of available SWM technologies, looking for one that could reduce landfill reliance, provide reliable and environmentally sound waste disposal, increase reuse of resources, and be economically acceptable. Representatives of companies made presentations to the Freeholders on mass-burn technology, RDF, pyrolysis, mixed waste composting, compaction, and other technologies. County consultants reviewed the waste reduction capacity and performance record of these technologies at other sites. The analysis, recorded in several volumes, identified four possibilities for Monmouth County: RDF, materials recovery with landfilling, materials recovery with incineration, and mass burning. In July 1988, the Board of Freeholders unanimously voted to proceed with a combined recycling-incineration system (1,700 tpd capacity). The recycling component, which involved a front-end separation process using magnets and hand sorting to remove targeted recyclable items and hazardous wastes, was selected despite Freeholders' knowledge that this alternative was more expensive than a mass-burn facility. In making this decision, the Freeholders believed they were complying with state directives for recycling, establishing long-term disposal capacity, and conserving increasingly limited open land in Monmouth County.

Despite the apparent depth of the technology assessment, some county and municipal officials believe it was a foregone conclusion that incineration would be chosen. In fact, opponents of the project continued to suggest alternatives to incineration.[10] In response to public opposition, Monmouth County again in early 1991 reviewed alternative technologies and again concluded that a materials recovery system and incineration best met county needs. Opponents then developed an elaborate "non-burn" plan that included materials recovery and composting (and possible landfilling of the composted material). The county conducted a formal point-by-point review of the alternative plan.

By early 1991, a vendor review process that selected Westinghouse and a preliminary health and environmental risk assessment had been completed. However, organized public opposition had surfaced, and changes in state guidance about county-level SWM activities had occurred. The state, with Governor Florio at the helm, was encouraging regional management of solid waste rather than the previous administration's policy that directed each county to handle its own garbage. Also, state government was emphasizing recycling and relegating WTE to an "option of last resort." In April 1990, the governor placed a four-month moratorium on incinerator construction, and it became increasingly clear that only regional incinerators would receive NJDEP approval.

The possibility of being forced to accept out-of-county trash and the growing public opposition left some on the Board of Freeholders wary and reluctant to allow the county to enter a contractual agreement with the vendor. Freeholders who still strongly supported the project were concerned about the delay and the other Freeholders' reluctance to proceed. For all these reasons, the Freeholders decided in February 1991 to bring the proposal to public referendum. Having done so, they signed a service agreement with Westinghouse to build and operate the facility to allow planning to proceed.

The level of activity was feverish in the months preceding the November referendum. Westinghouse campaigned in favor of the project with newspaper advertisements and glossy direct-mail leaflets, spending more than three times the opponents' expenditures (including legal fees related to the referendum incurred by Tinton Falls). County staff debated representatives of opponent groups and municipal officials opposing the WTE facility at numerous public forums held by various organizations throughout Monmouth County. One month before the election, Monmouth County announced preliminary results of a comparative health risk assessment that determined mixed waste composting to be 100 times more risky than incineration. Both sides also used fliers and newspaper advertisements to reach the general public. Opponents used a telephone campaign and the local cable television station for advertisements.

Fifty-six percent of the registered voters went to the polls in November 1991. However, only 47 percent of registered voters voiced an opinion on the SWM plan; 52 percent of those voters opposed the project. Immediately thereafter, the Freeholders exercised the "pull-out" clause and withdrew from the contract with Westinghouse.

The county since has organized a Recycling and Alternative Technologies Committee that includes citizens and elected officials who opposed the county's WTE facility. The committee is responsible for reviewing various SWM technologies and making recommendations to the county. Neither its activities nor the November 1991 referendum preclude the county from using WTE technology in the future. The vendor's contract stipulated that if the county signs a contract before 1997 with another WTE vendor, Westinghouse would receive compensation of $10 million. However, the county and Westinghouse negotiated a settlement in which the county paid Westinghouse $489,000 for planning expenses and the aforementioned clause was removed.

6.6.4.2 Participation. Numerous groups became involved in the debate over the Monmouth County incinerator. Those who opposed the WTE facility included local chapters of longstanding national and state environmental groups. One group, organized in 1988 to oppose the county's WTE facility, disbanded early because of infighting about technical issues. In the spring of 1990, local citizens organized a group, whose membership included hundreds of county residents, to oppose the project. Its leadership and membership were based in the Tinton Falls area, but through its own publicity efforts and general media coverage the organization and its position became widely known. It led the other groups in a well-orchestrated campaign against the county's proposed system. Another prominent opposition group was composed of 150 medical professionals, including physicians and dentists. As well-respected medical professionals, their arguments against the project, particularly those based on health concerns, were well received by the general public.

In early 1991, a group formed specifically to support the county's plan. The group, whose membership numbered above 100, argued that long-term, multifaceted solid waste planning was necessary immediately. The group's own financial analysis of the project agreed closely with county estimates. A local tax watchdog group and a coalition of academic, business, trade, and recycling organizations also supported the project.

Among the governmental and quasi-governmental groups who participated in decision making was NJDEP. Its review is required for all county SWM plans and amendments. Approval is based on technical considerations and adherence to state SWM policy, which became less supportive of WTE during the course of Monmouth's WTE planning. The county's solid waste advisory committee, composed of Freeholder representatives, waste haulers, and county staff, as well as the county's health risk assessment committee with citizen representation also provided guidance for the project.

Opportunities for public participation offered by the county included membership for an environmentalist on the Solid Waste Advisory Committee and representation by opposition groups on the Health Risk Assessment Committee. Numerous public hearings were held during the technology review process and for each version of the county's SWM plan. Meetings held before technology and site selection attracted few people; however, later hearings drew upward of 200 people. The greatest and most direct opportunity for public participation offered by the county came in November 1991, when the public referendum was held.

Early in the planning stages of the WTE facility, opponents received little media coverage. By 1990, opponent groups substantially increased their public visibility by planning and attending events other than those organized by the county. Various opponent groups, civic and environmental groups, and business organizations throughout Monmouth County held forums where county representatives, Westinghouse officials, and opposition group leaders addressed audiences about the SWM plan and answered questions. Rallies, signs, fliers, and booths at county fairs delivered opponents' viewpoints to the public. The lead opposition group gained much credibility by offering its own SWM plan that called for alternatives to incineration. Along with other groups and municipalities, it petitioned the county to reword the referendum to include the word "incinerator" and to remove the reference to its specific location.

Issues and concerns around which WTE opponents rallied included negative health and environmental effects, financial considerations, interference with recycling and waste reduction programs, adverse effects on property values, the likelihood of having to accept out-of-county garbage, and the county's selected WTE vendor, Westinghouse. These issues are discussed in Section 6.6.5.

6.6.4.3 Agreement Among the Participants. Early in the process of developing SWM plans, members of the Board of Freeholders apparently agreed that WTE was the method best suited for Monmouth County. The vote for adopting the SWM plan including WTE was unanimous. Later, three Freeholders (two of them new to the board) opposed possible regionalization of the facility and voted to bring the issue to referendum. After the state mandated that Monmouth's facility accept some out-of-county waste, one Freeholder moved to kill the project before the November election. However, no Freeholder seconded the motion, allowing the public to make the decision. Late in the decision-making process, Freeholders adopted one of three different positions: for WTE, against it, and "let the public decide."

It is difficult to characterize the level of agreement among opponents of the project, although apparently there was little disagreement. Considerable cooperation within and possibly among groups likely was required to produce an alternative SWM plan that all opponent groups supported. WTE facility opponents disagreed with the county staff and most officials on practically every aspect of the facility (except for the proposed front-end separation system for hazardous materials and recyclables), including the immediate need for one, its size, cost, and potential health effects. There also was serious disagreement about the wording of the referendum.

Apparently there was considerable disagreement among the members of the Health Risk Assessment Committee and as a result, members believe that the committee made little progress. Disagreements focused on health risk assessments of other WTE facilities and were exacerbated because the committee's facilitator was a non-local expert in risk assessment whom project opponents and some committee members viewed as completely biased in favor of the use and safety of incinerators. Though not formally disbanded, the committee ceased to meet in April 1991. Members of this committee learned of the preliminary results of the comparative risk assessment, released in the fall of 1991, along with the general public.

Negotiations among the disagreeing parties were not a part of the decision-making process. Few, if any, modifications were made to the SWM plan. The county, with its consultants, specified emissions standards to be met and determined facility size before issuing requests for proposals. When the county invited project opponents to provide input regarding the phrasing of the referendum, opponents construed it as an opportunity for negotiations. In actuality, both parties had predetermined—and polar—ideas about referendum wording and no negotiations to reconcile the difference occurred. Two municipalities that opposed the project tested the wording of the referendum in court, where the wording was upheld.

Once the specific technology was selected, refinements were made in health risk assessment associated with the SWM plan. Results of a preliminary comparative health risk assessment study were issued. The second study compared WTE and mixed waste composting and predicted that health effects of composting would be 100 times greater than those of incineration. The county revised its cost estimates (per ton tipping fees) after submitting its application to sell power, when it could better estimate its revenue. These figures coincidentally were produced shortly before the referendum, but caused skepticism among opponents.

6.6.4.4 Mitigation and Compensation. New Jersey law requires financial compensation to the city hosting a solid waste facility. Tinton Falls currently receives upwards of $2 million annually (an amount higher than that mandated by state law). The county offered additional financial compensation and to construct a public facility, i.e., a fire station, as a compensatory gesture to Tinton Falls.

6.6.4.5 Regulations and Laws. County officials and staff, along with their consultants, considered environmental regulation throughout the planning process. NJDEP and U.S. EPA permitting requirements were considered before the request for proposals was made, and companies unable to meet these standards were excluded from consideration. New Jersey regulations regarding the testing and disposal of incinerator ash are stricter than existing federal regulations. Each load must be tested, remain segregated, and, if it meets New Jersey criteria for hazardous waste (which also are stricter than U.S. EPA standards), must be disposed of as such. Air emissions estimates, developed by county consultants, are conservative. They are based on the throughput of the unsegregated waste stream even though the front-end separation process is designed to remove hazardous materials and metals that contribute to the toxicity of the air emissions and ash. Despite the conservatism of the estimates, they were within state and federal emissions standards. At no point were county officials or staff concerned that environmental regulations would affect the viability of the facility.

Changes in the state's interpretation of the PURPA motivated the county to sign an agreement with its vendor quickly in an attempt to be grand-fathered in under older power purchase regulations. Before 1989, the state's interpretation of PURPA caused utilities to purchase power at 110 percent of their avoided cost. The new interpretation, allowing an annual public bidding system to establish the market price for power, could result in substantially lower payment to the county for power produced at the WTE facility.

6.6.5 Decision-Making Issues

The key decision-making issue for county officials and staff was developing SWM capacity that would reduce reliance on landfills, provide environmentally sound waste disposal, be reliable (i.e., was proven to be reliable at other sites in the United States), recover resources, and be economically acceptable. The county staff and most officials believed that WTE with a front-end separation process was the technology that could meet these parameters.

Initially, key decision-making issues important to the public specifically focused on WTE incinerators rather than on SWM generally. The first issue to which the public reacted was the possibility for residents' health to be affected adversely by incinerator emissions. Following closely was the financial impact of the project on county residents. However, once opponents began to offer alternatives to incineration, the public framed issues in terms of broad SWM concerns. In particular, citizens wanted SWM activities to have minimal effects on the health of county residents and sought to keep solid waste disposal costs reasonable. The 125 additional acres of potential landfill space fostered a belief among some that any decision to proceed with incineration could be delayed.

6.6.5.1 Environmental and Technology Issues: Site Selection and WTE Technology.

Site selection. As was the case when MCRC first was built, county staff and officials believed that siting the facility at the Tinton Falls site was "logical" for several reasons. Its central location would minimize transportation costs and impacts. Land already owned by the county included sufficient space for the WTE facility, and a major power station nearby would allow easy hookup into the power grid. No alternative sites for the WTE facility were seriously considered. Site selection generally was not an issue for county officials or residents, although some residents were concerned that the site's proximity to newly developed residential areas would lower the value of those properties.

WTE technology. All parties involved agreed on the importance of minimizing adverse health effects of SWM activities. Project supporters and opponents disagreed, however, on whether WTE met this goal. The county's health risk assessment concluded that less than one additional cancer case per one million persons would result from the WTE facility (assuming no removal of recyclables or hazardous materials). Although a second preliminary health risk assessment concluded that the health risks of mixed waste composting and using compost on gardens, farms, and roadsides were 100 times greater than those from WTE, project opponents believed otherwise. Based on information gathered from community activists neighboring other incinerators, a national network of anti-incinerator activists, publications such as the *Citizen's Clearinghouse for Hazardous Wastes* and *Work on Waste*, mainstream national health associations, and the county and its consultants, opponents believed that using WTE technology would negatively affect the health of Monmouth County residents. An organization of local health professionals warned of health effects from air emissions of dioxin, lead, and mercury including respiratory problems, learning disabilities, and cancer. Opponents produced literature stating that the WTE facility would poison the air and have no mercury control. Because potential health effects on children were particularly important to opponents, this publication asked, will it be "your child or mine?"

Other environmental issues related to the use of WTE concerned the facility's size. The county and its consultants calculated the facility size—1,700 tpd with an average daily throughput of 1,500 tpd—based on average annual tonnage delivered to the county's landfill (in the mid-to-late 1980s). Because all county garbage is delivered to a county-operated facility, accurate tonnage data were available. As recycling rates increased and the recession began, the amount of waste going to the landfill (and that would go to the WTE facility) declined. The county retained the additional capacity (approximately 400 tpd) in the facility design because they anticipated population growth and an associated increase in solid waste production. Also the 400 tpd additional capacity would meet state directives (firm by late 1990) to regionalize SWM capacity. Because the county already controlled the flow of solid waste within its borders, a contract that excluded a "put-or-pay" clause (forcing the county to pay a predetermined amount per ton of waste not delivered to the facility) was accepted by Westinghouse.

The 400 tpd of excess capacity raised two issues among WTE opponents.

The first was that practices such as recycling and waste reduction might not be developed and implemented further because they would reduce the amount of fuel available for a WTE facility. The second issue was that the excess capacity would allow Monmouth County to import out-of-county garbage, causing local citizens to bear some financial burden and health risks for handling someone else's solid waste.

Westinghouse was chosen as the county's WTE vendor because of the degree of financial risk it accepted and because of its environmental guarantees. Westinghouse's environmental record became an issue of concern to opponents. Opponents highlighted garbage shortfalls, unexpected shutdowns, ash releases, and complaints from neighboring citizens at other Westinghouse incinerators. The corporation's association with numerous Superfund sites throughout the country and its involvement with nuclear weapons and waste disposal also were cited as drawbacks to accepting a Westinghouse facility. Additionally, opponents contended that Westinghouse's (the parent corporation) recent financial difficulties related to its involvement with nuclear energy development in the Philippines and the resulting lawsuit, significant losses in real estate, and cost overruns at other WTE facilities were reasons to oppose a Westinghouse project in Monmouth County. The implication was that Westinghouse management of a WTE facility could leave Monmouth County facing similar financial problems.

6.6.5.2 *Economic Issues.* Economic issues were secondary to technological issues, particularly reliability and waste-volume-reduction ability, in the county's selection of a SWM technology. Nevertheless, WTE proponents and opponents disagreed on the cost of alternative SWM methods. County-estimated composting costs (with landfilling) were $115 per ton; WTE opponents estimated $80 per ton. Other methods of solid waste disposal were not given such detailed analysis by either party for various reasons. For instance, state-mandated recycling already was being implemented. Further, implementation of additional source reduction activities, besides requiring long periods of time, might be dependent upon incentives or requirements provided in future federal legislation.

The county chose to own the facility and contract its construction and operation to a vendor. As a result, the county retained considerable control (e.g., monitoring and shut down) and could continue to use and own the facility after the 20-year financing period expired. Also, county ownership of a facility that generates electricity would qualify the bonds for tax-exempt status. The county planned a self-supporting facility, that is, tipping fees and revenues generated from the sale of power and recyclable items would be used to repay the bond issue that financed its construction and to pay Westinghouse's operator fee.

Opponents of the facility took issue with the county's assessment of the economic feasibility of using WTE technology. They predicted that tipping fees would double and that the 20-year cost of building, financing, and operating the facility would approach $1.5 billion instead of the $600 million estimated by the county. They argued that taxes would skyrocket as a result. The opposition's cost estimate apparently was based on general knowledge of costs and cost overruns at other sites, and not its own detailed cost analysis.

6.6.5.3 Public Attitudes and Participants' Relations. Before Monmouth County proposed its WTE facility, the general public knew little about solid waste disposal in Monmouth County. Neither siting and opening MCRC nor its 15 years of operation had drawn much public attention although newspaper coverage of county SWM plans began in early 1986. Public hearings regarding the SWM plan that considered a possible WTE facility at MCRC also were held. However, most respondents agreed that the WTE plan did not become general public knowledge until 1989. The highly visible campaigns for and against the WTE facility increased public awareness of solid waste issues and SWM in Monmouth County.

The general public's attitudes regarding SWM practices were surveyed shortly before the November referendum. A local newspaper found that 48 percent of the public favored composting, 29 percent favored incineration, and 10 percent favored continued landfilling. The remaining 13 percent were undecided. In addition to this formal survey, general public attitudes could be discerned through audience responses at the county's public hearings and independently held forums. Despite apparent public opposition to incineration, incumbent Freeholders who strongly supported the project were reelected by wide margins in November 1990 and 1991 elections.

Public leaders and elected officials (at the local and state level) adopted one of the three possible public stances toward WTE described previously: some favored using it, some opposed it, and others only reluctantly allowed their personal opinions to be known and supported the public's right to decide. The latter two positions, respondents suggested, were sometimes adopted because they were politically expedient. The most widely read newspaper in Monmouth County publicly opposed the project, and the leaders of the business community remained relatively silent on the issue.

Several participants in the research characterized the interactions among parties involved in the campaign as a manifestation of a classic clash of the powerful and the powerless. On one side was a large corporation wielding its power and financial clout. Alongside it were county officials, some of whom admittedly were paternalistic, trying to tell the public to accept what was best for it. On the other side was the seemingly powerless public about to be trampled by big business and government. Several respondents pointed out that skepticism of government and big business made the general public wary of the project. This mistrust was extended to the county's consultants, whom opponents labeled "hired guns."

The solid waste issue perhaps was the first to engender public mistrust of local government in New Jersey. This mistrust may have been part of a pattern of considerable mistrust of government in New Jersey—and the country—in recent years.

Difficult situations arose at public forums where the citizens sought answers to questions and where the county sought to allay fears. The Westinghouse representative was a foreign national who, according to respondents, had difficulty communicating with the public. County staff found it difficult to respond to broad charges and what they termed "leading" questions. Some people who attended the forums interpreted county staff behavior as showing a lack of preparation because of the staff's inability to provide immediate responses to some questions. A representative of the business community suggested that because of this apparent lack of preparation the county staff missed opportunities to allay doubts raised by opponents' claims of adverse health effects.

Other county actions fostered mistrust among the public and municipalities. For example, a request by Tinton Falls for access to data from monitoring wells around the landfill was denied by the county because the data (after being subjected to quality assurance controls) were available from the state. The municipality construed the denial as a county attempt to hide information. Changing facility tipping fee estimates and releasing comparative health risk assessment data shortly before the referendum were viewed suspiciously by opponents and some of the general public. County staff, in retrospect, suggested that the manner in which these information releases occurred hurt the county's image.

6.6.6 Improving the Decision-Making Process

No participant in the research expressed complete satisfaction with the decision-making process related to Monmouth County's WTE facility. All participants suggested that increased public participation would improve the process. While some respondents suggested increased and meaningful citizen representation on committees that contribute to the decision-making process, others recommended that the municipalities within the county should have some opportunity to contribute to the process.

Opinions about relying on public participation in the form of a referendum to decide such an issue varied, however. Some supporters and opponents of the project firmly believed that the public should decide. Others, having just been through the protracted ordeal, questioned whether the public could become informed well enough to make such a decision. All respondents agreed that if a referendum is held the public should be obligated to become informed; some argued that it is the county's responsibility to provide information and to provide increased opportunities for public involvement rather than to allow large segments of the public to remain inadequately informed.

Most participants were unsure whether such improvements would have affected the outcome of the solid waste decision-making process, but they believed the outcome would have better reflected an informed public's attitude.

6.7 ANALYSIS

The four case studies were compared to identify factors that influence communities' decisions to accept or reject waste-to-energy facilities. These factors were organized into two major categories: context and process. The decision-making context category is organized into two subcategories of information about counties: past waste management practices and demographic variables. The decision-making process category identifies who was involved, what happened, and how it happened and is organized into five subcategories: (1) proposed system, (2) siting process, (3) interaction among parties, (4) public participation, and (5) catalysts driving the project. Tables 6.1 and 6.2 summarize this information. Cross-cutting categories of factors related to context and process are the issues raised during the course of decision making.

Comparisons between case-study sites where WTE has been accepted to those where it has been rejected should consider the timing of proposed projects and the degree to which WTE was accepted or rejected. The timing of project initiation and implementation, as well as changes occurring on a national level during the 1980s, affected the decision-making process at each of the case-study sites. For example, the Broward County project began in 1982, fully three years before the other case-study projects were initiated and before the recycling ethic swelled in the mid-to-late 1980s. As a result, one area of controversy at other sites—competition between recycling and WTE facilities for a limited waste stream—was not an issue at Broward until late in project implementation. Also, national environmental groups, such as Greenpeace and the Sierra Club (Sierra Club, 1986, 1992) adopted anti-incineration stances, and national health organizations, such as the American Lung Association (ALA/ATS Government Relations Position, 1984) expressed serious concerns about incineration in the mid-to-late 1980s. Anti-incineration activists began to campaign nationwide, visiting numerous sites and establishing networks of local activists. These activities influenced the decision-making processes at the three sites initiated in 1985 or later.

Another consideration in cross-site comparisons is that decisions to proceed with WTE projects do not fall neatly into simple "acceptance" or "rejection" categories. There are differences in the degree to which WTE was accepted at each case-study site. At one extreme was Broward County, which has two WTE facilities now operating. WTE clearly was accepted at that site. Oakland County's mandate to proceed with WTE implementation is less clear. Although a public referendum narrowly approved WTE use,

Table 6.1 Summary of Decision-Making Context

	Accepted		Rejected	
	Broward, FL	Oakland, MI	Knox, TN	Monmouth, NJ
Waste Management				
Size of waste stream (approx. 1988)	4,400 tpd[1]	3,600 tpd	800 tpd	2,300 tpd
Environmental status of landfills in county	Mixed	Mixed	Good	Mostly good
Other combustion facility[1] in county	Yes, closed	Yes, closed	No	No
SW exported	Prohibited by law of recipient county (after 1980)	Some restrictions in county SWM plans	Yes	Yes
Key Demographic Variables				
Population 55+ (1990)	34.5%	19.4%	22.5%	20.9%
Population growth 1980–90	23%	7%	5%	10%
Projected population growth 1990–2010	35%	12%	15%	20%

[1]Acronyms: SW—solid waste; tpd—tons per day.

municipalities have failed to sign IGAs committing their waste to the county's system. Further, the county currently has no construction and service vendor because of Westinghouse's withdrawal. Monmouth and Knox counties are sites where WTE was rejected. Voters in Monmouth County rejected the county's WTE proposal by a very small margin. The Knox County project ended when Knoxville's mayor withdrew his support shortly before bond issuance. Except for the mayor's withdrawal, which was driven largely by concerns for political liability, the Knox County project might have proceeded unhindered.

Comparisons between case-study sites in this chapter largely are made in the context of the *outcome* of decision making—whether or not to proceed with the WTE facility. However, attention also is paid to the decision-making *process* itself. Examining the decision-making process does not presuppose that either WTE acceptance or rejection is the more desired outcome. It does, however, provide insights into process factors that influence the final WTE decisions, even though any one factor affecting the decision-making process may not lead to consistent outcomes. For instance, respondents uniformly recommended that the public be provided opportunities for involvement early in WTE planning—a process decision. The fact of early public involvement does not guarantee that a formal decision will be made to proceed with WTE. Early public involvement may, however, enhance public acceptability of the decision-making process while lack of it may amplify public concerns about WTE itself.

The following sections compare the decision-making contexts and the decision-making processes of the four case-study sites. For each factor, similarities and differences are analyzed to determine whether, how, and why that factor may have influenced the decision-making process or outcome. Major issues raised and addressed during the course of decision-making are summarized in the final section of this chapter.

6.7.1 Decision-Making Process

6.7.1.1 Proposed System. Case studies did not provide comparative information about the possibility that who initiates projects may constitute a factor affecting WTE decision making. Each case-study WTE proposal was initiated by county government officials or their designated planners. The Knox County project almost immediately became jointly sponsored and was to be jointly owned by the county and the city of Knoxville. All others proceeded under the sponsorship of a single government entity and, with the exception of Broward County, would be owned by the county. Broward selected a full-service vendor who would also own the facilities.

Selecting an ownership option and negotiating with vendors to provide service was arduous and one of the most time-consuming aspects of each case-study site's decision-making process. Comparable negotiations over

Table 6.2 Summary of Decision-Making Process

	Accepted		Rejected	
	Broward, FL	Oakland, MI	Knox, TN	Monmouth, NJ
Proposed System				
Proponent	County	County	County	County
Ownership	Vendor	County	County/City	County
Part of integrated SWM[1] system	No	Yes	Late	Yes
Proposed facility size	2–2,250 tpd[1]	2,000 tpd	900 tpd	1,700 tpd
Siting Process				
Systematic site identification	Yes	No	Yes	No
Compensation/mitigation	Very limited	Yes	Very limited	Yes
Site in an incorporated municipality	No	Yes	Yes, then No	Yes
Site in disproportionately minority area	No	Yes, then No	Yes, then No	No
Interaction Among Parties				
Past relation between county and municipalities	Average	Average to Poor	Poor	Good
Drafted ILAs with municipalities' input	Yes	Yes	N/A	N/A
State support for WTE	Yes	Yes, then No	Mixed	Yes, then No
Political agreement at county level	Yes	Not quite	Not quite	No
Consensus: county-municipalities	No	No	No	No

200

	Accepted		Rejected	
	Broward	Oakland	Knox	Monmouth
Public Participation				
Information provided to public	PR ad	Info. brochure, presentations to civic groups, Westinghouse PR ads	Forum	Forums, Westinghouse PR ads
Public involvement (other than referendum and hearings)	No	Advisory committee	Advisory committee	Advisory committee
Who decided to proceed or not	County Commission	Public referendum	City Mayor	Public referendum
Catalysts Driving Project				
State mandates for SW capacity	No	Yes	No	Yes
Financing deadlines	Yes (1984)	No	Yes (1986)	Yes (PURPA related)

[1]Acronyms: SWM—solid waste management; SW—solid waste; ILA—interlocal agreement; PR—public relations; tpd—tons per day.

costs and financial risk acceptance occurred with both municipal and vendor ownership. Facility ownership (assuming that the facility was sponsored and financed by a municipality) apparently was not a factor affecting the outcome of the decision-making process.

The size of the proposed facility relative to the size of the waste stream was a significant decision-making factor. Decisions about appropriate facility sizing include the size of the waste stream, projected changes in the amount of waste to be handled resulting from population growth or waste reduction and recycling, and economic feasibility, including capital expenditures and opportunities for vendor profit. Combined, Broward's two proposed facilities had a maximum daily throughput 100 tons greater than its average daily waste production. In contrast, though the proposed facility in Knox County had a capacity 100 tpd less than the final estimated waste stream size, waste stream estimates were sources of contention. Therefore, the proposed facility size was a source of contention. Oakland and Monmouth counties—where WTE was considered as part of integrated systems that included waste reduction, recycling, and composting—proposed WTE capacities much less than their current average daily waste production.

Decisions about facility sizing may have important implications for public acceptance of WTE because of resultant opportunities for waste importation and potential effects on other waste reduction methods, especially recycling. For example, the projected waste stream for the Monmouth facility, which diminished while facility planning was underway, resulted in 400 tpd of excess capacity. State policy required the county to use the excess capacity to process out-of-county waste. This forced regionalization was opposed by decision makers and segments of the public, alike.[11] There also was public concern about the possibility that WTE would reduce the viability of other waste reduction methods in Knox County, where facility size was based on estimated waste stream size, and Oakland County, where facility sizing accounted for recycling and other waste reduction methods. This concern suggests that the timing of WTE implementation relative to other waste reduction programs in addition to the size of the facility are factors affecting WTE decision making.

Case-study evidence suggests that merely placing WTE within the context of an integrated SWM system apparently does not affect the ultimate acceptance or rejection of WTE. Both WTE "acceptance" and "rejection" sites proposed WTE as a component of an integrated SWM system. Broward County was exceptional, however, because WTE planning largely preceded policies directing, and public knowledge of, integrated waste management systems. Planners at other case-study sites had to consider the effects of existing or planned recycling programs on proposed WTE facilities. In Knox County this consideration occurred only because of public outcry (that resulted in the establishment of limited curbside recycling and drop-off centers).

Respondents frequently suggested that the timing of waste management activities could influence the WTE decision-making process. Typically, respondents recommended implementing waste reduction, reuse, and recycling activities before WTE planning. This suggestion is amplified in recent literature about hierarchical waste management strategies for remedying the solid waste problems in America (Blumberg and Gottlieb, 1989b, pp. 203-211). Hierarchical waste strategies might have allowed a more realistic characterization of the size and nature of the waste stream to be handled by WTE and could have reduced the public apprehensions about recycling and the competition for limited quantities of waste in Knox, Monmouth, and Oakland counties. For example, in Monmouth County, where recycling is mandatory, concerns about WTE's effects on recycling were not paramount and apparently surfaced only after changes in the projected waste stream size resulted in the facility having 400 tpd of excess capacity. Therefore, it is possible that the inclusion of WTE in an integrated waste management system can affect what issues are raised in the course of WTE planning, as well as the timing and degree of concern about these issues.

6.7.1.2 Siting. Case-study comparisons showed no clear links between siting activities or site characteristics and WTE decision-making outcomes. For example, systematic site identification processes were undertaken by Broward County, where WTE was accepted, and by Knox County, where WTE was rejected. Both Oakland and Monmouth counties offered considerable financial compensation to the host communities, yet WTE was rejected at Monmouth. Whether proposed sites would be located in incorporated or unincorporated land also did not affect outcomes. Oakland and Monmouth counties have no unincorporated land. Knox County first selected a site in Knoxville. After that site was abandoned, Knox, like Broward County, intentionally selected a site on unincorporated county land.

Though siting literature suggests that a technically correct, systematic, and comparative siting process is essential to WTE facility siting (see, for example, Buhler, 1987), case studies suggest that participants can be satisfied that a proposed site is technically and environmentally suitable in the absence of multisite comparisons. For example, no multisite comparisons occurred in Monmouth County, but most participants agreed that the site chosen was environmentally and technically suitable for a WTE facility. Public and governmental acceptability of proposed sites is influenced by factors other than environmental and technical suitability. Broward, Oakland, and Knox counties' site-selection difficulties affirm literature findings that a site's political and public acceptability is equally as important as its environmental and technical acceptability (U.S. EPA, 1990c). Broward and Knox sought political acceptability by siting in unincorporated areas, while Oakland and Monmouth offered financial incentives to increase political acceptability.

Issues of environmental equity regarding the location of hazardous waste sites recently have received considerable attention (Bullard, 1990; Commission for Racial Justice, 1987; and General Accounting Office, 1983). None of the final locations proposed for WTE facilities at case-study sites were in areas where minority populations are disproportionately represented. However, the originally proposed sites of Oakland and Knox were in such areas. Oakland and Knox counties abandoned their original sites partly because of accusations that the counties were unduly burdening their minority population by proposing to site undesirable facilities in areas where relatively high proportions of minorities reside. Oakland's rationale for siting the facility at the original site was to make use of the steam at county buildings. Knox County's siting strategy emphasized a central location and easy transportation access.

6.7.1.3 Interaction Among Parties. Patterns of cooperation or mistrust that result from unrelated matters apparently affect WTE planning. In particular, patterns of mistrust tend to exacerbate dissatisfaction with the decision-making process. There are clear differences between Broward and the other case-study sites in the types of interaction that occurred and the level of agreement among participants. Broward's negotiations with its member municipalities occurred against a backdrop of generally satisfactory past relations with its municipalities and a tradition of interaction with the Broward League of Cities. In contrast, for example, Knoxville and Knox County have had a troubled relationship.

The member municipalities of each of the case-study counties participated differently in WTE planning. In Knox County, the only major city, Knoxville, became a project co-sponsor. In Monmouth, planning proceeded with very little consultation with Monmouth's municipalities. Although Broward and Oakland drafted interlocal agreements with their member municipalities, there were subtle differences in the interactive processes in the two counties. Interaction between Broward and its member municipalities occurred through the League of Cities, an organization that traditionally has represented the joint interests of Broward's municipalities. In Oakland, municipalities were represented by municipal officials and legal representatives in the drafting of interlocal agreements. These officials and representatives did not, however, represent the collective interest of all municipalities as the Broward League of Cities is mandated to do.

None of the case-study counties' member municipalities were completely supportive of the WTE project. For example, while Knoxville agreed to co-sponsor the Knox County's WTE project, the city council did not support siting the facility in the city, and ultimately the mayor withdrew his support for the project. At the other case-study sites, a small number of municipalities adamantly opposed the counties' WTE project. Oakland and Monmouth municipalities neighboring or hosting proposed WTE facilities generally opposed them. Municipalities that opposed the Broward project did not neighbor the proposed site. At least two of the municipalities that refused participation in Broward's WTE facilities have had poor relations with the county.

Unfaltering state support for WTE was clear only at the Broward County case study. In Oakland County there was a long delay in permitting because the state's permitting agency was restructured and because of a state review of mercury contamination. Changes in state support for WTE in New Jersey resulted in a temporary moratorium on incinerator planning activities and eventually forced regionalization of Monmouth's planned WTE facility. State support for Knox's WTE was likely, although the project folded before state support became apparent.

Having state-level support for WTE apparently influences WTE decisions. WTE planners and decision makers attempt to follow state guidelines for SWM whether or not such guidelines are encoded as law. As a result, state positions supporting WTE (often expressed only as goals) facilitate WTE adoption at the local level. Complete or partial withdrawal of state support for WTE slows the decision-making process when permits are delayed or moratoria are enacted. Also, the public might be swayed by the positions of state governments because it may perceive state staff to be better trained and more qualified than local government staff.

As with state support, unanimous, unfaltering support for WTE from county officials was evident only at Broward County. Elsewhere, some officials staunchly supported their respective WTE projects, while others called for reassessments of need, examinations of alternatives, and termination of the WTE projects. Having constant and unanimous support from county officials significantly influences the decision-making outcome by making facility acceptance more likely. There are several likely reasons why political support existed in Broward. Unlike the other case-study sites, Broward experienced very little turnover in key decision makers, i.e., county commissioners, during WTE planning and implementation. Because Broward's commissioners enjoyed some stability once elected, they might have thought that political liability resulting from decisions about WTE would have minimal effect on their political careers. Low turnover rates also provided continuity among the decision makers and prevented project planning from slowing because of the time new decision makers require to review past events and decisions. In contrast, the new mayor who took office in Knoxville during WTE planning altered the decision-making process and eventually withdrew from the Knox County project.

Perceptions of need for waste management capacity also might have contributed to agreement among Broward County commissioners. Closure of the county landfill (and projections of continuing population growth) might have made Broward's decision makers and the public perceive a dire need for a WTE facility. At the other sites where the public perceived no such urgency, they prompted decision makers to delay action.

Decisions about proceeding with WTE implementation were made by public referendum in Oakland and Monmouth counties, and by government officials in Broward and Knox counties. Although the decision-making process varied, the case-study sites demonstrate no tendency toward WTE acceptance or rejection based upon who makes the decision. It is likely, however, that decisions made by public referendum are generally more acceptable to the public than those made in other ways. A decision-making process that includes a public referendum is vastly different from one that does not primarily because it allows direct public participation. Another difference is that a referendum spawns massive campaigns in favor of and against WTE.

6.7.1.4 *Public Participation.* Although public information activities at the case-study sites were limited and occurred late in the decision-making process, case-study respondents uniformly agreed that the public must be informed about SWM issues and activities early in the planning process. There were, however, few recommendations about how this education process might occur or who should be responsible, suggesting that case-study decision makers are unsure about how public information programs should be implemented.

Similarly, there were strong, though not unanimous, recommendations for improving the decision-making process by involving the public in that process, but few concrete suggestions about how this involvement might be accomplished. Decision makers' knowledge of guidelines for WTE implementation (e.g., guidelines on permitting and contract negotiation published by U.S. EPA, 1979) may not have extended to guidelines for public participation that were available (e.g., suggestions provided by the Institute for Participatory Planning, 1981). Sources easily accessible to local decision makers became available only after years of WTE planning had occurred at the case-study sites (U.S. EPA, 1990c). (See Syme and Eaton, 1989, for a review of public participation literature.) This lack of familiarity may, in part, account for the lack of public involvement programs at the case-study sites.

Facilitating public participation in the decision-making process may not produce uniform decisions to adopt WTE, a point acknowledged by all respondents. However, dissatisfaction with decision making that generally excludes or makes public participation difficult exacerbates opposition to the decision. For instance, opposition to the Knox County project solidified partly because opponents perceived that early planning activities had been conducted in an almost clandestine manner and because they had trouble obtaining documentation about the proposed WTE facility. Employing a decision-making process acceptable to all parties might also make the outcome of such a process acceptable.

6.7.1.5 *Catalysts Driving the Project.* Regulations concerning SWM activities or project financing spurred project activities at each case study. For example, state mandates in Michigan and New Jersey required counties to plan or provide SWM capacity for a specified number of years. In the case of Oakland County these state regulations mandated unprecedented levels of county involvement in SWM. State mandates for county-level SWM planning did not affect activities in Broward and Knox counties.

Project financing and revenues regulations influenced the WTE decision-making process by establishing deadlines for the completion of certain activities if favorable financing or revenue arrangements were to be made. For example, both Broward and Knox counties hastily issued bonds to take advantage of their soon-to-expire, tax-exempt status. Monmouth County rushed to execute a power sales agreement before state reinterpretation of PURPA would significantly reduce revenue available from power sales.

6.7.2 Decision-Making Context

6.7.2.1 Waste Management. Ongoing and past SWM activities at the four case-study sites were reviewed to determine their effects on WTE decision making. The size of each county's waste stream reflects its population and economic activities, e.g., tourism or industry. Accordingly, Broward's waste stream is largest, and Knox's is smallest. On a per capita basis, however, Monmouth is the largest generator of waste. As a decision-making factor, waste stream size is important relative to the size of the proposed WTE facility (see Section 6.7.1.1).

Each of the case-study sites has hosted landfills and dumps in the past, but only Knox County no longer has an operating landfill within its bounds. At each of the sites, older landfills were closed because they could not meet more stringent state and federal regulation governing them and because retrofits were not economically feasible. Broward and Oakland are hosts to closed landfills listed as Superfund sites.

Municipally owned solid waste incinerators have operated in Broward and Oakland counties but were closed in the late 1970s and 1980s, respectively, because of failure to meet emissions standards. Neither Knox nor Monmouth has hosted municipal solid waste incinerators.

Solid waste exportation occurs and is restricted variously among the case studies. Shortly before WTE planning began in Broward, the county that had been importing Broward's waste prohibited waste importation but did not actively enforce its regulations. In Oakland, intercounty waste exportation is restricted by county SWM plans that require agreement between the importing and exporting counties. Current New Jersey policy encourages regionalization of waste facilities, and out-of-county and out-of-state waste exportation is allowed with NJDEP approval. However, Monmouth County historically has managed its solid waste without exportation. Tennessee does not restrict intercounty waste exportation, and after the privately owned Knox County landfill closed, all solid waste was exported to a privately owned landfill in a neighboring county.

The general SWM experience of sites where WTE has been accepted differs from that where WTE was rejected. It may be that, alone, none of the contextual factors at sites where WTE was accepted—contaminated land-fills, experience with incinerators, and limited opportunities for waste ex-portation—are significant enough to affect WTE decisions. In concert, however, the occurrence of these factors at case-study sites where WTE has been accepted suggests that such experience positively influences acceptance of WTE.

6.7.2.2 Key Demographic Variables. Demographic characteristics that vary among case-study sites are the age and growth of resident populations. Broward is distinguished from the remaining case-study sites because per-sons aged 55 and older represent over one-third of the population. At the other case-study sites, this cohort represents only between one-fifth and one-quarter of the population. It is uncertain what effect an elderly population has on WTE decision making, but it is likely that differing expectations among various age cohorts about participating in decision making and about the environment and environmental technology influence public accepta-bility of WTE. Other researchers have suggested that environmentalism is a concern primarily of the affluent young who also reject traditional au-thority in favor of participatory decision making (Milbrath, 1984; Jones and Dunlap, 1992).

Population growth in Broward County during the last decade (1980 to 1990) was 23 percent, more than double the growth at the other case-study sites and more than twice the U.S. average (U.S. Bureau of the Census, 1988b, 1992). Population growth projected for the period 1990 to 2010 is 35 percent compared to 20 percent at Monmouth, the case-study site with the second highest projected growth rate (Terleckyj and Coleman, 1990). Population growth trends probably contribute to perceptions of an imme-diate need for SWM capacity.[12] Because of past and projected rapid pop-ulation growth in Broward, the urgent need for additional SWM capacity was not a matter of disagreement between project proponents and oppo-nents as it was elsewhere.

6.7.3 Issues

During WTE planning, numerous issues were raised by WTE planners and other players for consideration by WTE decision makers, representatives of associated municipalities, non-governmental organizations, and the pub-lic. Whether these issues were addressed to the satisfaction of participants affects both the decision-making process and its outcomes. For example, members of the public who perceive that their concerns about potential adverse health effects have not been addressed adequately are unlikely to support WTE in a public referendum. This situation is outcome-related. The ways in which public concerns are addressed, for instance by modifying the decision-making process to include mitigation measures, is process-related.

The issues raised at each case-study site were similar, and most were a source of disagreement between WTE proponents and opponents. Such disagreement was the product of lack of information, mistrust of available information or the sources of information, and conflicting viewpoints held by credible organizations. Issues at the case-study sites included those related to waste management, health and the environment, finance, and process itself. These issues are listed below.

Waste Management Issues
- Immediacy of the need for SWM capacity
- Need to reduce reliance on landfills
- WTE's effects on recycling and other waste reduction programs

Health and Environmental Issues
- Impacts of WTE relative to other waste management options (e.g., landfilling and composting)
- Potential adverse human health effects
- Potential adverse environmental effects of emissions (e.g., to water and wildlife)

Financial Issues
- Projected waste disposal costs
- Property value depreciation

Processual Issue
- Access to formal decision-making process

One issue on which most participants at each case-study site agreed was the need to reduce reliance on landfills. This issue is related to participants' perceptions that landfills have significant potential for adverse health and environmental effects and that alternatives such as recycling are more environmentally benign waste management options than landfilling. During WTE planning, participants at each case-study site, with the exception of Broward County, disagreed about the potential impacts of WTE on the viability of recycling and other waste reduction programs. At Monmouth this disagreement became an issue of contention because of the excess 400 tpd of capacity. (This issue arose at Broward County after facility construction was underway.)

The immediacy of the need for additional waste management capacity contributed to the WTE decision-making context (see Section 6.7.2) and also contributed to WTE decision-making outcomes. Agreement among participants about the dire need for SWM capacity significantly influenced Broward County's adoption. Participants elsewhere, particularly in Oakland

and Knox counties, opposed WTE because they did not see an urgent short-term need for SWM capacity; they thought that a critical need would not occur for several years.

Respondents who participated in formalized WTE planning and decision making generally identified waste management issues as the most critical issues in WTE decision-making, particularly the need for SWM capacity and to reduce reliance on landfills. In contrast, WTE opponents at each of the case-study sites tended to identify health and environmental impacts and waste disposal costs as the most important issues.

WTE project opponents and proponents at all four case-study sites disagreed about each of the health and environmental issues previously listed. In each case opponents perceived the health and environmental risks of WTE to be unacceptable, even though project proponents, using detailed health and environmental risk assessments, characterized them as negligible or minor. Communicating the results of scientifically based risk assessments is difficult (Konheim, 1989; Luderer, 1990), particularly in the absence of a trusting relationship between the public and an individual responsible for the risk assessment. Where trust is lacking, the counterappeals of WTE opponents can effectively sway public opinion (Konheim, 1989). This situation occurred in Monmouth County where the public trusted better an organization of local medical professionals who opposed WTE than they did an unfamiliar, non-local scientist leading the health risk assessment committee. Although the process of addressing health and environmental issues may affect some aspects of decision making, the issues have their greatest influence on the outcome of decision making.

Two unrelated financial issues arose at the case-study sites. The first was how WTE project costs would affect waste disposal costs, and how, in turn, waste disposal costs would affect municipal tax rates or citizens' costs for waste disposal services. Projected tipping fees at the case-study sites often were revised because of changes in estimates of project revenues or upward revisions of project costs. The consequence was concern among municipal officials and the public about uncontrollable project costs necessitating additional taxes or increased disposal fees.

The second financial issue, unrelated to project costs, was the adverse impact that WTE facilities might have on the value of neighboring properties. Many respondents who were proponents of WTE asserted that residents' fear of decreasing property values was the underlying cause for opposition to WTE. However, opposition to the case-study WTE facilities, with the possible exception of Knox County, was broad enough to suggest that other concerns, particularly health and financial issues, were predominant.

The final issue relates to the conduct of the formal decision-making process, that is, the set of formalized procedures that lead to a decision about WTE. In general, representatives of groups and municipalities at the case-study sites perceived that they had insufficient access to early stages of the formal decision-making process. In contrast, many of the respondents actually involved in the formalized decision-making process perceived that meetings and hearings provided the public ample access to the formalized decision-making process. Public referenda at two sites and the introduction of a new, key decision-maker at the third site provided greater public access to the final stages of the decision-making process than was afforded early on at these three sites.

6.8 SUMMARY AND FUTURE OUTLOOK

This chapter has examined the decision-making contexts, processes, and outcomes at four case-study sites to determine what factors have influenced WTE decision making. Key factors have been identified by comparing their occurrence at the case-study sites, by considering respondents' recommendations, and by examining relevant literature.

These factors can influence either the decision-making process, its outcome, or both. Process and outcome are not mutually exclusive aspects of decision making. For example, the inextricable link between how a decision is made and what decision is made suggests that any factor related to the decision-making process may in turn affect the outcome. The following is a list of key decision-making factors categorized according to whether they most significantly affect the decision-making process or the decision-making outcome.

Key Decision-Making Factors: Process
- Provisions for public information
- Provisions for and the type of public involvement
- Municipalities' involvement
- Planning WTE as a component of an integrated SWM system

Key Decision-Making Factors: Outcome
- Perceptions of urgent need for facility
- State's support for WTE
- Public support for WTE
- Elected officials' support for WTE
- Concern about environmental and health risks
- Concern about increased solid waste disposal costs

Factors within categories, particularly the outcome-related factors, are uniquely intertwined. For example, concern about environmental and health effects contributes to state, public, and elected officials' support for WTE; public support for WTE contributes to elected officials' support for WTE;

and state support for WTE contributes to public and elected officials' support.

The limited number of case studies allows only tentative estimates of trends that might occur in WTE decision-making processes during the next several years. One likely change is that decisions about WTE increasingly will be made only in the context of integrated (or partly integrated) SWM systems. Voluntary or mandatory recycling programs, waste separation programs, vegetative composting, and other waste reduction programs are already operating in many municipalities and their relationship to WTE will have to be considered during WTE planning. Further, the popularity of recycling programs relative to WTE likely will demand that the former be implemented before the latter is planned.

Another probable trend is that WTE decision-making processes increasingly will include public information and public involvement programs from their inception. The case studies present only limited evidence of this trend; the WTE programs introduced in the mid–1980s offered more public information and opportunities for public involvement than the program introduced in the early 1980s. In addition, increased public concern about solid waste issues and public demands for participatory decision-making may encourage this trend. Also, during the late 1980s updated and easily accessible SWM guides became available to local decision makers (U.S. EPA, 1989, 1990c). These guides include recommendations about public information and involvement programs and emphasize that such programs should be fundamental elements of all SWM programs. Last, at both sites where WTE proposals were rejected, the SWM planning activities that ensued have included broad-based citizen participation. Although neither site has reconsidered WTE, each has developed a new strategy for SWM planning that includes increased public participation.

Based on the occurrence and intensity of public opposition at the case-study sites and anti-incineration stances of prominent national medical and environmental associations, it is likely that considerable public opposition to WTE proposals will continue. This opposition may be mitigated by changes in the decision-making processes, such as those discussed above, that will make the process, and thus the outcome of the process, more publicly acceptable.

NOTES

1. See Chapter 2 for a detailed discussion of environmental issues.

2. Representatives of Broward County Commission declined interviews with the researchers, although one commissioner performed a cursory review of the case study. Information about the opinions and activities of county commissioners was obtained from publicly available materials (reports, minutes, news articles) and through other participants in the research.

3. WMI submitted two proposals to Broward County for WTE facilities. One proposal met the county's specifications for size. The other proposal was for a larger facility to be sited on WMI's landfill site in northern Broward County. That WMI already had broached the topic of using its property to site the WTE facility likely led to these negotiations with the county after Pompano Beach's actions.

4. In fact, by mid–1992 Broward County staff determined that the county was delivering waste at a rate that would result in a 138,500 ton shortfall and a $7.5 million penalty by year's end. WMI was importing waste from Dade and Monroe counties charging as little as $35 per ton compared to the $62.50 per ton tipping fee for Broward's waste. To avoid a year-end penalty, Broward negotiated a deal with Dade County wherein Dade would send a minimum of 350,000 tons per year for the next 10 years. Tipping fees would be $42.50 during the first year, $50 during the second, and equal to Broward's for the remaining years. Largely because of Hurricane Andrew–generated waste, the county's 1992 put-or-pay fine was approximately $1 million and the Dade County deal was not executed.

5. Oakland County was selected as a case-study site prior to Westinghouse's withdrawal. Research about Oakland County proceeded because the county met the researchers' definition of WTE approved site: a formalized decision to proceed with WTE had been made. After Westinghouse's withdrawal, Oakland County reexamined its options ranging from completely withdrawing from SWM planning to pursuing the WTE component of its plan with Ogden Martin Systems, the runner-up bidder in the original vendor selection process. In August 1992, county staff, with Ogden Martin's knowledge and cooperation, drafted a memorandum of understanding by which Ogden Martin would become the county's WTE vendor. With the election approaching, the county commission took no action on the memorandum of understanding. In early 1993, the commission began to reexamine the SWM issue.

6. Restrictions on importing wastes across state lines were struck down in the U.S. Supreme Court in 1992. The applicability of this ruling to cross-county transport is undetermined.

7. The county has since won the lawsuit on appeal.

8. Subsequently, another public relations firm was hired with the approval of the commission.

9. The Monmouth County Reclamation Center—named such because when it opened ferrous materials were removed from the waste stream—frequently is called the Tinton Falls Reclamation Center and the Tinton Falls landfill.

10. Representatives of groups opposing the project declined opportunities to participate in this research. Consequently, information about the groups, their activities, and their opinions is derived from publicly available materials (including reports, fliers, and other documents they produced) and from other participants in the research.

11. It is possible that, regardless of facility size, Monmouth's WTE plant would have been required by state policy to accept some out-of-county waste.

12. Recall that this study's aggregate analysis concluded that there is no significant difference between counties that have considered and not considered WTE on the basis of population growth. See Chapter 4.

Chapter 7

The Socioeconomics of Waste-to-Energy: Conclusions

7.1 THE MOTIVATION FOR THIS STUDY

Municipal solid waste (MSW) incineration was adopted by many U.S. communities during the 1980s to manage their growing quantities of MSW. Although less than 1 percent of all U.S. MSW was burned to retrieve its heat energy in 1970, WTE grew to account for 16 percent of MSW in 1990, and many experts forecasted that WTE would be used to manage as much as half of all U.S. garbage by the turn of the century.

Those forecasts now are challenged by recent WTE project cancellations, and the long-run viability of WTE is in question. A total of 248 WTE projects in various stages of planning were canceled during the 1982 to 1990 time frame. Only 8 projects were scratched between 1982 and 1984, while 207 were abandoned between 1986 and 1990. To put these cancellations in perspective, consider that there were only 140 operational U.S. facilities in 1990 and that the total WTE capacity that was abandoned between 1986 and 1990 exceeded the total operational WTE capacity in 1990.

Why have these cancellations occurred, and what, if anything, do they tell us about the long-run viability of WTE in the United States? This study has taken an in-depth look at these questions by addressing numerous socioeconomic factors that have played a role in the decisions of communities that have considered WTE as a component of their solid waste management (SWM) strategies. More specifically, a three-pronged approach was adopted to investigate (1) the relationships between key socioeconomic characteristics and a municipality's decision to consider and accept or reject WTE, (2) the potential impacts of recent changes in financial markets on the viability of WTE, and (3) the WTE decision-making process and the socioeconomic parameters that are most important in the municipality's decision.

The first two objectives were met by the collection and analysis of aggregate data on all U.S. WTE initiatives between 1982 to 1990. The latter objective was met by way of four in-depth case studies—two directed at communities that have accepted WTE and two that have canceled WTE projects. In addition, this study has presented background information on the current status of WTE in the United States, the structure of the WTE industry, and the potential for energy production from WTE. Also presented was a discussion of why WTE has become so controversial, including background information on environmental and health issues, regulatory uncertainties, and uncertainties about alternatives to WTE.

This final chapter summarizes the major findings of this work, both in terms of why WTE facilities have been adopted or canceled and in terms of the outlook for WTE in the coming decades.

7.2 WHY IS WASTE-TO-ENERGY SO CONTROVERSIAL?

WTE controversies tend to cluster around three major issues about which there is much disagreement. First is the issue of potential environmental and health consequences of WTE. Second, regulations that affect WTE are changing or are expected to change in the near future. Third, the costs and availabilities of alternatives to WTE are changing, which makes the relative viability of WTE difficult to assess.

No attempt has been made in this work to confirm or refute the various arguments about the potential health and environmental effects of WTE. The main arguments and concerns have, however, been summarized with the intent of understanding the issues that regularly come into play when considering WTE. Three main environmental/health questions persist: (1) the implications of atmospheric emissions—particularly from furans, dioxins, and heavy metals; (2) appropriate ash management—focusing on whether incinerator ash can be managed along with other municipal waste in municipal waste landfills, or if ash requires a more protective and expensive monofill; and (3) the environmental consequences of alternatives to WTE—landfilling, composting, recycling, and source reduction.

Studies suggest that the severity of the environmental and health problems associated with WTE is, to a great extent, a matter of perspective. Numerous studies have been cited that suggest that the environmental and health risks are small if available technology is used and operated correctly. When viewed in relation to other sources of emissions, these studies suggest that threats posed by WTE are relatively minor. The public and some environmental and health organizations, nonetheless, view the environmental and health risks as severe; and some scientists agree that under some circumstances the problems can be serious. A lack of sufficient operator training and facility operation under conditions that do not conform to specification requirements have been of concern to many WTE opponents.

While WTE has been the focus of much attention, it is interesting to note that the environmental and health effects of alternatives, especially recycling and composting, have received much less attention. Recycling and composting now are coming under increased scrutiny, and some scientists speculate that these alternatives to landfilling and WTE are not as environmentally benign as the public reaction suggests. Composting, for example, is viewed by some as being equally or more damaging than WTE because potentially hazardous materials are made "bioavailable" without sufficient follow-on controls. Possibly most important in the controversy about health and environmental risks are, however, a fundamental public mistrust of some sources of information about WTE, uncertainty about available information, and a concern that health and environmental risks, however small, will be borne inequitably.

Another source of controversy is a very uncertain regulatory environment. In the environmental and health areas, the current controversy over the Resource Conservation and Recovery Act (RCRA) (which may change requirements for ash disposal and alter the "playing field" with respect to WTE and alternatives) and the Clean Air Act Amendments (CAAA) (which will require updated U.S. Environmental Protection Agency [U.S. EPA] rules for municipal waste combustors) are most important. Although the U.S. EPA recently issued a statement that incinerator ash is not a hazardous waste, the coming RCRA debate in the Congress and pending litigation in the U.S. Supreme Court suggest that the controversy about ash disposal is far from over. In addition to persisting environmental uncertainties about the leachability of incinerator ash, ash disposal is also important from an economic perspective in that disposal as a hazardous waste is an order of magnitude more expensive than disposal in conventional MSW landfills. Although it is unlikely that the federal government will require ash to be disposed of in RCRA Subtitle C hazardous waste landfills, it is quite possible that less restrictive ash monofills will be mandated—with uncertain cost implications. In the absence of clear federal rules on ash disposal, several states have already required special ash monofills.

The CAAA also will impose a greater financial burden on WTE in that facilities soon will be required to meet rules based on Maximum Achievable Control Technology (MACT) as compared to the less-strict, recently issued emission rules based on Best Demonstrated Technology (BDT). The WTE industry claims that likely new standards can be met, but the implications for costs remain uncertain.

Added to the uncertainties posed by environmental regulations are financial uncertainties and burdens derived from the Tax Reform Act of 1986 (TRA86) (which, among other things, limits federally tax-exempt financing for WTE and other local projects) and the Public Utility Regulatory Policies Act (PURPA) (which presents uncertainties about how much a WTE operator will be paid for power produced). Additional uncertainties are derived from the host of legislative initiatives at the federal and state levels to promote alternatives to WTE and uncertainty about which level of government ultimately will define the "rules of the game." In short, regulatory and legislative uncertainties make the selection of WTE—or the selection of most alternative technologies or approaches to waste management—particularly risky at this time.

A third set of issues that make WTE controversial concern the costs and availabilities of alternatives to WTE. Although landfill numbers have declined in recent years, current and future landfill capacity is more uncertain. Small landfills are being replaced by larger facilities that take advantage of economies of scale, particularly important when meeting the new and more environmentally restrictive U.S. EPA rules for landfill operation. Landfill costs are expected to escalate as a result of these new rules, but there is uncertainty about how much.

The future availabilities and costs of recycling and composting also have been questioned. Although many communities and states have adopted goals of recycling, composting, and source reducing 25 to 50 percent of their waste streams, some experts question if these goals can be met. Questions persist about which materials should be collected for recycling, which recycling technology is least costly, and which approach elicits the highest participation rate. In many less populated areas, meeting these ambitious recycling goals will be difficult and may carry a cost that is much higher than either landfilling or WTE. And although the public has expressed a willingness to pay more for recycling and composting, the local decision maker must decide on an appropriate premium. Ultimately, communities are likely to find that while recycling is a crucial component of their integrated approach to waste management, it is, in fact, only one component. Landfilling and/or waste incineration will be necessary, at minimum, to supplement recycling, composting, and source-reduction efforts. In the foreseeable future, the question for communities will not be whether landfilling and/or WTE are needed, but rather the extent of the roles these conventional management approaches will play in their integrated waste systems.

WTE is controversial and poses risks for the local decision maker. Nonetheless, municipal waste management remains, for the most part, the responsibility of local government. Local decision makers ultimately must select from an extremely complicated set of MSW choices, the current and future pros and cons of which often are unknown and increasingly out of their control.

7.3 AN OVERVIEW OF WTE IN THE UNITED STATES

This study has presented numerous statistics about the size and composition of WTE in the United States. The study also traces how key parameters have changed over time, e.g., the size of facilities, types of WTE technologies used, and geographical locations of facilities. As previously stated, WTE is a relatively new technology in the United States, with only two of the current facilities beginning operations in the 1960s and 114 starting during the 1980s. The South has the largest number of existing facilities, while the majority of advanced-planned facilities are located in the Northeast.

The WTE industry structure has also been discussed. In 1990 there were less than 10 full-service WTE companies in the United States, although numerous additional companies were involved in one or more WTE projects during the 1980s. Many factors have contributed to the decline in the number of firms, including the generally depressed nature of the WTE market in recent years and increasing barriers to market entry. Long lead times are required to negotiate a contract, obtain funding, and site a facility, thus limiting the industry to large diversified firms that can wait many years for payoffs. Perceived technical, environmental, and financial risks associated with WTE also encourage communities to contract with large established companies. In addition, many communities now require an integrated waste management system—including waste collection, recycling and composting programs, and ash disposal—that often can be provided at lower cost by large, vertically integrated firms. The four largest firms in the industry have accounted for 51 percent of all capacity constructed in the United States (in terms of tons per day). Using the same measure, the top four firms account for about 65 percent of all WTE facilities being constructed or in the advanced stages of planning. WTE firms recently have come under attack for their failure to elicit support for their technologies from all segments of host communities. The WTE industry's defensive posture with respect to environmental and other opposition groups has been recognized within their industry and by outside observers as hindering the overall decision-making process.

One of the main arguments in support of WTE is the replacement of conventional forms of energy. This study has presented estimates and projections of energy production from WTE in recent years and the coming two decades. Base, high, and low scenarios were derived from estimates and projections about the quantity of MSW produced, the average Btu value of MSW, and the percentage of MSW managed by WTE. WTE is estimated to have produced about 0.3 quads of total energy in 1990 and is projected in the base case to produce 0.6 quads and 1.2 quads of energy in the years 2000 and 2010, respectively. The high-case scenario places WTE energy output at 0.8 quads in 2000 and 1.8 quads in 2010. WTE results in 0.5 quads and 0.7 quads in the same years in the low-case scenario. The base-case scenario suggests that WTE will account for only about 0.6 percent of total U.S. energy consumption in 2000 and about 1.1 percent in 2010. However, viewed in terms of energy consumed in the generation of electricity, the numbers appear more significant. For example, only about 1.25 quads of petroleum and 2.87 quads of natural gas were used for electricity generation in 1990. Given that all WTE facilities in the advanced-planning stage will generate electricity exclusively or cogenerate electricity with steam, WTE could become a major player in the electric power sector.

7.4 THE SOCIOECONOMICS OF WTE FROM AN AGGREGATE PERSPECTIVE

Chapter 4 of this study presented the results of intensive data collection and analysis of information about each existing, planned, and canceled WTE project. Numerous potential relationships between decisions about WTE and socioeconomic characteristics were examined.

This work has identified 354 counties that have had WTE initiatives during the 1982 to 1990 period. Almost 71 percent of all WTE initiative counties were in metropolitan areas. Interest in WTE does not appear to be solely a metro-oriented activity, however. While 35 percent of metro counties have had a WTE initiative, only 4 percent of non-metro counties were involved with WTE. Nonetheless, because of the large number of non-metro initiatives, this 4 percent still gives rise to a sizable number of non-metro counties (102) with WTE initiatives. In 1990, there were almost two-and-a-half times as many metro counties (80) as compared to non-metro counties (33) with operating facilities. The study finds that relatively more metro counties (54 percent) have scratched WTE initiatives than non-metro counties (47 percent).

The study concludes that non-metro counties have scratched relatively more facilities than metro counties—42 percent of all initiatives in non-metro counties and 37 percent in metro counties. Relative to counties without WTE initiatives, counties with WTE initiatives generally are wealthier, more educated (i.e., percent completing high school), less blue-collar (i.e., percent of workers in manufacturing, mining, and construction), less rural (i.e., percent of population in a rural environment), and have a higher percentage of individuals in what is called the "family formation" stage (i.e., 22 to 39 years old). Counties that have WTE initiatives are more likely to have access to existing recycling programs and material recovery facilities (MRFs) than counties with no WTE initiative. There is no identifiable relationship between the availability of landfills (measured in terms of number of landfills per capita) and the decision to consider WTE. Surprisingly, there is no significant difference between WTE and non-WTE counties in terms of population growth. As compared to counties with no WTE initiatives, counties that have WTE initiatives face significantly higher costs for municipal waste disposal; they typically have a larger percentage of citizens that belong to environmental groups; and they are more likely to be out of attainment with respect to one or more U.S. EPA atmospheric criteria pollutants. Communities in states with strong environmental regulations and incentives and goals for recycling are also more likely to have considered

WTE than other communities. Communities that have considered WTE facilities have average populations of about 522,000; populations in communities that have not had WTE initiatives average 129,000. Metropolitan counties that have actively considered WTE tend to have larger and less rural populations than counties that have not considered WTE. The study finds that these same conclusions generally are true for WTE initiatives in non-metropolitan counties.

Therefore, the results of the aggregate analysis suggest a variety of differences between counties that have formally considered WTE initiatives and those counties that have not. Possibly much more important, however, is the finding that there are virtually no aggregate socioeconomic differences between counties with existing WTE facilities and counties that have canceled WTE projects. In other words, when only those counties that have had WTE initiatives are considered, there are no significant differences between communities that see those initiatives through to completion and those communities that cancel their projects at some point in the planning process. If particular socioeconomic factors have contributed to the cancellations of WTE projects during recent years, they are factors other than those considered in this segment of our study.

7.5 A FOCUS ON FINANCIAL ISSUES

Chapter 5 of this work focused specifically on the financial trends during the 1980s and early 1990s that may have contributed to WTE project cancellation and altered the relative attractiveness of waste incineration. Three major trends were assessed. First was the rapidly escalating costs of WTE facilities, primarily in response to requirements for increasingly sophisticated environmental controls and the movement toward large mass-burn facilities. Second, federal tax policy took a major turn in 1986 with the enactment of the Tax Reform Act (TRA86), which placed limits on the local government's ability to finance WTE and other projects with federal tax-exempt financing. Third, increasing demands for other environmental infrastructure, local and state tax and expenditure limitations, and difficulties in accessing national capital markets hindered some financial packages.

Chapter 5 also presented a discussion of the various financial instruments that have been or could be used to finance WTE facilities. These instruments are placed in three categories: (1) traditional debt, which includes general-obligation bonds, tax-exempt revenue bonds, and taxable revenue bonds; (2) state and federal grant programs; and (3) innovative market approaches, including third-party credit enhancements, letters of credit, leasing arrangements, and variable-rate municipal debt.

Data collected for this study show that the cost of WTE facilities has increased sharply. When adjusted for inflation, the capital costs of existing and advanced-planned facilities increased from an average of $43.8 million in 1982 to $52.4 million in 1990. More revealing, the mean adjusted cost of advanced-planned facilities increased by 40.6 percent between 1982 and 1990, from $62.1 million to $87.3 million.

During the same time frame, the federal government imposed new restrictions on the types of local debt that could qualify for federal tax-exempt status and placed unified volume caps on each state's allotment of tax-exempt private-activity bonds. To qualify as tax-exempt bonds under TRA86, the bonds must be classified as (1) governmental bonds (on which there are no limits), or (2) private-activity bonds that also are "qualified bonds" for solid and hazardous waste facilities (which are subject to unified volume caps). Governmental bonds are problematic in that the municipality must retain an almost proprietary interest in the facility, forego its share of the tax benefits, and observe the restrictions on private use of facilities imposed by TRA86. Furthermore, to be classified as "qualified bonds," tax-exempt bonds must meet a host of restrictions. To the extent that tax-exempt bonds cannot be used to finance WTE facilities, the total cost of project financing will be higher.

The higher cost of facilities and restrictions on tax-exempt financing have come at a time local governments face other environmental expenditures. For example, it is projected that by the year 2000 municipalities will need to issue about $18.8 billion in municipal bonds for wastewater, drinking water, and solid waste projects, or approximately double the level of bonds issued for these facilities in the 1980s. Although capital markets can accommodate this increased demand, large capital-intensive environmental projects can crowd out other local investments due to the "lumpy" expenditure stream of these facilities. The extremely large capital outlays required for some WTE facilities may force some communities to make hard decisions about where they allocate their limited credit lines. Communities may be forced to make trade-offs between funding environmental infrastructure and more traditional activities, such as housing and education.

Although financial problems exist, this study finds that, in general, municipalities are successfully adjusting to altered financial conditions by taking a four-pronged approach to finance WTE projects. First, local jurisdictions are using a combination of several financing mechanisms in their financial packages. Second, jurisdictions are increasingly using local-sector resources for financing (e.g., city and county revenues and taxable revenue bonds). Third, as traditional debt options become less viable because of restrictions imposed by legislation, such as TRA86, innovative and new methods of finance are being used. Fourth, private-sector participation is being used more extensively. Private-sector participation allows local-sector resources to be reallocated elsewhere for other public good consumption.

In terms of the impacts of financial changes on WTE project cancellations, the results are somewhat mixed. Study findings show that most successful

WTE projects utilize multiple and innovative forms of finance. Surprisingly, innovative methods of finance, which are designed primarily to lower the community's level of financial risk, were not present in any of the financial packages put together or considered for facilities that eventually were canceled. It is unclear, however, if the absence of multiple and innovative financing mechanisms was a contributor to the failure of the projects, or if these projects simply did not get far enough down the development path to consider these innovative and possibly less obvious financing strategies. To the extent that public opposition arose to the WTE project on the basis of increased financial risk to the community, the absence of innovative approaches may have played a role in project cancellation. An analysis of the available data shows that a large share of the proposed financing for abandoned projects was to be public financing.

Unified volume caps may have hindered WTE project development, but the magnitude of the problems those caps imposed is not clear. For example, six of the nine states that contributed more than 49 percent of all WTE project cancellations came close to fully using their caps; and more than $750 million in solid-waste financing requests were denied in 1991 as a result of the unified volume caps. However, some states that had several cancellations did not use a high percentage of their allowed caps.

There is little doubt that the restrictions imposed by TRA86 played a significant role in escalating the rate at which WTE projects were introduced in the mid- to latter 1980s. Some projects that might have developed at a more leisurely pace were no doubt "moved along" to avoid the impending financing restrictions of TRA86. If TRA86, in fact, resulted in a surge in the number of WTE projects being considered in the mid- to latter 1980s, a follow-on argument is that the number of cancellations also increased even if the probability of a project making it through to operation remained unchanged. Further, to the extent that projects were hurried in their development, a case can be made that some projects met cancellation because they were simply "pushed too fast." In this case, changes in financial markets may have contributed indirectly to some WTE project cancellations.

The fundamentals of the long-term bond market are generally positive over the next decade, and, therefore, capital markets should show little strain in funding future expenditures for local environmental projects, such as WTE. The question is whether local jurisdictions will have the financial ability and, in some cases, the political will to take on higher levels of debt burden. Large, capital-intensive WTE facilities can crowd out other local investments, and some small communities may face obstacles in accessing capital markets.

On the positive side, innovative financial instruments increasingly are available that overcome to some extent the financial obstacles imposed during the 1980s. Adjustments on the parts of capital markets and communities to new financial realities are likely to improve the financial viability of capital-intensive projects, such as WTE facilities. Although financing constraints will continue to be problematic, especially for those communities with questionable credit ratings, financial constraints are not expected to be a "show-stopper" as the overall viability of WTE is determined in the 1990s.

7.6 A FOCUS ON THE DECISION-MAKING PROCESS: CASE-STUDY RESULTS

Our aggregate analyses of socioeconomic and financial conditions do not draw strong conclusions about differences between communities that begin a WTE project and follow that project through to completion and communities that abandon a project somewhere in the planning process. Socioeconomic parameters do not differ markedly between the two groups. And, while certain financial trends do seem to be partially responsible for the increased rate of project abandonment in the late 1980s, financial constraints do not appear to be the primary force motivating project cancellations. The major challenge faced by proponents, as well as opponents, of WTE may be negotiating the "treacherous waters" of the decision-making process itself.

To better understand the process by which communities make decisions about WTE and identify factors that may contribute to project cancellation, this study undertook four detailed case studies. At two sites—Oakland County, Michigan, and Broward County, Florida—a WTE project was approved, and in the case of Broward County two WTE facilities now are operational. At the two other sites—Monmouth County, New Jersey, and Knox County, Tennessee—planned WTE facilities were canceled. Questions of particular interest in the case studies included the sequence of decision events; the participation of different groups in different steps of the decision process; the degree of agreement at each decision step; the effects of mitigation and compensation at different stages of implementation; the effectiveness of different siting procedures; public attitudes about WTE technologies, costs, environmental impacts, and the decision-making process; and any difficulties that may arise when several governmental jurisdictions are forced to cooperate or form compacts to site a facility. Chapter 6 of this study provided a detailed discussion of the case studies and their results.

Several general findings result from the case studies. The decision to accept or reject a project tends not to fall neatly into simple "acceptance" or "rejection" categories. There are degrees of acceptance and rejection. At one extreme is Broward County, where WTE clearly was accepted and two facilities now are operational. Oakland County's mandate to proceed with WTE implementation is less clear. Although a public referendum narrowly approved WTE use, municipalities have failed to sign intergovernmental agreements committing their waste to the county's system. Further, the county currently has no construction and service vendor due to the recent withdrawal of Westinghouse. Monmouth and Knox counties rejected WTE, but at different stages and in different ways. In Monmouth County, voters rejected a WTE proposal by a very small margin—about the same as the margin by which Oakland County accepted its project. The Knox County project ended when Knoxville's mayor withdrew his support shortly before bond issuance. Except for the mayor's withdrawal, which was motivated in part by political considerations, the Knox County project might have proceeded unhindered.

The timing of project initiation and implementation, as well as changes occurring on a national level during the 1980s, affected the decision-making process at each of the study sites. For example, the Broward County project began in 1982, fully three years before the other case-study projects were initiated and before the recycling ethic swelled in the mid- to late 1980s. As a result, one area of controversy at other sites—competition between recycling and WTE for a limited waste stream—was not an issue at Broward until late in project implementation. The mid- to late 1980s also marked the emergence of anti-incineration stances by some national environmental and other groups. Anti-incineration activists began to campaign nationwide, visiting numerous sites and establishing networks of local activists. These activities influenced the decision-making process at the three sites initiated in 1985 and after.

Although comparisons between case studies were made largely in the context of the outcome of the decision, i.e., whether or not to proceed with the project, attention also was paid to the decision-making process itself. Examining the decision-making process does not presuppose that either WTE acceptance or rejection is the more desired outcome. It does, however, provide insights into process factors that influence the final WTE decision, even though any one factor affecting the decision-making process may not lead to consistent outcomes.

While our small sample size does not support strong conclusions about the WTE population as a whole, the following preliminary findings do stand out. First, selecting among ownership options and negotiating with vendors to provide services were arduous and some of the most time-consuming aspects of decision making at the case-study sites. However, facility ownership apparently was not a strong factor affecting the outcome of the decision-making process.

Second, the size of the proposed facility relative to the size of the waste stream was a significant decision-making factor. Sizing decisions affect facility costs. Such decisions also have important implications for public acceptability of WTE because of resultant opportunities for waste importation and potential effects on other waste management methods, especially recycling. Study findings suggest that the timing of WTE project implementation relative to other waste reduction and recycling programs were factors that affected WTE decision making.

Third, case-study comparisons indicate that there is no clear link between siting activities or site characteristics and the outcome of WTE decision making. For example, systematic site identification processes were undertaken by Broward County, where WTE was accepted, and by Knox County, where WTE was rejected. Both Oakland and Monmouth counties offered considerable financial compensation to their host communities, yet WTE was rejected at Monmouth. Further, though siting literature suggests that a technically correct, systematic, and comparative siting process is essential to siting a WTE facility, case-study siting activities reveal that participants can be satisfied that a proposed site is technically and environmentally suitable in the absence of multisite comparisons.

Fourth, there were clear differences between Broward and the other case-study sites in the types of interaction that occurred and the level of agreement among participants. Broward's negotiations with its member municipalities occurred against a backdrop of generally satisfactory past relations with its municipalities and a tradition of interaction with the Broward League of Cities. In contrast, for example, Knox County and Knoxville have had a troubled relationship. None of the case-study counties' member municipalities were completely supportive of the WTE project, and patterns of mistrust that resulted from unrelated matters affected WTE planning.

Fifth, having state-level support for WTE apparently influences WTE decisions. WTE planners and decision makers attempt to follow state guidelines for SWM whether or not the guidelines are encoded as law. As a result, state positions supporting WTE (often expressed as goals) facilitate WTE adoption at the local level. Complete or partial withdrawal of state support for WTE slows the decision-making process when permits are delayed or moratoria are enacted. Also, the public may be swayed by the positions taken by state governments because the public may perceive state staff to be better trained and more qualified than local government staff. Likewise, having constant and near-unanimous support from county officials positively influences the decision-making outcome.

Sixth, shared perceptions of the urgent need for waste management capacity are likely to have contributed to agreement in Broward County. Closure of the county landfill and rapid population growth may have made Broward's decision makers and the public perceive a dire need for a WTE facility. At the other sites the public perceived no such urgency and prompted decision makers to delay action.

Seventh, case-study respondents uniformly agreed that the public must be informed about SWM issues and activities early in the planning process. There were strong recommendations for improving the decision-making process by involving the public, but few concrete suggestions about how this involvement might be accomplished. Facilitating public participation in the decision-making process will not produce uniform decisions to adopt WTE, a point acknowledged by all respondents. However, dissatisfaction with a decision-making process that generally excludes or makes public participation difficult may exacerbate opposition to the decision.

Eighth, the case studies uncovered evidence that state and federal regulations hastened project activities at each study site. For example, both Broward and Knox counties hastily issued bonds to take advantage of soon-to-expire tax-exempt status. Monmouth County rushed to execute a power sales agreement before state reinterpretation of PURPA would significantly reduce revenues available from power sales. However, decisions about proceeding with WTE facilities at the case-study sites appear to have been unaffected by the uncertain environmental regulatory environment.

Finally, the general SWM experiences of sites where WTE has been accepted differ from those where WTE was rejected. It may be that, alone, none of the contextual factors at sites where WTE was accepted—e.g., contaminated landfills, experience with incinerators, and limited opportunities for waste exportation—are significant enough to affect WTE decisions. In concert, however, the occurrence of these factors at case-study sites where WTE has been accepted suggests that the constellation of such factors positively influences WTE acceptance.

7.7 SUMMARY CONCLUSIONS

This study has addressed a broad set of socioeconomic issues that may have contributed to decisions about WTE projects in the United States during the latter 1980s and early 1990s, focusing on issues that influenced the numerous cancellations of those projects. Also considered are technology, environmental, health, energy, and regulatory issues that may have played a role in WTE acceptance and rejection and are likely to be key issues as the overall viability of WTE is determined in the latter 1990s and beyond.

Conclusions of this study are numerous and varied. Several summary findings are, however, particularly significant in the assessment of WTE project outcomes and the overall viability of WTE. First, municipal waste management in the United States is likely to become more problematic in the coming decades as all waste management options face barriers related to their applicability to a larger percentage of the waste stream, their social acceptance, and their affordability. Second, despite many scientific studies suggesting that the health and environmental impacts from WTE are minimal, both in absolute terms and in relation to other common sources of emissions, public concern and opposition to WTE on the basis of environmental and health risks are pervasive. Such concern and opposition have played a major role in the communities' decisions about WTE. At the heart of these issues is the matter of which information to believe and which information providers to trust. Third, on the basis of our aggregate socioeconomic analysis, there are marked differences between communities that initiate a WTE project and those communities that have not yet considered WTE. Socioeconomic differences do not, however, correlate with decisions either to proceed with or cancel a WTE project. Fourth, the study's financial analysis identifies several trends that made WTE financing more difficult in the latter 1980s. That analysis concludes that financial barriers were neither *the* predominant reason for WTE project cancellation nor are they likely to be "show stoppers" in the coming decade. Fifth, the case studies identify numerous complexities that community leaders and decision makers must address when making decisions about WTE or most other methods to manage municipal waste. Once a WTE project has been initiated, the decision to proceed with or abandon that project appears to depend largely on the dynamics of the decision-making process and the interactions among concerned parties. Future research should build upon case studies conducted thus far to identify methods to assist communities in making decisions about what the public and governmental leaders acknowledge to be one of our most divisive and complex waste issues.

Appendixes

Appendix A: Air Emissions for Common Waste Management Strategies (Pounds per Ton of MSW at the Curb—Total for 20 Years)

	Strategy (see Key)										
	1	2	3	4	5	6	7	8	9	10	11
Air Emissions											
Particulates	0.02	0.086	0.07	0.05	0.46	0.02	0.08	0.05	0.02	0.47	0.47
Carbon monoxide	0.79	1.47	1.33	2.06	23.24	0.94	1.55	2.09	0.94	23.39	23.94
Hydrocarbons	0.08	0.08	0.08	0.08	2.32	0.09	0.09	0.09	0.09	2.34	2.34
Nitrogen oxides	0.32	5.1	4.1	2.64	9.30	0.38	4.7	2.47	0.38	9.36	9.36
Methane	14.34	0.00	0.00	2.29	13.82	13.05	0.00	2.06	5.16	12.47	0.00
Carbon dioxide	437	1650	1320	1460	421	397	1485	1313	157	379	1440
Water	188	1140	912	970	180	171	1026	872	68	164	992
NMOC	0.75	0.00	0.00	0.12	0.72	0.68	0.00	0.11	0.37	0.65	0.00
Dioxin/furan (10^{-6} lb)	NA	0.014	0.011	0.0038	NA	NA	0.012	0.0034	NA	NA	0.011
Sulfur dioxide	NA	2.45	1.96	1.10	NA	NA	2.21	0.99	NA	NA	2.13
Hydrogen chloride	NA	1.40	1.12	0.26	NA	NA	1.26	0.24	NA	NA	1.22
Metals (10^{-6} lb)											
Antimony	NA	NA	NA	ND	NA	NA	NA	ND	NA	NA	NA
Arsenic	NA	4.1	3.3	ND	NA	NA	3.69	ND	NA	NA	3.6
Cadmium	NA	8.0	6.4	ND	NA	NA	7.2	ND	NA	NA	6.9
Chromium	NA	19	15	87	NA	NA	17	78	NA	NA	16.5
Lead	NA	10	8.0	320	NA	NA	9	288	NA	NA	8.7
Mercury	NA	230	184	55	NA	NA	207	50	NA	NA	200
Nickel	NA	17	14	64	NA	NA	15	57	NA	NA	14.8
Zinc	NA	NA	NA	170	NA	NA	NA	153	NA	NA	NA
Total Metals (10^{-6} lb)	NA	288	230	696	NA	NA	259	626	NA	NA	251

Source: National Renewable Energy Laboratory, 1992

Notes: ND=Not detected; NA=Not analyzed; NMOC=Non-Methane Organic Compounds

Key:
1 = Landfill with Gas Recovery
2 = Mass Burn
3 = On-Site MRF + Mass Burn
4 = RDF for Direct Firing
5 = Yard Waste Composting + Landfill
6 = Curbside MRF + Landfill
7 = Curbside MRF + Mass Burn
8 = Curbside MRF + RDF for Direct Firing
9 = Curbside MRF + RDF for Composting
10 = Curbside MRF + Landfill + Yard Waste Composting
11 = Curbside MRF + Mass Burn + Yard Waste Composting

Appendix B: Case Studies: Waste-to-Energy Facilities Protocol

Preface: The results of this study will be used by researchers at Oak Ridge National Laboratory to investigate decision making affecting the development, as well as abandonment of, proposed Waste-to-Energy (WTE) facilities in various communities in the United States. Your identity will be kept confidential. If you wish, we will notify you as to the availability of the final results of the study and tell you how to obtain a copy.

Section I. Demographic Information

1. Gender___Male___Female 2. Age_____

3. Race___White___Black (African-American)___Hispanic___Oriental-Asiatic

4. Name_____

5. Occupation _____

6. Job/position title _____

7. Organization/role_____

Section II. Context Factors Checklist

1. Community

    — characterization of community (development, industry, economy)

    — development plans...vision of future (ideal vs. real)

2. Waste management policies and practices

    — how wastes handled currently

    — service region

    — rationale behind decisions

    — reliability

— safety

— environmental impact

— operator training

— overall management

3. Previous siting controversies:

    — waste facilities

    — other industrial/noxious facilities

    — central issues:

        — environmental concerns

        — land use

        — site availability

        — site suitability

        — low income/racial minority communities

Section III. Decision Making Process (sequence of events; respondents' perceptions; when and if things become issues...opportunities and constraints; who is involved)

1. Sequence of events

    — who was proponent

    — when initiated by proponent

    — when discovered by community...by respondent

    — how was decision reached

2. Participation (at each stage)

— what groups are involved [new vs. established organizations; civic vs. environmental groups;

    local, regional, or external groups (sought or required)]

— types (public or private; via public meetings, negotiation, protest)

— why did the groups first get involved (issues)

3. Degree of agreement (at each stage)

— among what parties (e.g., community and proponent, different stakeholders)

— public or private agreements

— negotiation

— formal or informal agreements

— iterations (what required, how long a period of time, what result)

4. Mitigation (at different stages)   Issues in Section IV

— what methods

— how idea originated

— offered to whom (regional or local)

— offered by whom (regional, local or external)

5. Compensation (at different stages)   Issues in Section IV

— what form

— to whom

— by whom

6. Regulations and laws: role and effect on viability of WTE (at different stages)

— what agencies had permitting jurisdiction

— EPA Municipal Waste Combustor (MWC) guidelines   Issues in Section IV

— Clean Air Act of 1990 (restrictions on atmospheric emissions from MWCs)

— Resource Conservation and Recovery Act of 1980s landfill disposal rules

— Public Utility Regulatory Policy Act (PURPA)

— 1986 Tax Law Changes (financing rules)

Section IV. Decision Making Issues (personal view vs. community view; effects on viability of WTE)

A. Key issues

— at different points in time

B. Environmental and technology issues

1. Siting selection

— where (characterize; suitability, neighboring populations)

— alternatives (where...characterize)

— basis for selection (criteria; who selected site)

— responses to selection (local, regional)

2. Proposed WTE facility and technology (here or elsewhere)

— reliability

— safety

— environmental impact

— operator training

— overall management

— a reasonable size facility?

3. Waste management and environmental practices and regulations

— recycling requirements and their impacts   Topic introduced in Section III

— emissions requirements and their impacts

— landfill disposal requirements and their impacts

— ash management requirements and their impacts

— interstate transport restrictions and their impacts

C. Public/community issues

  1. Public attitudes

    — general public

    — elite public (organizational leaders, public officials, powerful people)

    — how became aware of public attitudes

  2. Proponent/public (local, regional)/municipality relations:

    — trust and confidence

    — if mistrust, what caused it, when begun

  3. Mitigation   Topic introduced in Section III

    — what was offered...by whom

    — mitigating adverse economic/environmental impacts through specific measures (e.g. operator training, pollution control

    — permitting, permit enforcement, local control, supervision, monitoring of the facility

    — restriction on garbage importing

  4. Compensation   Topic introduced in Section III

    — insuring property values against depreciation

    — compensation for adverse impacts in the form of direct payments or other policies

    — payment of host fees to the local community or region

D. Economic issues

  1. Disposal costs

    — recycling

    — source reduction

    — landfill

2. Financing alternatives

  — what alternatives considered

  — (financial) risks of each alternative

3. Effect of the Tax Reform Act of 1986 (tax-exempt status of industrial development bonds

  for WTE projects)

  — economic viability of WTE facility

4. Effect of Public Utility Regulatory Policy Act (PURPA)

  — power generation

  — economic viability of WTE facility

  — if no restriction on power generating capacity, effect on viability of WTE facility

  — customer for power identified

Section V. Conclusion

1. How was the decision making process regarding the proposed WTE facility resolved?

  — if failure to site: other facility; interim decision; future projections; site no facility

  — if decide to site: what conditions

2. How could the decision making process be improved?

  — toward what end(s)

3. Was the correct decision made?

4. Is there anything else you would like to tell us about WTE decision making?

Bibliography

Abert, J. G., 1985. *Municipal Waste Processing in Europe: A Status Report on Selected Materials and Energy Recovery*. UNDP/World Bank Integrated Resource Recovery Rep. Ser. No. 4 (WBTP–37), World Bank, Washington, D.C.

Advisory Commission on Intergovernmental Relations, 1990. *Significant Features of Fiscal Federalism*. Vol. 1, Washington, D.C.

ALA/ATS Government Relations Position, 1984. *Waste Disposal or Reuse*. American Lung Association and American Thoracic Society. Washington, D.C., December 7.

Alexeeff, George V., Melanie A. Marty, and Michael J. Lipsett, 1989. "Comments on Permitting of Resource Recovery Facilities." *Risk Analysis*, Vol. 9, No. 2, pp. 153–155.

Allard, S. J., 1989. "Regulation Can Affect Bond Costs." *Waste Age*, Vol. 20, No. 11, pp. 140–144.

Allen, Phillip, Peter Foye, and Thomas M. Henderson, 1990. "Recycling and Incineration: Not Mutually Exclusive in Broward County, Florida." *Government Finance Review*, Vol. 6, October, pp. 7–11.

Aquino, J. T., 1991. "NSWMA Releases Expanded Tipping Fee Survey." *Waste Age*, Vol. 22, No. 12, pp. 24–28.

Aquino, J. T., 1992a. "The Waste Industry in France, Part One." *Waste Age*, Vol. 23, No. 1, pp. 61–62.

Aquino, J. T., 1992b. "The Waste Industry in France, Part Two." *Waste Age*, Vol. 23, No. 2, pp. 55–58.

Aquino, J. T., 1992c. "Waste-to-Energy: Not Only Surviving But Growing." *Waste Age*, Vol. 23, No. 4, pp. 179–182.

Argonne National Laboratory, 1987. *Energy from Municipal Waste: Opportunities for the Southwest*. ANL/CNSV-TM–173.

Bailey, J., 1991a. "Major Venture for Recycling Loses a Partner." *Wall Street Journal*, November 7, pp. B1, B7.

Bailey, J., 1991b. "Some Big Waste Firms Pay Some Tiny Towns Little for Dump Sites." *Wall Street Journal*, December 3, pp. A1, A9.

Ballentine, J. G., 1992. "The Structure of the Tax System Versus the Level of Taxation: An Evaluation of the 1986 Act." *The Journal of Economic Perspectives*, Vol. 6, No. 1, pp. 59–68.

Bartone, Carl R., 1990. "Economic and Policy Issues in Resources Recovery from Municipal Solid Waste." *Researches, Conservation and Recycling*, Vol. 4, pp. 7–23.

Barzel, Dari, 1988. "Financing Programs for Local Government Agencies: A Regional Approach." *Government Finance Review*, August, pp. 7–12.

Bealer, Robert C., and Donald Crider, 1984. "Sociological Considerations of Siting Facilities for Solid Waste Disposal." In S. K. Majumdar and E. W. Miller (eds.): *Solid and Liquid Wastes: Management, Methods and Socioeconomic Considerations*. The Pennsylvania Academy of Science, Easton, pp. 364–376.

Binder, J. J., and D. H. Minott, 1989. "Siting a Resource Recovery Facility: Community Decision-Making, Risk Education, and Multi-facet Compensation." In *International Conference on Municipal Waste Combustion*. Conservation and Protection, USEPA, Research Triangle Park, North Carolina, and Environment Canada, Ottawa, Canada, pp. 8B21–8B46.

Bland, Robert L., and Chilik Yu, 1987. "Municipal Bond Insurance: An Assessment of Its Effectiveness at Lowering Interest Costs." *Government Finance Review*, Vol. 3, June, pp. 23–26.

Blankenship, J., 1992. "How a Waste Reduction/Composting Plant Came to Broward County." *BioCycle*, Vol. 33, No. 3, p. 47.

Blumberg, Louis, and Robert Gottlieb, 1989a. "Saying No to Mass Burn." *Environmental Action*, Vol. 20, pp. 28–30.

Blumberg, Louis, and Robert Gottlieb, 1989b. *War on Waste: Can America Win Its Battle with Garbage?* Island Press, Washington, D.C.

Boldt, Harold, 1988. "Reducing Interest Costs with an Interest Rate Swap in Columbia, Missouri." *Government Finance Review*, Vol. 4, June, pp. 23–26.

Bosworth, B., and G. Burtless, 1992. "Effects of Tax Reform and Labor Supply, Investment, and Saving." *The Journal of Economic Perspectives*, Vol. 6, No. 1, pp. 3–26.

Brickner, Robert H., 1987. "Combustion Technologies for Municipal Solid Waste." In *Energy from Solid Waste: An Option for Local Government*. Kentucky Energy Cabinet, Louisville, Kentucky, pp. 11–25.

Broiles, Steven A., 1988. "A Suggested Approach to Overcome California's Inability to Permit Urban Resource Recovery Facilities." *Risk Analysis*, Vol. 8, No. 3, pp. 357–366.

Brown, M. D., and K. Jarvie, 1989. "The Future of Waste-to-Energy." *Solid Waste & Power*, Vol. 3, No. 3, pp. 12–22.

Buhler, Franchot, 1987. "Energy from Municipal Waste: Siting Considerations." In *Energy from Solid Waste: An Option for Local Government*. Kentucky Energy Cabinet, Louisville, Kentucky, pp. 45–49.

Bullard, Robert D., 1990. *Dumping in Dixie: Race, Class, and Environmental Quality*. Westview Press, Boulder, Colorado.

Bullard, Robert D., 1991. "Environmental Racism in America." *Environmental Protection*, June, pp. 25–26.

Burr, Michael T., 1990. "Doing Your Homework." *Independent Energy (USA)*, Vol. 20, No. 4, pp. 34–36.

Carter, M. D., and W. H. Davis, 1989. "Public Participation in the SERRF Project." *Solid Waste & Power*, Vol. 3, No. 3, pp. 54–56.

Chen, Philip M., Gina D. France, and Stephen E. Howard, 1990. "Financing Solid Waste Disposal Systems." In Frank Kreith (ed.): *Integrated Solid Waste Management: Options for Legislative Action*. Genium Publishing Corporation, Schenectady, New York, pp. 139–154.

Chertoff, Lawrence, and Diane Buxbaum, 1986. "Public Perceptions and Community Relations." In William D. Robinson (ed.): *The Solid Waste Handbook*. John Wiley & Sons, New York.

Chilton, Kenneth, and James Lis, 1992. *Recycling for Recycling's Sake*. Center for the Study of American Business, Washington University, St. Louis, Missouri, June.

Clarke, M. J., 1989. "Minimizing NO_x." *Waste Age*, Vol. 20, No. 11, pp. 132–138.

Clay, Nicole, 1987. "The San Diego Experience in Resource Recovery." In *Energy from Solid Waste: An Option for Local Government*. Kentucky Energy Cabinet, Louisville, Kentucky, pp. 203–205.

Commission for Racial Justice, 1987. *Toxic Wastes and Race in the United States: A National Report on the Racial and Socio-Economic Characteristics of Communities with Hazardous Waste Sites*. United Church of Christ, New York.

Cook, Richard J., 1989. "Municipal Solid Waste Incineration Ash Management: A State Perspective." *Risk Analysis*, Vol. 9, No. 1, pp. 9–11.

Council for Solid Waste Solutions (CSWS), 1991. "Communities with Access to PET Recycling." Data base, Washington, D.C., November.

Curlee, T. Randall, 1986. *The Economic Feasibility of Recycling: A Case Study of Plastic Wastes*. Praeger, New York.

Curlee, T. Randall, 1987. "Source Reduction and Recycling as Municipal Waste Management Options: An Overview of Government Actions." Oak Ridge National Laboratory, Oak Ridge, Tennessee, draft report prepared for the Office of Policy Planning and Evaluation, U.S. Environmental Protection Agency, October.

Curlee, T. Randall, 1989. "The Feasibility of Recycling Plastic Wastes: An Update." *Journal of Environmental Systems*, Vol. 18, No. 3, pp. 193–211.

Curlee, T. Randall, 1991. "The Potential for Energy from the Combustion of Municipal Solid Waste." *Journal of Environmental Systems*, Vol. 20, No. 4, pp. 303–322.

Curlee, T. Randall, and Sujit Das, 1991. "Identifying and Assessing Targets of Opportunity for Plastics Recycling." *Resources, Conservation and Recycling*, Vol. 5, pp. 343–363.

Curtis, C., G. Brenniman, and W. Hallenbeck, 1992. "Cost Calculations at MSW Composting Sites." *BioCycle*, Vol. 33, No. 1, pp. 70–74.

Davis, Scott S., 1992. "Financing a Recycling/MSW Composting Facility." *BioCycle*, Vol. 33, No. 2, pp. 54–56.

Denison, R. A., and E. K. Silbergeld, 1988. "Risks of Municipal Solid Waste Incineration: An Environmental Perspective." *Risk Analysis*, Vol. 8, No. 3, pp. 343–355.

Diaz, Luis F., G. M. Savage, and Clarence G. Golueke, 1982. *Resource Recovery from Municipal Solid Wastes.* Vol. II. CRC Press, Boca Raton, Florida.

Dickson, Elizabeth L., and George D. Friedlander, 1988. "The Impact of Tax and Expenditure Limitations on the Quality of Municipal Bonded Debt." *Government Finance Review,* February, pp. 13–17.

Edwards, Melissa, 1990. "Solid Waste Incineration." Waste Management Research and Education Institute, The University of Tennessee, Knoxville, Tennessee, December.

Energy Information Administration, 1986. "Historical Plant Cost and Annual Production Expenses for Selected Electric Plants." DOE/EIA–0455(86), Washington, D.C.

Energy Information Administration, 1990. *International Energy Outlook: 1990.* DOE/EIA–0484(90), U.S. Department of Energy, Washington, D.C.

Energy Information Administration, 1991. *Monthly Energy Review.* U.S. Department of Energy, Washington, D.C., March, p. 33.

Environmental Financial Advisory Board, 1990. *Environmental Tax Policy Statement.* Washington, D.C., May 21.

Environmental Financial Advisory Board, 1991a. *Private Sector Incentives Advisory.* Washington, D.C., January 30.

Environmental Financial Advisory Board, 1991b. *Small Community Financing Strategies for Environmental Facilities.* Washington, D.C., August 9.

Environmental Financial Advisory Board, 1991c. *Private Sector Participation in the Provision of Environmental Services: Barriers and Incentives.* Washington, D.C., October 29.

Environmental Financial Advisory Board, 1991d. *Public Sector Options to Finance Environmental Facilities.* Washington, D.C., November 25.

Fabozzi, Frank J., T. Dessa Fabozzi, and Irving M. Pollack, 1991. *The Handbook of Fixed Income Securities.* 3d ed. Business One Irwin, Homewood, Illinois.

Farber, P. S., 1992. "Advanced CEMs Test Air Emissions." *Environmental Protection,* Vol. 3, No. 4, pp. 12–14, 16–19.

Federal Register, 40 CFR Parts 51, 52, and 60. Standards of Performance for New Stationary Sources and Final Emission Guidelines; Final Rules.

Federal Register, 40 CFR Part 60. Emission Guidelines: Municipal Waste Combustors. Subpart Ca. Code of Federal Regulations, July 1, 1992 edition.

Federal Register, 40 CFR Part 81. Air Quality Designations and Classifications; Final Rule. November 6, 1991.

Federal Register, 40 CFR Parts 257 and 258. Solid Waste Disposal Facility Criteria; Final Rule. October 9, 1991.

Federal Reserve Bulletin, 1965–1990. Board of Governors of the Federal Reserve System, Washington, D.C.

Feenberg, Daniel R., and James M. Poterba, 1991. "Which Households Own Municipal Bonds? Evidence from Tax Return." *National Tax Journal,* Vol. 44, No. 4, Part 1, pp. 93–104.

Florini, Karen, Richard A. Denison, and John Ruston, 1990. "An Environmental Perspective on Solid Waste Management." In Frank Kreith (ed.): *Integrated Solid Waste Management: Options for Legislative Action.* Genium Publishing Corporation, Schenectady, New York, pp. 173–195.

Fortune, Peter, 1991. "The Municipal Bond Market, Part I: Politics, Taxes, and

Yields." Federal Reserve Bank of Boston, *New England Economic Review*, September/October, pp. 13–36.

Fortune, Peter, 1992. "The Municipal Bond Market, Part II: Problems and Policies." Federal Reserve Bank of Boston, *New England Economic Review*, May/June, pp. 47–64.

Frillici, P. W., and S. C. Schwarz, 1991. "BACT, MACT, and the Act: What's Going On?" *Waste Age*, Vol. 11, No. 1, pp. 65–72.

General Accounting Office, 1983. "Siting of Hazardous Waste Landfills and Their Correlation with Racial and Economic Status of Surrounding Communities." GAO/RCED–93–168, June 1.

Gershman, Harvey W., 1987. "Finding Markets and Negotiating a Successful Project?" In *Energy from Municipal Waste: Opportunities for the Southwest*. ANL/CNSV-TM-173. Argonne National Laboratory, Argonne, Illinois, pp. 124–141.

Glenn, J., 1991. "Sorting the Mix at Materials Recovery Facilities." *BioCycle*, Vol. 32, No. 7, pp. 30–37.

Glenn, J., 1992a. "The Garbage Stops Here (at the State Line)." *BioCycle*, Vol. 33, No. 3, p. 40.

Glenn, J., 1992b. "1992 Nationwide Survey, The State of Garbage in America." *BioCycle*, Vol. 33, No. 4, pp. 46–55.

Glenn, J., 1992c. "The State of Garbage in America, Part II." *BioCycle*, Vol. 33, No. 5, pp. 30–37.

Glenn, J., 1992d. "Efficiencies and Economics of Curbside Recycling." *BioCycle*, Vol. 33, No. 7, pp. 30–34.

Glenn, J., 1992e. "Maturation of Materials Recovery Facilities." *BioCycle*, Vol. 33, No. 8, pp. 34–39.

Glenn, J., and D. Riggle, 1991a. "The State of Garbage in America." *BioCycle*, Vol. 32, No. 4, pp. 34–38.

Glenn J., and D. Riggle, 1991b. "The State of Garbage in America, Part I." *BioCycle*, Vol. 32, No. 5, pp. 30–35.

Glenn, J., and R. Spencer, 1991. "Solid Waste Composting Operations on the Rise." *BioCycle*, Vol. 32, No. 11, pp. 34–37, 80–84.

Gold, Steven D., 1991. "Changes in State Government Finances in the 1980s." *National Tax Journal*, Vol. 44, No. 1, pp. 1–19.

Gottlieb, Robert, 1990a. "The Incineration Option." In *Solid Waste Management: Planning Issues and Opportunities*. American Planning Association, Planning Advisory Service Report Numbers 424/425, pp. 18–20.

Gottlieb, Robert, 1990b. "The Rise and Eclipse of Incineration." In *Solid Waste Management: Planning Issues and Opportunities*. American Planning Association, Planning Advisory Service Report Numbers 424/425, pp. 2–6.

Government Advisory Associates, 1982, 1984, 1986–87, 1988–89, 1991. *Resource Recovery Yearbooks*, New York.

Gravelle, J. G., 1992. "Equity Effects of the Tax Reform Act of 1986." *The Journal of Economic Perspectives*, Vol. 6, No. 1, pp. 27–44.

Guntou, John, and Kathy Aho, 1988. "Variable-Rate Debt and Minneapolis' Debt Management Policy." *Government Finance Review*, April, pp. 13–16.

Gursky, S., 1992. "Refractories Contribute to Environmentally Sound Solutions." *Waste Age*, Vol. 23, No. 3, pp. 34–38.

Gutfeld, Rosp, 1992. "Dioxin's Health Risks May Be Greater than Believed, EPA Memo Indicates." *Wall Street Journal*, October 16, p. B9.

Hall, B., and Mary Lee Kerr, 1991. *1991–1992 Green Index: A State-by-State Guide to the Nation's Environmental Health.* Island Press, Washington, D.C.

Hatfield, T. H., 1989. "A Formal Analysis of Attitudes Toward Siting a Hazardous Waste Incinerator." *Journal of Environmental Management*, Vol. 29, No. 1, pp. 73–81.

Herman, Tom, 1992. "With Flood of 'Calls' on Muni Bonds, Higher Yields Will Be Washed Away." *Wall Street Journal*, June 3, pp. 1–2(c).

Hershkowitz, Allen, 1987. "Burning Trash: How It Could Work." *Technology Review*, Vol. 90, July, pp. 26–34.

Hershkowitz, Allen, and Eugene Salerni, 1987. *Garbage Management in Japan: Leading the Way.* INFORM, Inc., New York.

Hilgendorff, Christine C., 1989. "Emerging Trends in Solid Waste Finance." *Solid Waste & Power*, Vol. 3, No. 2, pp. 12–17.

Holtz-Eakin, Douglas, 1991. "Bond Market Conditions and State-Local Capital Spending." *National Tax Journal*, Vol. 44, No. 4, pp. 105–120.

Hough, Wesley C., and John E. Petersen, 1983. *Creative Capital Financing.* Municipal Finance Officers Association, Chicago.

Institute for Participatory Planning, 1981. *Citizen Participation Handbook for Public Officials and Others Serving the Public.* 4th ed. Laramie, Wyoming.

Integrated Waste Services Association, 1992a. "Recent Development in the Science of Municipal Waste Combustion Ash." Washington, D.C., April.

Integrated Waste Services Association, 1992b. "Recent Public Opinion Polls." *Update*, Vol. 1, No. 1, p. 3.

Integrated Waste Services Association, 1992c. "European Pragmatism." *Update*, Vol. 1, No. 2, p. 2.

Integrated Waste Services Association, 1992d. "Study on MWC Metals Emissions." *Update*, Vol. 1, No. 2, p. 1.

Jacobs, Harvey E., Jon S. Bailey, and James I. Crews, 1984. "Development and Analysis of a Community-Based Resource Recovery Program." *Journal of Applied Behavior Analysis*, Vol. 17, No. 2, pp. 127–145.

Jones, Kay H., 1987. "What are the True Air Toxics Risks Associated with Resource Recovery Projects?" In *Energy from Solid Waste: An Option for Local Government.* Kentucky Energy Cabinet, Louisville, Kentucky, pp. 61–66.

Jones, Kay H., and James Walsh. 1988. "On the Regulation of Municipal Solid Waste Resource Recovery Incinerators." *Risk Analysis*, Vol. 8, No. 3, pp. 379–382.

Jones, Kay H., and J. Walsh, 1989. "The Need to Involve the Public in Waste-to-Energy Projects." *Solid Waste & Power*, Vol. 3, No. 4, pp. 20–25.

Jones, R. E., and Riley E. Dunlap, 1992. "The Social Bases of Environmental Concern—Have They Changed Over Time?" *Rural Sociology*, Vol. 57, No. 1, pp. 28–47.

Kelsay, Michael, 1992. Data on Financing of Waste-to-Energy Facilities. Collected for use in his Ph.D. dissertation, University of Tennessee, Department of Economics (dissertation in progress).

Kentucky Energy Cabinet, 1987. *Energy from Solid Waste: An Option for Local*

Government. Proceedings of a conference held May 13–15, 1987, at Louis-ville, Kentucky.

Kenyon, Daphne A., 1991. "Effect of Federal Volume Caps on State and Local Borrowing." *National Tax Journal*, Vol. 44, No. 4, Part 1, pp. 81–92.

Kenyon, Daphne A., and Dennis Zimmerman, 1991. "Private Activity Bonds and the Volume Cap in 1990." *Intergovernmental Perspectives*, Summer 1991, pp. 35–37.

Keohane, John, 1988. "The Federal Government and State/Local Government Se-curities: A Short History of Reciprocal Immunity." *Government Finance Review*, June, pp. 7–11.

Kilgore, M., 1988. "WTE Developers: What Are They? Who Are They?" *Solid Waste & Power*, Vol. 2, No. 4, pp. 23–28.

Kiser, J.V.L., 1989. "... The Rest of the Story Is Good!" *Waste Age*, Vol. 20, No. 11, pp. 45–52.

Kiser, J.V.L., 1991a. "Municipal Waste Combustion in the United States: An Over-view." *Waste Age*, Vol. 22, No. 11, pp. 27–30.

Kiser, J.V.L., 1991b. "The Future Role of Municipal Waste Combustion." *Waste Age*, Vol. 22, No. 11, pp. 33–38.

Kiser, J.V.L., 1992a. "Municipal Waste Combustion Ash: Recent Developments." *Environmental & Waste Management World*, Vol. 6, No. 5, pp. 1–7.

Kiser, J.V.L., 1992b. "Municipal Waste Combustion in North America: 1992 Up-date." *Waste Age*, Vol. 23, No. 11, pp. 26–36.

Kiser, J.V.L., and D. B. Sussman, 1991. "Municipal Waste Combustion and Mer-cury: The Real Story." *Waste Age*, Vol. 22, No. 11, pp. 41–44.

Klass, D. L., 1990. "The U.S. Biofuels Industry." In D. L. Klass (ed.): *Energy from Biomass and Wastes XIV*. Institute of Gas Technology, Chicago, Illinois, pp. 1–46.

Kolb, J. O., and J. E. Wilkes, 1988. "Power Generation from Waste Incineration." *Oak Ridge National Laboratory*, ORNL/TM–10484, June.

Konheim, Carolyn S., 1988. "Risk Communication in the Real World." *Risk Anal-ysis*, Vol. 8, No. 3, pp. 367–373.

Konheim, Carolyn S., 1989. "Communicating with the Public About Risks." *Solid Waste & Power*, Vol. 3, No. 3, pp. 36–44.

Kreith, Frank, 1992a. "Solid Waste Management in the U.S. and 1989–1991 State Legislation." *The International Journal*, Vol. 17, No. 5, pp. 427–476.

Kreith, Frank, 1992b. "Technology and Policy of Waste Management." Consulting engineer, Boulder, Colorado, presented at the Air and Waste Management Association's Annual Meeting, Kansas City, Missouri, June 21–26.

Lewis, Stephen G., 1987. "Resource Recovery Facility Development: Steps to Suc-cessful Implementation." In *Energy from Solid Waste: An Option for Local Government*. Kentucky Energy Cabinet, Louisville, Kentucky, pp. 35–40.

Lovely, Mary E., and Michael J. Wasylenko, 1992. "State Taxation of Interest Income and Municipal Borrowing Costs." *National Tax Journal*, Vol. 45, No. 1, pp. 37–52.

Luderer, Lynn M., 1990. *Communicating with the Public about Environmental Health Risks: A Case Study of Waste-To-Energy*. DOE/IR/05/106–T146. U.S. Department of Energy.

Lueck, G. W., 1991. "South Florida Embraces Waste-To-Energy." *Waste Age*, Vol. 22, No. 11, pp. 54–56.

McLoughlin, Thomas, and Catherine Holstein, 1989. "Does Bond Insurance Make Sense?" *Government Finance Review*, December, pp. 37–38.

Macoskey, Kristian, 1992. "A Comparative Evaluation of Metal Emissions and Human Health Risks from Inhalation of Metals Emitted from Waste and Coal Combustors." ADW Technologies, paper presented at the Air and Waste Management Association's annual meeting, Kansas City, Missouri, June 21–26.

Magee, R., 1988. "Plastics Incineration in Municipal Solid Waste Incineration." Paper presented at the RecyclingPlas III Conference, Washington, D.C., May 25–26, sponsored by the Plastics Institute of America.

Markowitz, P., 1991. "Winning Strategies for Curbside and Dropoff." *BioCycle*, Vol. 32, No. 4, pp. 39–41.

Mattheis, Ann H., 1988. "NIMBYism Prevails in Illinois." *Waste Age*, Vol. 19, No. 3, pp. 159–174.

Meade, K., 1992. "Plastics Recycling: Caught in a Bottleneck." *Waste Age*, Vol. 23, No. 8, pp. 38–48.

Metcalf, Gilbert, 1991. "The Role of Federal Taxation in the Supply of Municipal Bonds: Evidence from Municipal Governments." *National Tax Journal*, Vol. 44, No. 4, Part 1, pp. 57–70.

Michael, Joel, 1987. "Tax Incremental Financing: Local Redevelopment Finance After Tax Reform." *Government Finance Review*, October 17–21.

Migden, Janine L., 1990. "State Policies on Waste-to-Energy Facilities." *Public Utilities Fortnightly*, Vol. 126, Sept. 13, pp. 26–30.

Milbrath, Lester W., 1984. *Environmentalists: Vanguard for a New Society*. State University of New York Press, Albany.

Mishkin, Andrew E., 1987. "Resource Recovery for Municipalities in the Southwest: Major Legal Issues and Their Impacts." In *Energy from Municipal Waste: Opportunities for the Southwest*. ANL/CNSV-TM–173. Argonne National Laboratory, Argonne, Illinois, pp. 105–123.

Mitchell, Constance, 1992, "Bond Insurers Nearing Their Capacity for Backing Some Municipalities' Debt." *Wall Street Journal*, June 1, pp. 1, 21(c).

Moore, Richard J. T., and Michael A. Pagano, 1985. *Cities and Fiscal Choices*. Duke University Press, Durham, North Carolina.

Muilenburg, Robert W., 1990. "Balancing the Debate: A Case Study in Combating Misinformation." *Solid Waste & Power*, Vol. 4, No. 1, pp. 32–37.

National Conference of State Legislatures, 1990. *Solid Waste Management: 1989–1990 State Legislation*. 2nd ed. Washington, D.C.

National Renewable Energy Laboratory, 1992. NREL/TP–431–4988, Data Summary of Municipal Solid Waste Alternatives: Executive Summary. SRI International, Menlo Park, California, August.

National Solid Wastes Management Association, 1991. "Special Report: Recycling in the States." Washington, D.C., September.

National Solid Wastes Management Association, 1992. "The Cost to Recycle at a Materials Recovery Facility." Special Report, Washington, D.C.

New Jersey State Advisory Council on Solid Waste Management, 1992. *Municipal Solid Waste Composting*, March 25.

Newkirk, N., K. Probst, J. Wyner, et al., 1990. "Hazardous Waste Sites and the Rural Poor: A Preliminary Assessment." *Sparks Commodities, Inc.*, pp. iv-ix.

Newsday, 1989. *Rush to Burn: Solving America's Garbage Crisis.* Island Press, Washington, D.C.

Newton, Kathy C., 1991. "Beyond Ankle-Biting: Fighting Environmental Discrimination Locally, Nationally, and Globally." *The Workbook*, Vol. 16, No. 3, pp. 98–110.

New York State Energy Research and Development Authority, 1987. *Results of the Combustion and Emissions Research Project at the Vicon Incinerator Facility in Pittsfield, Massachusetts.* Report 87–16, prepared by Midwest Research Institute, June.

Office of Technology Assessment, 1989. *Facing America's Trash: What Next for Municipal Solid Waste?* Congress of the United States, U.S. Government Printing Office, Washington, D.C.

Ollis, R. W., Jr., 1992. "Financing Recycling Programs." *Waste Age*, Vol. 23, No. 3, pp. 65–68.

Pearl, D., 1991. "Neighborhoods Resist Recycling Plants." *Wall Street Journal*, October 14, pp. B1.

Petersen, John E., 1991. "Innovations in Tax-Exempt Instruments and Transactions." *National Tax Journal*, Vol. 44, No. 4, Part 1, pp. 11–28.

Pierce, Lawrence W., 1987. "Selling the Bonds Before the Bond Sale: Elements of a Successful Bond Referendum." *Government Finance Review*, June, pp. 7–11.

Pompelia, M., 1989. "No$_x$: How Much of a Concern?" *Waste Age*, Vol. 20, No. 11, pp. 123–128.

Popp, Paul O., Norman L. Hecht, and Rick E. Melberth, 1985. *Decision-Making in Local Government: The Resource Recovery Alternative.* Technomic Publishing Company, Lancaster, Pennsylvania.

Pryde, Joan, 1990. "Volume Limit Helps Small States, but Larger Ones Feel Cramped." *The Bond Buyer*, June 14.

Pryde, Joan, 1991. "Bond Hungry: Volume Caps Devoured by Environmental and Energy Projects." *Muniweek*, May 28.

Raloff, Janet, 1993. "Cleaning Up Compost: Municipal Waste Managers See Hot Prospects in Rot." *Science News*, Vol. 143, January 23, pp. 56–58.

Rathje, William, and C. Murphy, 1992. *Rubbish! The Archaeology of Garbage, What Our Garbage Tells Us About Ourselves.* Harper Collins, New York.

Redd, A., 1992. "World's First Automobile Disassembly Plant." *BioCycle*, Vol. 33, No. 2, pp. 82–83.

Repa, E. W., and S. K. Sheets, 1992. "Landfill Capacity in North America." *Waste Age*, Vol. 23, No. 5, pp. 18–28.

Richards, Dick, Robert Gould, Dan Kelly, Margaret M. Sachs, and Dennis Dreher, 1990. *Waste-to-Energy Commercial Facilities Profiles: Technical, Operational, and Economic Perspectives.* Noyes Data Corp., Park Ridge, New Jersey.

Richmond, Philip, 1987. "The Tulsa Resource-Recovery Project: From Start to Start-up." In *Energy from Municipal Waste: Opportunities for the Southwest.*

ANL/CNSV-TM–173. Argonne National Laboratory, Argonne, Illinois, pp. 206–211.

Robinson, W. D., 1986. *The Solid Waste Handbook, A Practical Guide.* John Wiley & Sons, Inc., New York.

Russell, Stuart H., 1982. *Resource Recovery Economics: Methods for Feasibility Analysis.* Marcel Dekker, Inc., New York.

SERI, 1990. *The Potential of Renewable Energy: An Interlaboratory White Paper,* SERI/TP–260–3674, Golden, Colorado. Prepared for the Office of Policy, Planning, and Analysis, U.S. Department of Energy.

Sierra Club, 1986. Sierra Club Policy, Solid Waste Management. San Francisco, California.

Sierra Club, 1992. Sierra Club Policy, Solid Waste Management. San Francisco, California.

Skibiski, K. C., 1992. "Gaining Public Support by Design." *BioCycle,* Vol. 33, No. 8, pp. 60–61.

Slemrod, J., 1992. "Did the Tax Reform Act of 1986 Simplify Tax Matters?" *The Journal of Economic Perspectives,* Vol. 6, No. 1, pp. 45–59.

Smith, Randolph B., 1990. "Cleaner Incinerators Draw Less Fire." *Wall Street Journal,* May 31, pp. B1, B10.

Smith, Ray F., 1988. "Certificates of Participation for Lease Financing." *Government Finance Review,* December, pp. 25–28.

Solid Waste Report, 1992a. "Solid Waste Management Tops State Environmental Issues." Vol. 23, No. 6, February 10, p. 54.

Solid Waste Report, 1992b. Vol. 23, No. 20, May 18, p. 198.

Solid Waste Report. 1992c. Vol. 23, No. 23, June 11, p. 219.

Solid Waste Report. 1992d. Vol. 23, No. 24, June 18, p. 228.

Spector, Jeremy A., 1989. "Tax-Exempt Financing for Solid and Hazardous Waste Facilities." *Tax Notes,* May 29.

Steisel, Norman, 1987. "The Promise of Resource Recovery: Lessons from the New York Experience in Gaining Public Approval." In *Energy from Municipal Waste: Opportunities for the Southwest.* ANL/CNSV-TM–173. Argonne National Laboratory, Argonne, Illinois, pp. 180–193.

Society of the Plastics Industry, Inc., 1992. "Plastic Bottles Reach Recycling Rate of 14 Percent in 1991." *Plastic Bottle Reporter,* Vol. 10, No. 3, pp. 1 and 4.

Steuteville, R., 1992. "Economic Development in the Recycling Arena." *BioCycle,* Vol. 33, No. 8, pp. 40–44.

Stevens, P. L., J. S. Henderson, and R. Tulli, 1990. "Indianapolis Resource Recovery Facility: Community Efforts and Technology Required for a Successful Project." *Journal of Engineering for Gas Turbines and Power,* Vol. 112, No. 1, pp. 31–37.

Sundberg, Ronald E., 1988. "Effects of WTE Facility Financing on Community Credit Ratings." *Solid Waste & Power,* Vol. 2, No. 4, pp. 44–49.

Sweetnam, R. J., Jr., 1989. "Trends in Waste-To-Energy." *Waste Age,* Vol. 20, No. 11, pp. 39–41.

Syme, Geoffrey J., and Elizabeth Eaton, 1989. "Public Involvement as a Negotiation Process." *Journal of Social Issues,* Vol. 45, No. 1, pp. 87–107.

Tauscher, Deborah M., 1989. "Municipal Waste Incineration: An Issue of Concern." *The Journal of Environmental Sciences* (March/April), pp. 18–25, 66–67.

Terleckyj, N. E., and C. D. Coleman, 1990. *Regional Economic Growth in the United States: Projections for 1991–2010*. 1990 Regional Economic Projections Series, Volume III. NPA Data Services, Inc., Report No. 90–R–3. Washington, D.C.

Travis, Curtis C., and Holly A. Hattemer-Frey, 1989. "A Perspective on Dioxin Emissions from Municipal Solid Waste Incinerators." *Risk Analysis*, Vol. 9, No. 1, pp. 91–97.

Turbeville, Wallace C., 1990. "Cutting Facility Financing Costs." *Waste Age*, May, pp. 41–48.

United States Conference of Mayors, 1990. *Incineration of Municipal Solid Waste: Scientific and Technical Evaluation of the Art*. Coalition on Resource Recovery and the Environment, Washington, D.C., February 1.

U.S. Bureau of the Census, 1983. *County and City Data Book, 1983*. U.S. Government Printing Office, Washington, D.C.

U.S. Bureau of the Census, 1988a. County Statistics File 3 (Co-Stat 3). U.S. Department of Commerce, Washington, D.C.

U.S. Bureau of the Census, 1988b. *County and City Data Book, 1988*. U.S. Government Printing Office, Washington, D.C.

U.S. Bureau of the Census, 1991. *County Government Finances: 1989–90*. Series GF/90–8. U.S. Government Printing Office, Washington, D.C.

U.S. Bureau of the Census, 1992. *1990 Census of Population and Housing, Summary Tape File 1A*. CD Rom.

U.S. Department of Energy, 1991a. *National Energy Strategy: Powerful Ideas for America*. DOE/S–0082P. Washington, D.C., February.

U.S. Department of Energy, 1991b. *National Energy Strategy: Executive Summary, 1991*. DOE/S–0083P. Washington, D.C.

U.S. Environmental Protection Agency (EPA), 1979. *Resource Recovery Management Model*. Office of Solid Waste Management, Washington, D.C., September.

U.S. EPA, 1987. *Municipal Waste Combustion Study, Report to Congress*. EPA/530–SW–87–021a.Washington, D.C., June.

U.S. EPA, 1989. *Decision-Maker's Guide to Solid Waste Management*. EPA/530–SW–89–072. Office of Solid Waste, Washington, D.C.

U.S. EPA, 1990a. *A Preliminary Analysis of the Public Costs of Environmental Protection: 1981–2000*. Prepared by Apogee Research, Inc., Washington, D.C.

U.S. EPA, 1990b. *Characterization of Municipal Solid Waste in the United States: 1990 Update*. EPA/530–SW–90–042. Prepared by Franklin Associates, Ltd.

U.S. EPA, 1990c. *Sites for Our Solid Waste: A Guidebook for Effective Public Involvement*. Office of Solid Waste.

U.S. EPA, 1992a. *Characterization of Municipal Solid Waste in the United States: 1992 Update*. Prepared by Franklin Associates, Ltd., July, Final Report.

U.S. EPA, 1992b. *Environmental Equity: Reducing Risk for All Communities*. Office of Policy, Planning, and Evaluation, Washington, D.C.

Update, 1992. "Study on MWC Metals Emissions." Integrated Waste Services Association, Vol. 1, No. 2, Washington, D.C.

Van Fleet, H., 1989. "Tulsa, Oklahoma—A WTE Success Story." *Solid Waste and Power*, Vol. 3, No. 4, pp. 45–48.

Varello, P., and K. Burton, 1992. "Steady Growth Predicted for WTE." *Integrated Waste Services Association*, Vol. 1, No. 1, p. 3.

Velzy, Charles O., 1990. "Incineration's Role in Integrated Solid Waste Management." In Frank Kreith (ed.): *Integrated Solid Waste Management: Options for Legislative Action*. Genium Publishing Corporation, Schenectady, New York, pp. 102–120.

Visalli, Joseph R., 1989. "The Similarities of Environmental Impacts from all Methods of Managing Solid Wastes." Presented at the Conference on Hazardous and Municipal Solid Waste Minimization. Meetings of the Air and Waste Management Association, Providence, Rhode Island, February 7–8.

Walsh, J., 1990. "Sanitary Landfill Costs, Estimated." *Waste Age*, Vol. 21, No. 3, pp. 50–54.

Waste Age, 1989. "Easy on the Peanut Butter." Vol. 20, No. 11, November, pp. 36–37.

Waste Age, 1991. "EPA Issues New Combustion Regs." Vol. 22, No. 3, March.

Waste Age, 1992a. "Interstate Movement Report." Vol. 23, No. 4, pp. 12, 16.

Waste Age, 1992b. "States Increase Recycling Laws, but Shift Focus from Separation." Vol. 22, No. 9, pp. 20, 124.

Wiedemann, Peter M., Holger Schutz, and Hans P. Peters, 1991. "Information Needs Concerning a Planned Waste Incineration Facility." *Risk Analysis*, Vol. 11, No. 2, pp. 229–235.

Williams, S., 1991. *Trash to Cash: New Business Opportunities in the Post-Consumer Waste Stream*. Investor Responsibility Research Center, Inc., Washington, D.C.

Wise, D. H., 1990. "How Big a Role for Railroads?" *Waste Age*, Vol. 21, No. 3, pp. 64–68.

Woods, R., 1991a. "Curbing Household Hazardous Waste." *Waste Age*, Vol. 22, No. 9, pp. 84–90.

Woods, R., 1991b. "Ashes to . . . Ashes?" *Waste Age*, Vol. 22, No. 11, pp. 46–52.

Woodward, A., 1992. "Financing Waste-To-Energy Plants." *Energy Economics*, July, pp. 233–236.

Yaffe, Harold J., and Jonathan Wooten, 1984. "The Development and Financing of the Northeast Massachusetts (NESWC) Resource Recovery Project: A Tale of Twenty-Two Cities and Towns." *Proceedings of the 1984 National Waste Processing Conference*. American Society of Mechanical Engineers, New York, pp. 102–110.

Zimmerman, Dennis, 1990. *The Volume Cap on Tax-Exempt Private Activity Bonds: State and Local Experience in 1989*. Advisory Commission on Intergovernmental Relations, Washington, D.C.

Zimmerman, Dennis, 1991. *The Private Use of Tax-Exempt Bonds*. The Urban Institute Press, Washington, D.C.

Zimmerman, Dennis, 1992. "POINT: Advisory Board's Proposal to Reclassify Environmental Bonds May Open Pandora's Box." *MuniWeek*, January 13.

Index

ABB Resource Recovery Systems, 41, 62 n.6
Act 641, Michigan, 160, 161–162, 164, 166–167, 168
Air emissions controls, 106. *See also* WTE (waste-to-energy)
Air quality, 63; non-attainment counties, 85
Air Products and Chemicals, Inc., 42
Alaska, 65
AMBAC (American Municipal Bond Assurance Corporation), 132 n.7
American Lung Association, 197
American Ref-Fuel Company, 41, 42
Anaerobic digestion, 30
Anti-incineration activism, 197. *See also* WTE (waste-to-energy) and *specific case studies*
Aquino, J. T., 27
Ash: disposal, 13–15; disposal fees, 40; environmental and health risks, 13–15; management, 136; MSW-to-ash ratio, 20; as a percentage of incoming MSW, 40; public concerns about, 15; regulations, 19–20; toxicity characteristics, 34 nn.7, 9
Auburn Hills, Michigan, 158, 160, 162, 165, 166

Bailey, J., 27
BDT (Best Demonstrated Technology), 19, 217

Bealer, R. C., 137
BIG (Bond Investors Guaranty Insurance Corporation), 132 n.7
Blumberg, L., 136
Bottle-deposit laws, 87
Broiles, S. A., 137
Broward County, Florida, 141, 144–156, 197, 224–227; decision-making process, 145–146, 147–152, 155–156, 204; and EPA, 146, 149, 151, 152; facility and waste stream size, 145, 152, 153–154, 202; financial and economic issues, 146, 148–149, 152, 154–155; health and safety issues, 151, 153; interlocal agreements, 149–150, 151; litigation, 149, 150, 151, 152; permitting, 146, 149, 150; pollution control equipment, 146, 149, 150, 151, 152; public attitudes, 153, 155–156; public participation, 150–152; regulations and laws, 152; site selection, 148, 153, 203–204; tipping fees, 152, 154–155, 213 n.4; vendor selection, 148; waste flow agreements, 149–150; waste management alternatives, 146–147, 148, 151, 152, 153–154; waste management issues, 145–147, 151
Broward County Commission, 145, 147, 148, 151, 212 n.2

Broward League of Cities, 145, 149–150, 151, 204
Browning-Ferris Industries, 42
Buxbaum, D., 139, 143

CAA (Clean Air Act), 19, 20, 38, 106
CAAA (Clean Air Act Amendments), 19, 20, 32, 35 n.28, 217
Case studies: approach, 141; data collection, 141, 143–144; selection of sites, 141; summary conclusions, 224–227. See also specific case studies: Broward County, Florida; Know County, Tennessee; Monmouth County, New Jersey; Oakland County, Michigan
Catchment area, 70
Chertoff, L., 139, 143
Chilton, Kenneth, 16
Clarke, M. J., 12
Clean Water Action, 151
Combustion engineering, 41, 62 n.6
Comparisons of means, definition, 70
Composting: cost, 218; environmental and health risks, 16–17, 217; number of programs, 2; percentage of MSW managed by, 2, 28; public perceptions, 27
Concentration ratio, defined, 62 n.7
Contingent liability, 101
Cook, R. J., 136
Costs. See Composting; Financing; Landfill; Recycling; WTE (waste-to-energy); specific case studies
Council for Solid Waste Solutions, 28, 77, 78
County, classification, 76
Credit enhancements, 100, 103, 121; third-party, 99, 101–103, 124
Crider, D., 137
Curlee, T. Randall, 54, 58

Davie, Florida, 146, 148. See also Broward County, Florida
Debt, municipal, 99, 118; innovative, 98–99, 101–106, 124, 125, 130; traditional, 98–101
Decision-making: context, 197, 207–208; outcomes, 135, 199, 208–209, 211–212; process, 135, 197, 199, 202–207, 208–209, 211–212. See also specific case studies
Denison, R. A., 13, 136
Detroit, Michigan, 163. See also Oakland County, Michigan
Diaz, Luis F., 32
DRA84 (Deficit Reduction Act of 1984), 109, 152

Electricity generation costs, 34 n.15
Energy Information Administration, 61
Environmental concern, local climate, 66, 83–89
Environmental controls, 97, 120, 131 n.1
Environmental Defense Fund, 21
Environmental equity, 203–204. See also Knox County, Tennessee; Oakland County, Michigan
Environmental Financial Advisory Board, 120, 133 n.19
Environmental protection, costs, 98, 106, 120, 131 n.1, 133
Environmental quality, state indexes, 83–84
EPA (U.S. Environmental Protection Agency), 2, 4, 5, 14, 19, 20, 21, 23, 24, 26, 27, 28, 37, 45, 47, 49, 54, 98, 217; equity capital, 121, 123, 125; guide for public involvement, 137–138; guide to solid waste management, 136, 137, 138–139. See also Broward County, Florida; Monmouth County, New Jersey
Everglades, 153. See also Broward County, Florida

Federal Energy Regulatory Commission, 22
FGIC (Financial Guaranty Insurance Company), 132 n.7
Financing: adjustable-rate securities, 125, 131, 132–133; aversion, 102, 129, 130; barriers, 97; bond insurance, private, 103, 130; bonding banks, 98, 100–101, 121;

bonds, general-obligation, 99, 118, 125, 130; bonds, governmental, 110; bonds, municipal, 98; bonds, qualified, 112; bonds, revenue, 100, 118, 120–122; certificate of participation, 105, 132 n.13; constraints, 125, 131; county tax policy, 120; federal tax policy, 108–120; fiscal policy, federal, 97, 101; fixed-rate, 105; floating-rate, 105; government revenue, 93; government revenue, local, 121, 124; grant programs, 98, 100, 121, 124; interest rate, 99; interest-rate swap, 105–106, 133 n.15; intergovern-mental aid, 97; leasing, 103–105, 121, 125, 130, 132 n.11; limitations on tax benefits, 109–110; loan guarantees, 98, 121, 124; LOC (letters of credit), 103, 121, 124, 130; local, 97–99, 121, 124, 125; mechanisms, 98–106; prime rate, 105; risk, 97, 99, 131; state guarantees, 100; state mandates, 120; tax benefits, 104; tax exempt, 97, 100, 108–110, 118, 123, 125, 130; trends, 97–107, 120; user fees, 120; variable-rate securities, 105, 121; volume caps, 110, 113, 118, 130, 131, 133 n.21; yield ratio, 110. *See also* Broward County, Florida, financial and economic issues; Knox County, Tennessee, financial and economic issues; Monmouth County, New Jersey, financial and economic issues; Oakland County, Michigan, financial and economic issues; TRA86 (Tax Reform Act of 1986)
Florida Department of Environmental Regulation (DER), 146, 147, 148, 149, 151
Florida Solid Waste Management Act, 147, 154
Florini, K., 136
Fluidized bed combustion, 30
Foster Wheeler Power Systems, Inc., 41, 172, 176
Franklin Associates, 45, 47, 49, 54

Furans, 10, 11, 12, 13, 14, 168. *See also* WTE (waste-to-energy), atmospheric emissions

GAA (Government Advisory Associates), 14, 19, 22, 26, 30, 39–41, 51, 64, 123
Glenn, J., 2, 26, 27, 28, 46, 79, 81, 87
Gold, Steven, 120
Golueke, Clarence G., 32
Gottlieb, R., 136
Greenpeace, 83, 151, 197

Hall, B., 84, 88
Hattemer-Frey, Holly A., 12, 136
Hawaii, 65
Health and safety. See WTE (waste-to-energy); *specific case studies*
Hecht, N. L., 138
Hershkowitz, Allen, 49
Hierarchical waste management strategies, 203
Household hazardous waste, 11, 16, 33–34 n.1

IDB (Industrial Development Bond), 109, 121–122, 123, 125, 130
Incineration, with heat recovery. See WTE (waste-to-energy)
Incineration, without heat recovery. *See* WTE (waste-to-energy)
Independent cities, 65
Industrial base, 63, 76; employment, 76
Integrated waste management, 136, 138–139
Integrated Waste Services Association, 14
IRB (industrial revenue bond), 100, 118, 130

Japan, WTE in, 37, 61 n.1
J. J. Kenny Index, 105
Jones, Kay H., 13, 136

Kelsay, Michael, 113, 123
Kenyon, Daphne, 113, 118
Kerr, Mary Lee, 84, 88
Kidder, Peabody, Inc., 41, 42

Kiser, J.V.L., 11, 22, 23, 54, 136
Klass, D. L., 58
Knox County, Tennessee, 141, 171–
   183, 199, 224–227; citizens'
   advisory committee, 175, 177; city-
   county antagonism, 172, 182, 204;
   decision-making process, 172, 174–
   180, 182–183; environmental equity,
   178, 180, 204; facility size, 174,
   202; financial and economic issues,
   172, 174, 176–177, 179, 181, 182,
   183; health and safety issues, 181;
   litigation, 178; mitigation, 179;
   permitting, 172, 176, 178; pollution
   control equipment, 180; public
   attitudes, 181–182; public
   opposition, 173, 176, 177–178, 180,
   182; public participation, 178, 182;
   regulations and laws, 179–180; site
   selection, 172, 175–176, 180, 203–
   204; tipping fees, 181; vendor
   selection, 176; waste disposal
   capacity, 180; waste flow
   agreements, 175; waste management
   alternatives, 173, 176, 202; waste
   management issues, 173, 174, 183;
   waste stream size, 174–175
Knoxville, Tennessee, 172, 175, 176,
   204. See also Knox County,
   Tennessee
Knoxville City Council, 174, 175, 177
Knoxville Metropolitan Planning
   Commission, 172, 174, 175, 176,
   177
Konheim, C. S., 137
Kreith, Frank, 16, 28, 33

Landfill, 63, 77, 80–81; capacity, 35
   n.21, 63, 80–81; closures, 26; costs,
   27; environmental and health risks,
   16–17; legislation, 2; number of
   facilities, 2, 26, 35 n.21; percentage
   of MSW managed by, 2, 26; public
   opinion, 2; siting, 2, 27; tipping fees,
   2, 80; tipping fees by region, 27;
   total capacity by region, 26
Leading Edge Reports, 58
Legislative mandates, 63

Levy, Steven, 54
LIBOR Rate, 105
Lis, James, 16
Los Angeles County, 65
Luderer, L. M., 137
Lumpy capital, 97, 98

Macoskey, Kristian, 11
MACT (Maximum Achievable Control
   Technology), 19, 217
Madison Heights, Michigan, 159, 165.
   See also Oakland County, Michigan
Mass-burn facilities, 30–31, 75, 97.
   See also WTE (waste-to-energy),
   mass-burn)
MBIA (Municipal Bond Investors
   Assurance Corporation), 132
MCRC (Monmouth County
   Reclamation Center), 185, 187, 192,
   195, 213 n.9
Melberth, R. E., 138
Mercury, 153, 158, 162, 163, 168,
   193
Metropolitan counties, 65–66; density,
   72; growth, 71; non-attainment, 86;
   rural, 75
Michigan Department of Natural
   Resources (DNR), 158, 162, 163,
   164
Michigan Solid Waste Management
   Act. See Act 641, Michigan
Military installations, 65
MKSWA (Metropolitan Knox Solid
   Waste Authority), 172, 174–180,
   181
Modular systems, 31, 75. See also
   WTE (waste-to-energy), modular
   systems
Monmouth County, New Jersey, 141,
   183–197, 199, 224–227; decision-
   making process, 183–184, 186–192,
   196–197; EPA, 191; facility size,
   184, 187, 193–194, 202; financial
   and economic issues, 189, 190, 191,
   192, 194–195; freeholders, 183–
   184, 187, 188, 190; health and
   safety issues, 188, 189, 190, 191,
   192, 193, 196; Health Risk

Assessment Committee, 190, 191;
mitigation and compensation, 191;
moratorium on incinerator
construction, 188, 205; permitting,
185, 191; pollution controls, 185,
192; public attitudes, 185, 192,
195–196; public opposition, 184,
186, 188, 189, 190, 191, 192, 194–
196; public participation, 188, 189–
190, 196; public referendum, 184,
188–189, 190, 191, 196; public
support, 189; regulations and laws,
185, 186, 187, 191–192; site
selection, 187, 192–193, 203–204;
Solid Waste Advisory Committee,
189–190; technology assessment,
187, 188; tipping fees, 194, 196;
vendor selection, 183–184, 194;
waste flow concerns, 193–194, 202;
waste management alternatives,
185–186, 187, 188, 190, 192; waste
management issues, 184–187, 188,
191, 192, 194, 202
Montenay Power Corporation, 41
MRFs (materials recovery facilities),
number of facilities, 28, 78, 79
MSW (municipal solid waste): average
Btu value, 49–51; defined, 45;
general background, 7 n.2;
generation in Europe, 49; hazardous
waste in, 11, 16; historical and
projected quantities, 45–49;
interstate transport, 34 n.18;
management cost as a percent of
average household income, 26;
management cost as a percent of
municipal budget, 26; per capita
generation, 47–49; projected impacts
of source reduction, 46; public
opinion, 1; quantity estimates, 2, 62
n.10; in relation to GNP, 45–46. See
also Household hazardous waste
Multiple regression analysis, 70, 92

National Energy Strategy, 58
National Planning Association, 95
National Solid Wastes Management
Association, 15, 24, 29

National Wildlife Federation, 84
Naval Weapons Center, New Jersey,
185, 186
New Jersey Department of
Environmental Protection (NJDEP),
185, 187, 189, 191
New Jersey Emergency Solid Waste
Task Force, 186
New Jersey Solid Waste Management
Act of 1975, 185, 187
New Jersey State Advisory Council on
Solid Waste Management, 16
New Jersey Wetlands Protection Act,
185
Non-attainment counties, 85
Non-metropolitan counties, 66;
density, 72; growth, 71; non-
attainment, 85; rural, 75
NSPS (New Source Performance
Standards), 19, 23, 106, 133; cost of
WTE compliance, 19

Oakland County, Michigan, 141, 156–
171, 197, 213 n.5, 224–227;
decision-making process, 158, 161–
167, 170–171; environmental equity,
160, 167, 204; financial and
economic issues, 163, 169; health
and safety issues, 168–169;
intergovernmental agreements, 158,
161, 163, 164, 165, 166, 199, 204;
litigation, 167; mitigation and
compensation, 166; permitting, 162,
166–167, 205; pollution control
equipment, 159, 168; public
attitudes, 169–170; public
opposition, 159, 160, 164–165, 167,
168; public participation, 164–165;
public referendum, 158, 163–164,
170; regulations and laws, 159, 161,
166–167; site selection, 161, 162,
167–168, 203–204; tipping fees,
169; vendor selection, 162; waste
flow agreements, 161, 163; waste
management alternatives, 159–160,
161–162, 167, 202; waste
management issues, 158–160, 161–
162, 164

Oakland County Commission, 158
Ogden Martin Systems, Inc., 41, 42, 62 n.6
Ogden Projects, Inc., 24–25
OTA (Office of Technology Assessment), 7 n.2, 26, 29, 45, 51, 136

PAB (private activity bond), 100, 110, 112; qualified, 110, 112; tests, 112
Paper, impact on heat value of MSW, 51
Pembroke Pines, Florida, 146, 147. See also Broward County, Florida
Plastics: atmospheric emissions from incineration, 12, 34 n.5; impact on heat value of MSW, 51; recycling, 35 nn.23–24, 77
Pompano Beach, Florida, 146, 147, 148, 151, 153. See also Broward County, Florida
Pontiac, Michigan, 160, 162, 167–168. See also Oakland County, Michigan
Popp, P. O., 138
Population: age, 63, 76; density, 63, 70; education, 76; growth, 70; per capita income, 63; rural, 70; settlement patterns, 66, 70–76
Pryde, Joan, 118
Public opinion, 17. See also Composting; Landfill; Recycling; WTE (waste-to-energy); specific case studies
PURPA (Public Utility Regulatory Policies Act), 21, 38, 192, 217
Pyrolysis, 30

Quayle, Dan, 23

Raloff, Janet, 16
RCRA (Resource Conservation and Recovery Act), 17, 19, 20, 21, 23, 27, 45, 217
RDF (refuse-derived fuel): design capacity, 30; technical reasons for aversion to, 32; technologies, 31–32, 97. See also WTE (waste-to-energy)
Reading Energy Company, 41

RECA (Revenue and Expenditure Control Act of 1968), 109
Recycling: challenges facing, 2–3; in combination with WTE, 28, 40–41; costs, 2, 28–29; environmental and health risks, 16–17, 217; percentage of MSW managed by, 2, 28; possible limitations on use, 28; programs, 2, 28, 63, 77–79; public perceptions, 27; state goals, 2; state incentives, 87; state laws, 24; state mandates, 83, 86–88. See also MRFs (material recovery facilities); Plastics, recycling
Reilly, William, 21
Repa, E. W., 26, 27
Reuter, Inc., 146, 147
Rhode Island, ban on WTE, 25
Rhode Island Solid Waste Management Corporation, 24
Riggle, D., 81, 87
Rochester Hills, Michigan, 159, 165, 168
RRRASOC (Resource Recovery and Recycling Authority of Southwest Oakland County), 159
Ruston, J., 136

Savage, G. M., 32
Sheets, S. K., 26, 27
Sierra Club, 84, 197
Silbergeld, E. K., 13, 136
Siting. See Broward County, Florida, site selection; Knox County, Tennessee, site selection; Monmouth County, New Jersey, site selection; Oakland County, Michigan, site selection; WTE (waste-to-energy), facility siting
Socioeconomic, WTE aggregate analysis, 63–95
SOCRRA (Southeast Oakland County Resource Recovery Authority), 158–159, 163
Solar Energy Research Institute, 58
Source reduction, state goals, 2
Standard and Poors, 132 n.9
Statistical, significance test criteria, 72–73

Superfund, 147, 159
Sussman, D. B., 11
Sweetnam, R. J., Jr., 41

Tinton Falls, New Jersey, 184, 185,
191, 192. *See also* Monmouth
County, New Jersey
Tipping fees. *See* Costs; Landfill; WTE
(waste-to-energy); *specific case
studies*
TLDA (Tennessee Local Development
Authority), 132 n.3
TRA86 (Tax Reform Act of 1986), 21,
22, 34 n.17, 97, 110, 113, 121, 130,
132, 179, 217, 221–223; two-part
test, 112. *See also* Financing
Traitement Industriel Des Residus, 44
Travis, Curtis C., 12, 136
TRB (taxable revenue bond), 100. *See
also* Financing
Treasury Bill Rate, 105

Unified volume caps, 223. *See also*
Financing
United States Conference of Mayors,
12, 13, 14, 15
University of Tennessee, 175
Urban Institute, 118
U.S. Advisory Commission on
Intergovernmental Relations, 118
U.S. Department of Energy, 22, 58
U.S. Department of Housing and
Urban Development, 175

Velzy, C. O., 136
Visalli, Joseph R., 17

Waste Age, 13
Waste importation/exportation, 207.
See also specific case studies
Waste management alternatives, 136,
202–203, 207. *See also* Composting;
Pyrolysis; Recycling; Source
reduction; *specific case studies*
Westinghouse Electric Corporation, 41,
42, 158, 162, 163, 164, 165, 183,
188–189, 190, 194, 199
Wheelabrator Technologies, Inc., 41,
42, 146, 148

Williams, S., 14, 20
WMI (Waste Management, Inc.), 146,
147, 148, 154, 159, 213 n.3
Woodward, A., 120
WTE (waste-to-energy): abandoned
facilities, 64; acceptance and
rejection, 139, 197–198, 199, 206;
adoption/cancellation related to
socioeconomic factors, 220–221;
alternative technologies, 29–33;
atmospheric emissions, 10–13;
barriers to future use, 5;
cancellations, 4, 64, 66, 125, 130–
131, 133 n.20, 215; capacity, 37;
capacity by region, 39; capacity by
technology type, 39; capital costs,
106; case-study summary
conclusions, 224–227; catalysts
driving decision-making process,
206–207; chronological framework
for case studies, 139–140;
compensation, 137; concentration
ratios, 42; current status of the
industry, 38–41; decision making,
135–214; decisions and facility size,
225–226; decisions and impacts of
federal regulations, 227; decisions
and local government interaction,
226; decisions and ownership
options, 225; decisions and
perceived need, 226; decisions and
public involvement, 226–227;
decisions and siting activities, 226;
decisions and state-level support,
226; description of mass-burn
facilities, 30–31; design size, 70, 75;
developmental technologies, 30;
dioxins, atmospheric emissions, 10,
11, 12, 13, 14, 153, 168, 193;
economies of scale, 70; energy type
produced, 39; energy produced as a
function of technology type, 62
n.11; energy produced in relation to
total energy consumption, 61; energy
production, 219–220; environmental
and health regulations, 19–21;
environmental and health risks, 10–
15, 17, 216; environmental controls,

32–33, 34 n.6, 40; environmental issues, 136, 210; in Europe, 4, 37; facilities, classification, 64; facilities, design capacity, 107; facility and waste stream size, 202, 207; facility costs, 26, 221–222; facility siting, 138, 203–204; factors leading to controversy, 216–218; financial and economic issues, 137, 209, 210, 221–224; health and safety concerns, 208–209, 210; history of, 37–38; history of adoption, 61 n.2; industry structure, 41–44, 62 n.9, 219; initiative county, definition, 64; issues facing, 9; in Japan, 37, 61 n.1; legal issues, 137; legislative and regulatory uncertainties, 17–18; market potential in Europe, 62 n.8; mass-burn, 107; modular system design capacity, 30; modular systems, 107; number of facilities, 4, 38–39, 215; operating facilities, 64, 66; percentage of MSW managed by, 4, 215; prices paid for electricity, 22, 39; projections of future use, 5, 51–56; proposed moratoriums, 25; public opinion, 9; public participation, 137–139, 199, 206, 212; quantity of energy produced, 44–61; recycling programs in conjunction with, 23; regulations influencing financial viability, 21–23; state mandates, 24–25; tipping fees, 25–26, 41. *See also* Ash; Broward County, Florida, regulations and laws; Financing; Knox County, Tennessee, regulations and laws; Monmouth County, New Jersey, regulations and laws; Oakland County, Michigan, regulations and laws; Pyrolysis; *specific case studies*

Zimmerman, Dennis, 113, 118

About the Authors

T. RANDALL CURLEE is an economist and Head of the Energy and Global Change Analysis Section in the Energy Division of Oak Ridge National Laboratory. In addition to congressional testimony and serving on several national advisory panels on the topic of municipal waste management, Dr. Curlee is widely published in various areas of waste management and resource allocation. He has also contributed several chapters to books on the subject of waste management and is the author of *The Economic Feasibility of Recycling: A Case Study of Plastic Waste* (Praeger, 1986).

DAVID L. FELDMAN is a political scientist and Senior Research Associate at the Energy, Environment and Resources Center at the University of Tennessee-Knoxville. He also serves as Senior Editor of *Forum for Applied Research and Public Policy*. Dr. Feldman has led studies on the implications of SARA Title III for risk communication and public involvement in risk management and is widely published in the fields of waste management in the United States and Europe, global environmental policy, and water resources management. He is the author of *Water Resources Management: In Search of an Environmental Ethic* (1991).

MICHAEL P. KELSAY is currently an Assistant Professor at Indiana-Purdue University at Fort Wayne in the School of Public and Environmental Affairs. Dr. Kelsay has an extensive background in the areas of municipal waste management and finance. While at the University of Tennessee's Energy, Environment, and Resource Center in Knoxville, Tennessee, he worked on a variety of solid and hazardous waste projects for the State of Tennessee and the U.S. EPA. Prior to going to the University of Tennessee, Dr. Kelsay was President and Chief Executive Officer of Argentine Savings and Loan

in Kansas City, Kansas. He is the author of book chapters and other publications on waste management and tax policy and has made numerous
professional presentations on the financial aspects of waste management.

SUSAN M. SCHEXNAYDER, an anthropologist, is a research associate of
the University of Tennessee's Energy, Environment, and Resource Center
subcontracted to Oak Ridge National Laboratory's Energy Division. Ms.
Schexnayder has extensive interviewing and social impact assessment experience. She has examined community preferences at Superfund sites for
the U.S. EPA, conducted social and cultural resource impact assessments
for environmental impact statements for several federal agencies, and produced sociodemographic portions for U.S. Department of Energy safety
analysis reports.

DAVID P. VOGT is an economist in the Energy and Economic Analysis
Section of Oak Ridge National Laboratory. His research interests are in the
development of analysis tools that focus on providing a consistent national
and regional perspective of the potential impacts of alternative policy
choices. Much of his work has addressed the potential constraints on regional development and/or adverse impacts due to energy shortage or shifts
in energy supply patterns. Dr. Vogt has developed several nationally recognized regional modeling systems for the U.S. Department of Energy, the
Federal Emergency Management Agency, and the U.S. National Guard.

AMY K. WOLFE, an anthropologist in Oak Ridge National Laboratory's
Energy Division, specializes in decision-making issues relating to technology
and the environment as well as social impact assessment. Dr. Wolfe's publications—book chapters, journal articles, and technical reports—center on
perceptions of technologies and their risks, risk communication, and methods for social impact assessment. Journals in which she published and served
as guest editor or co-editor include *The Environmental Professional* and
Practicing Anthropology.